Be Home Here

Mala Iqbal

Designed by Grace Sullivan.

Published by Passe-Partout Books in New York City.

ISBN 978-0692303344

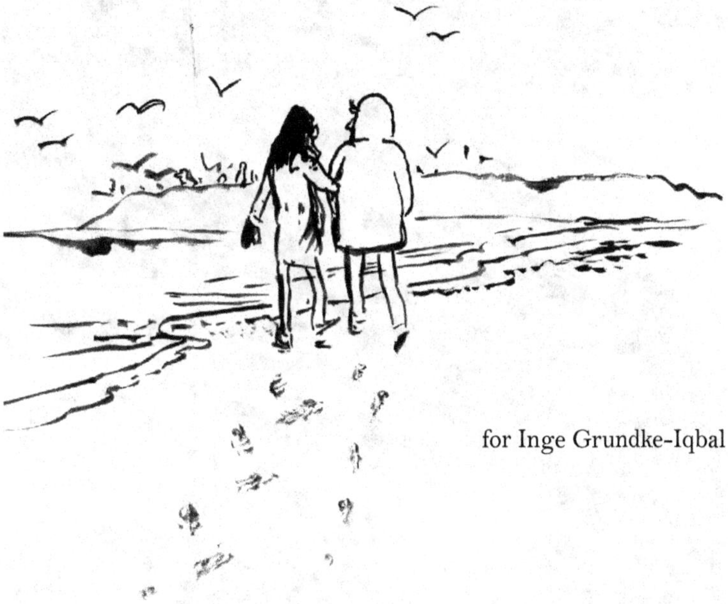

for Inge Grundke-Iqbal

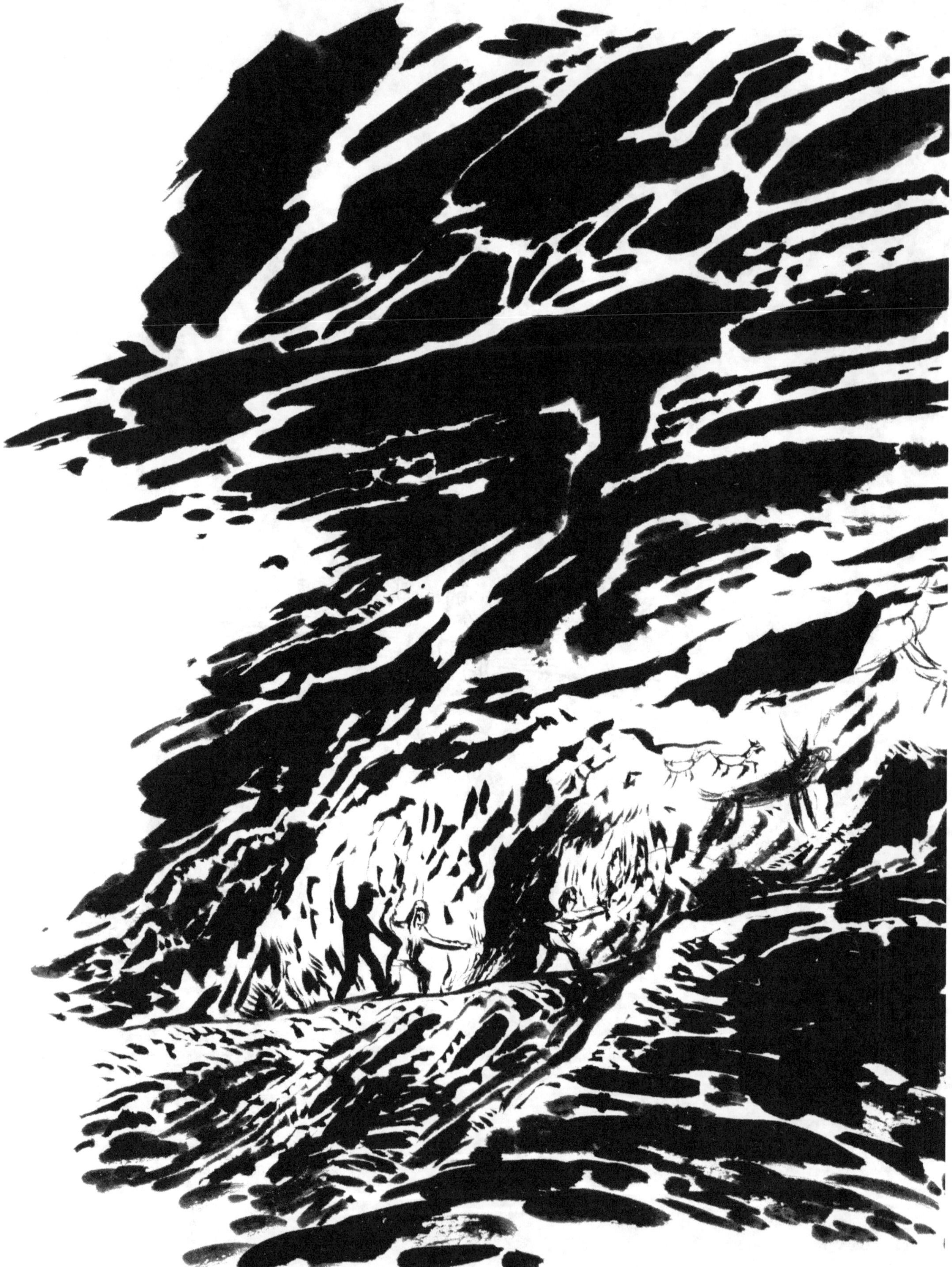

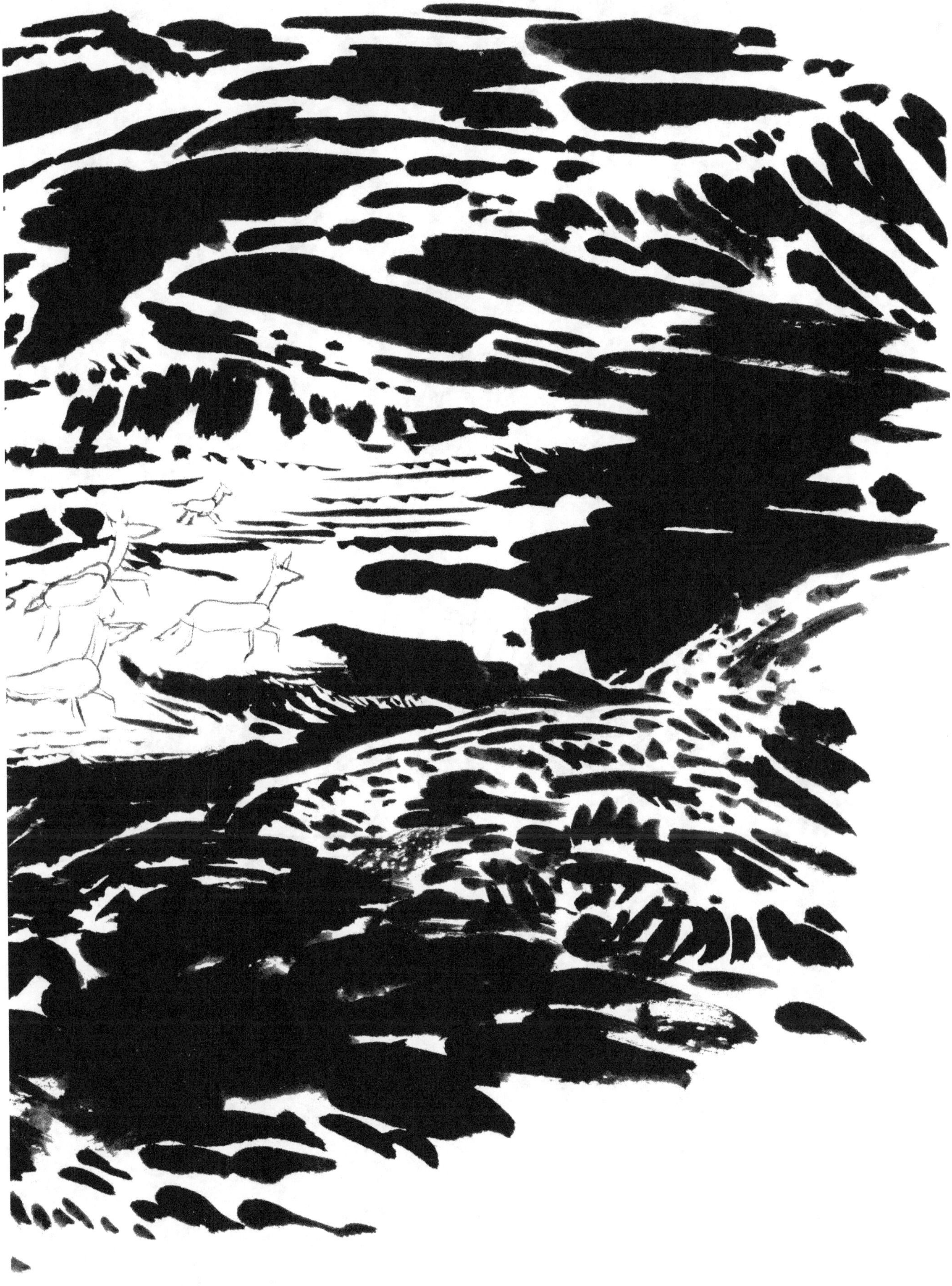

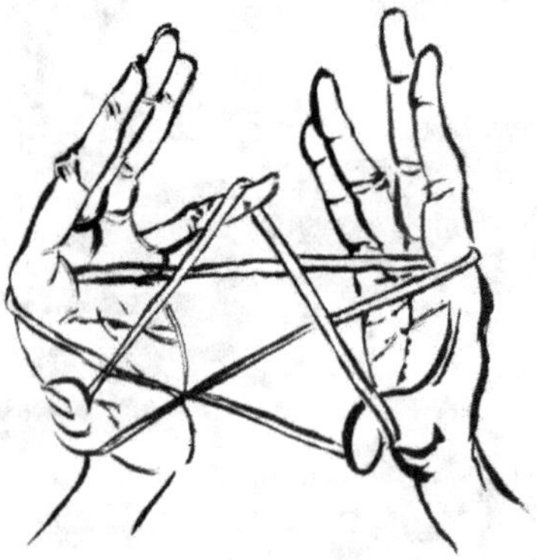

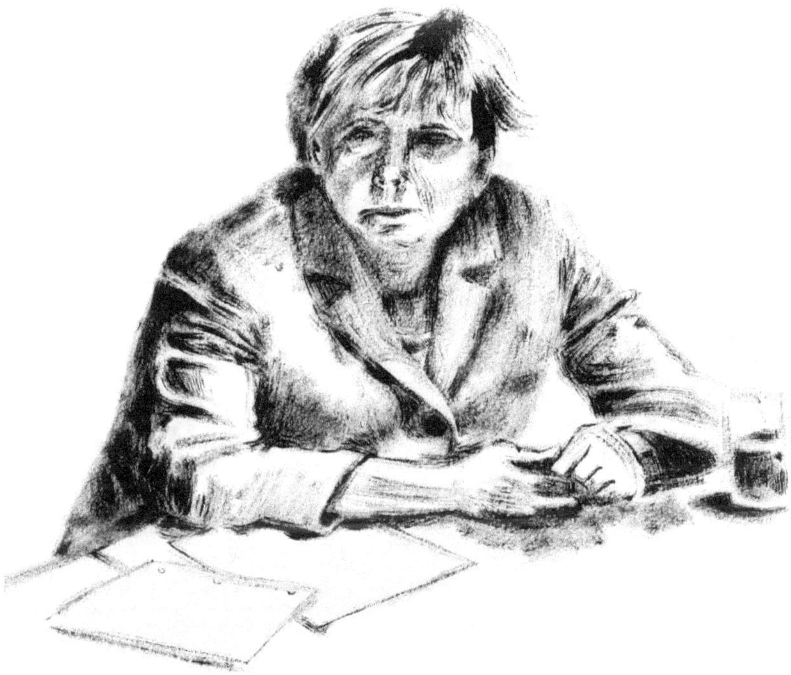

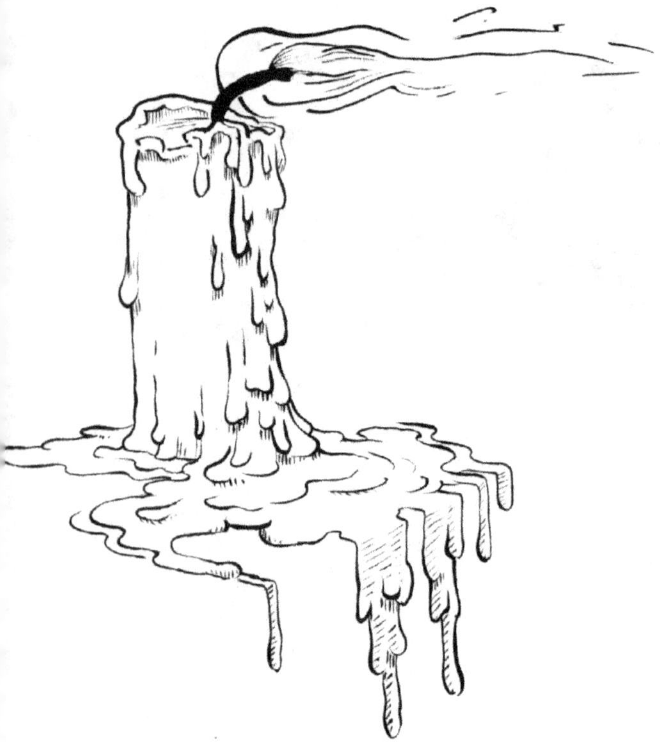

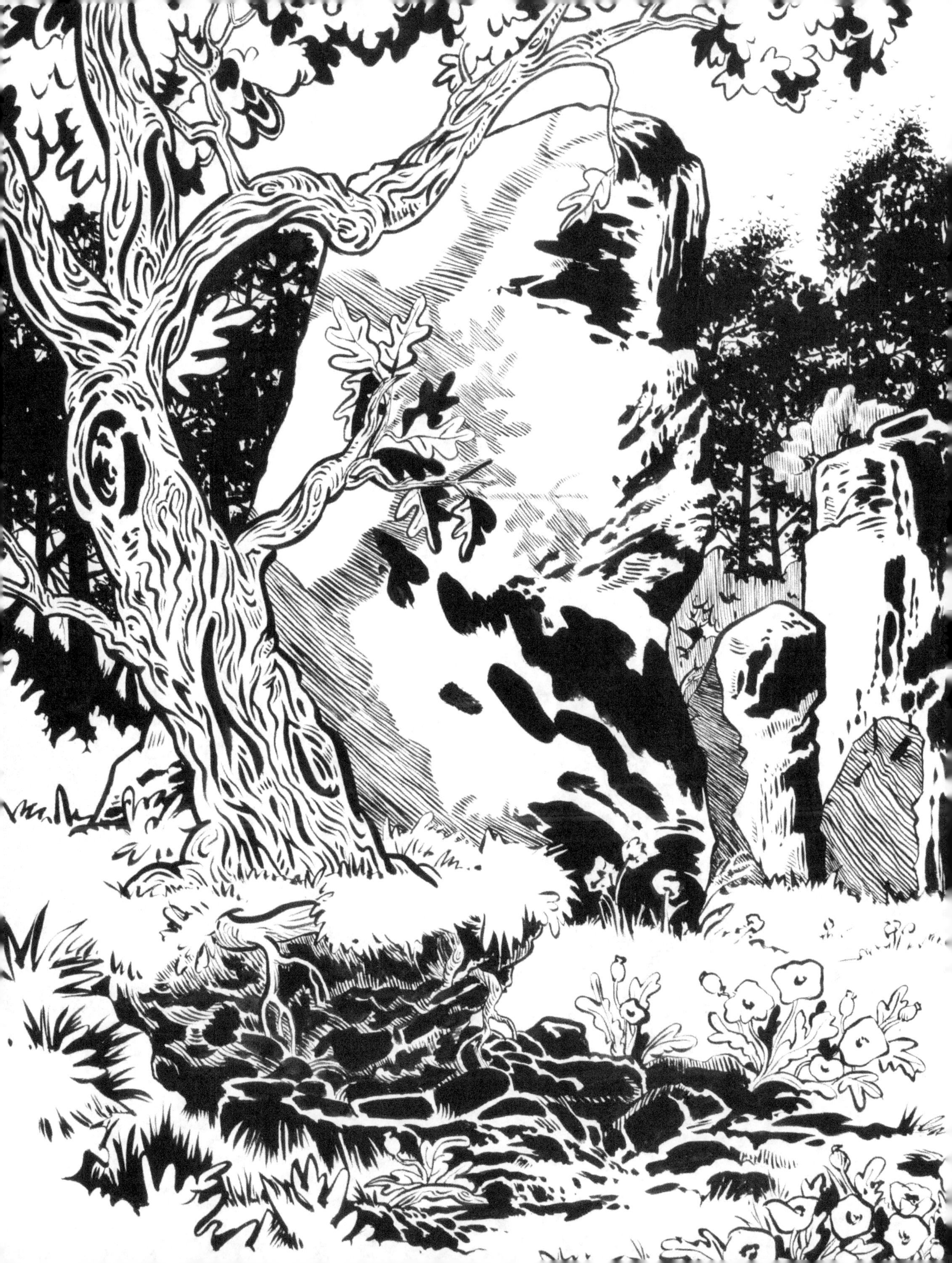

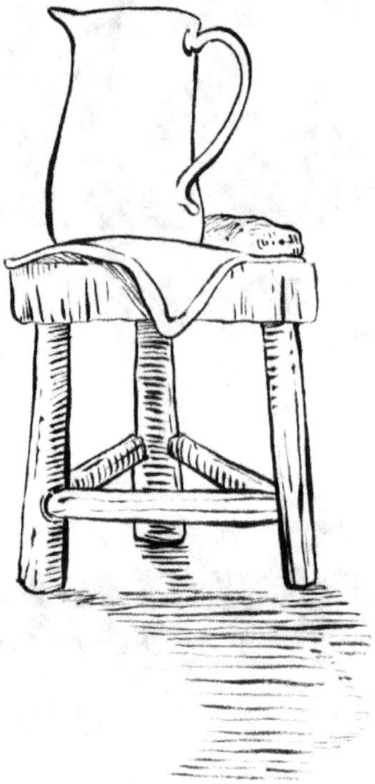

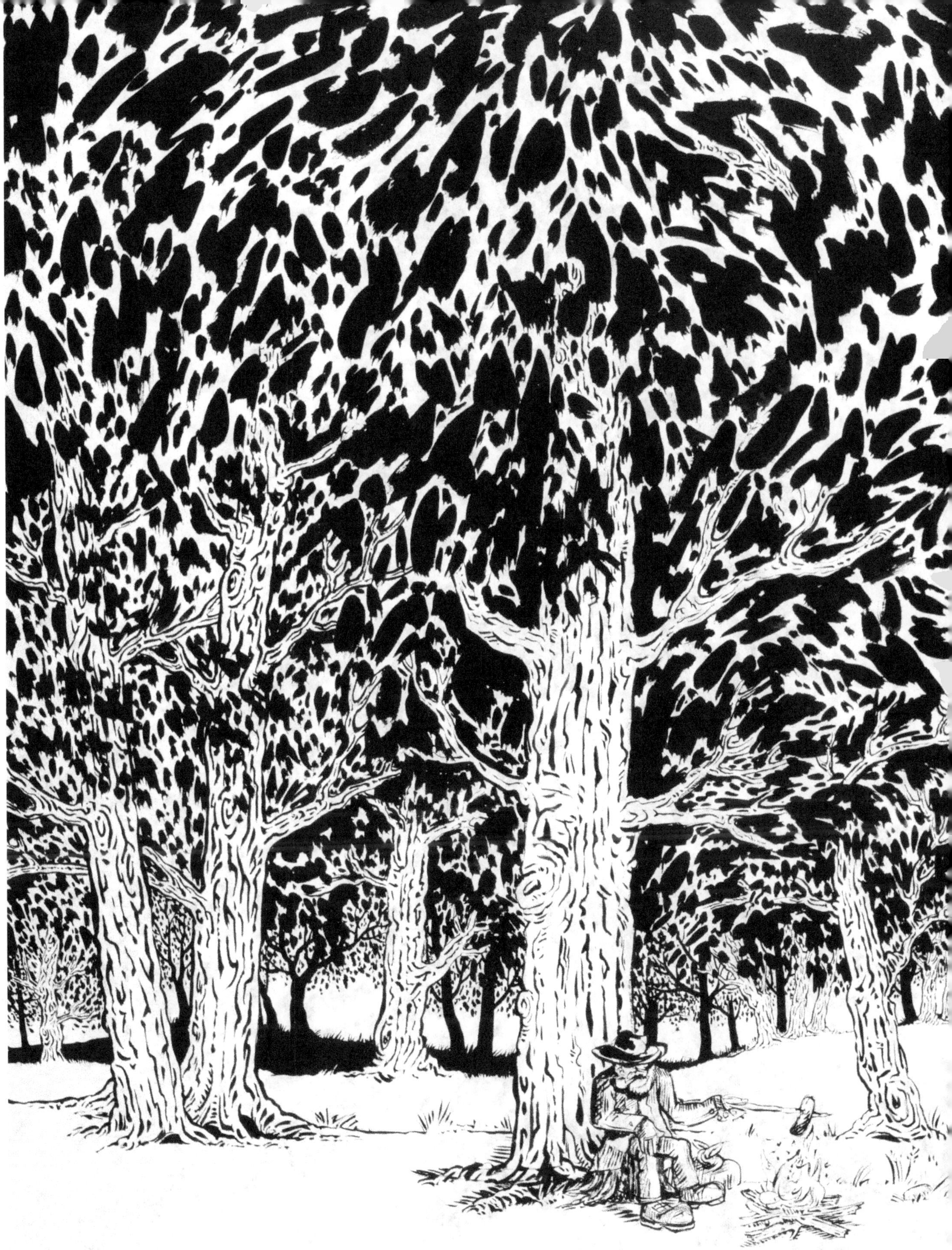

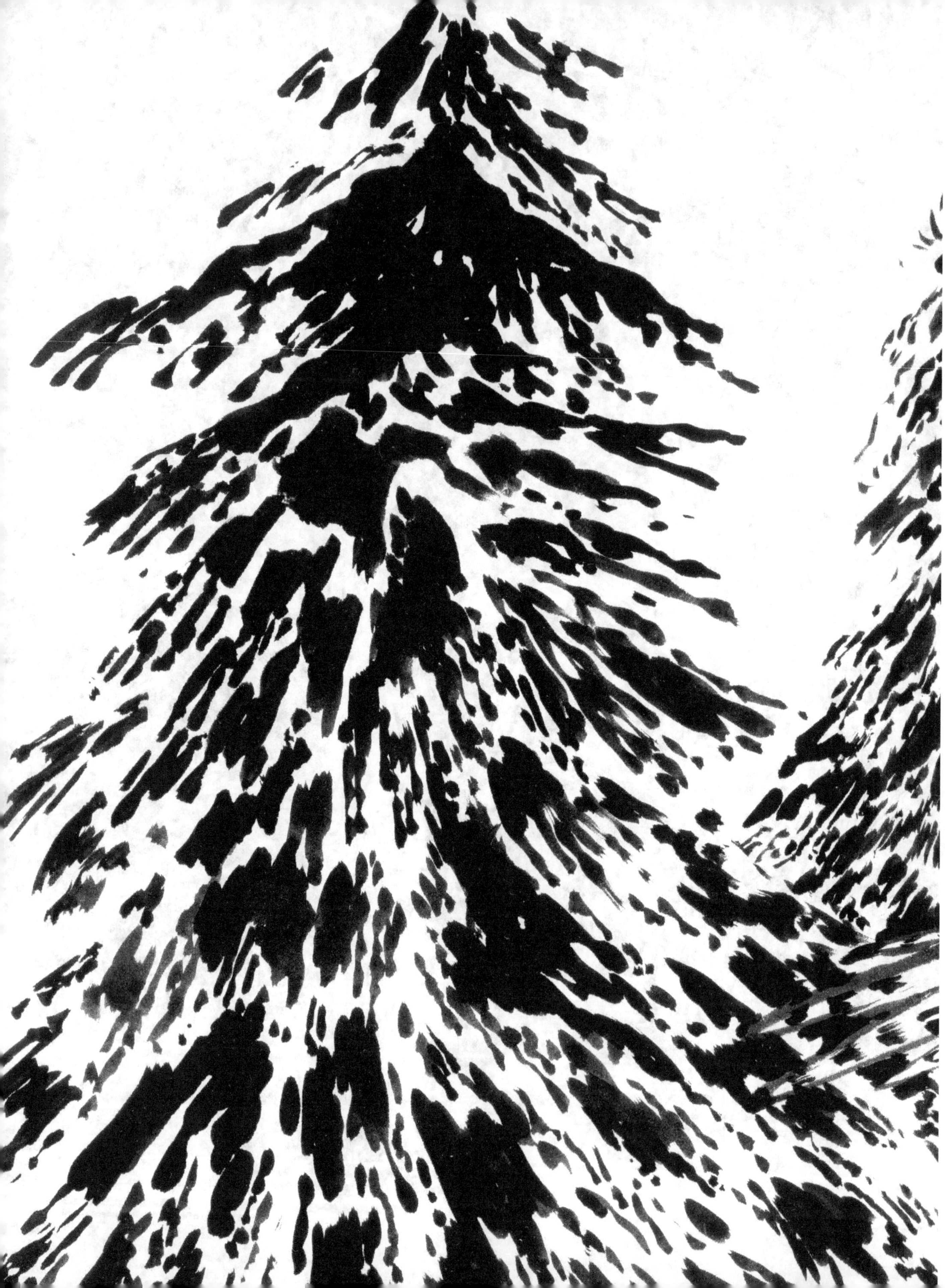

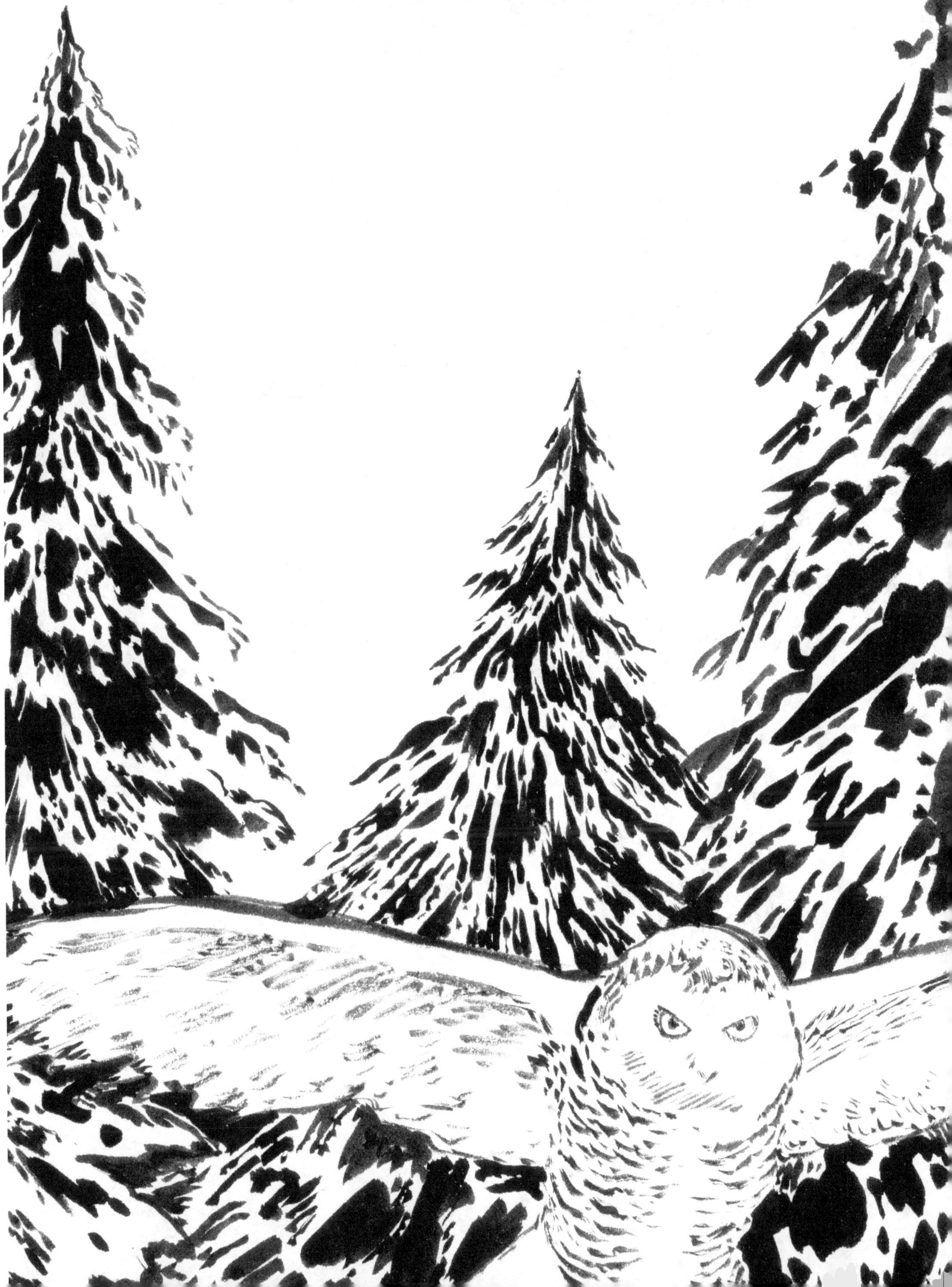

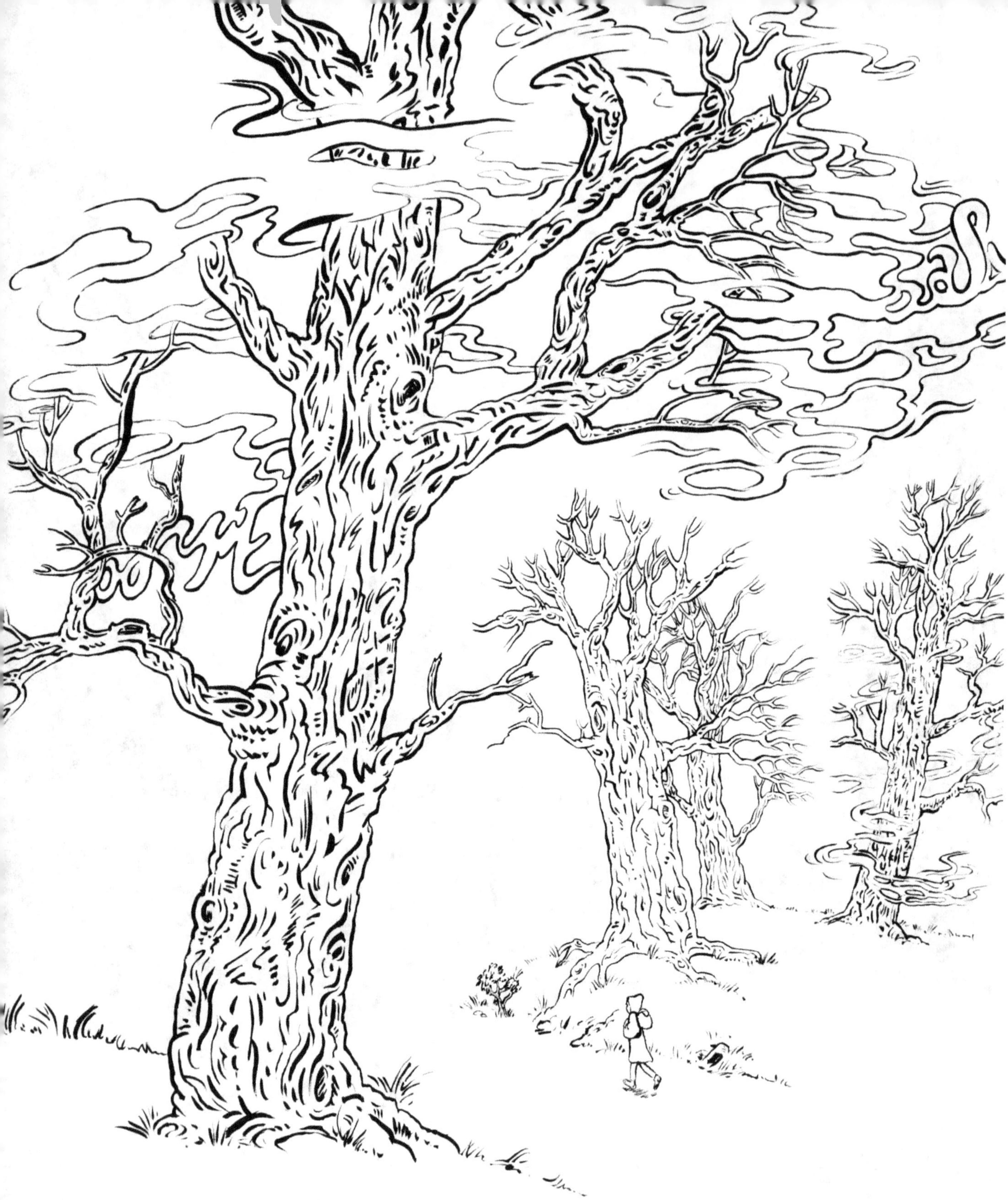

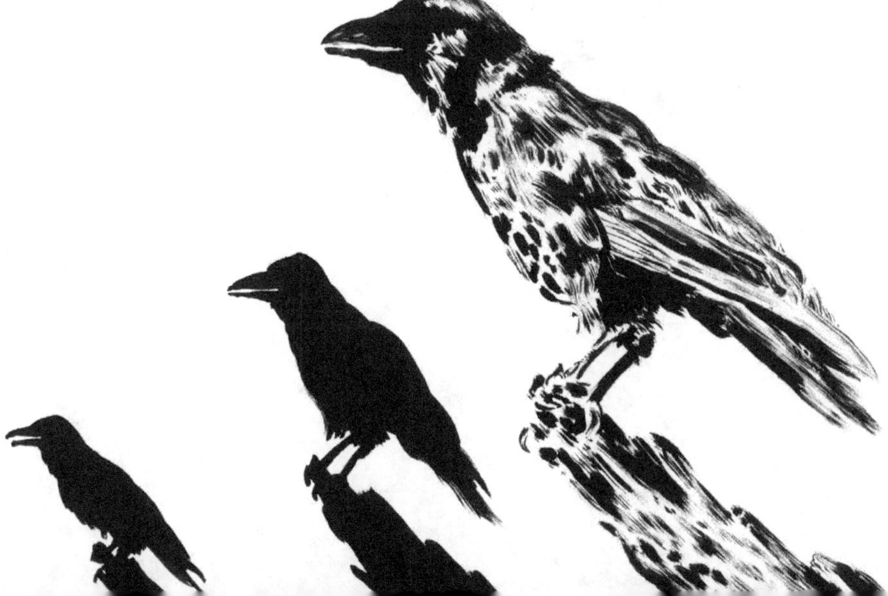

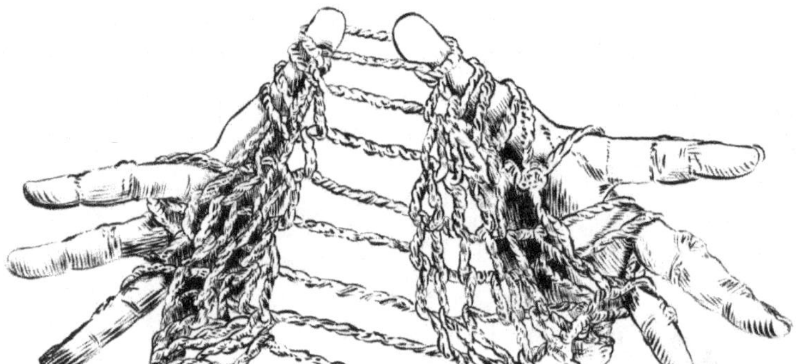

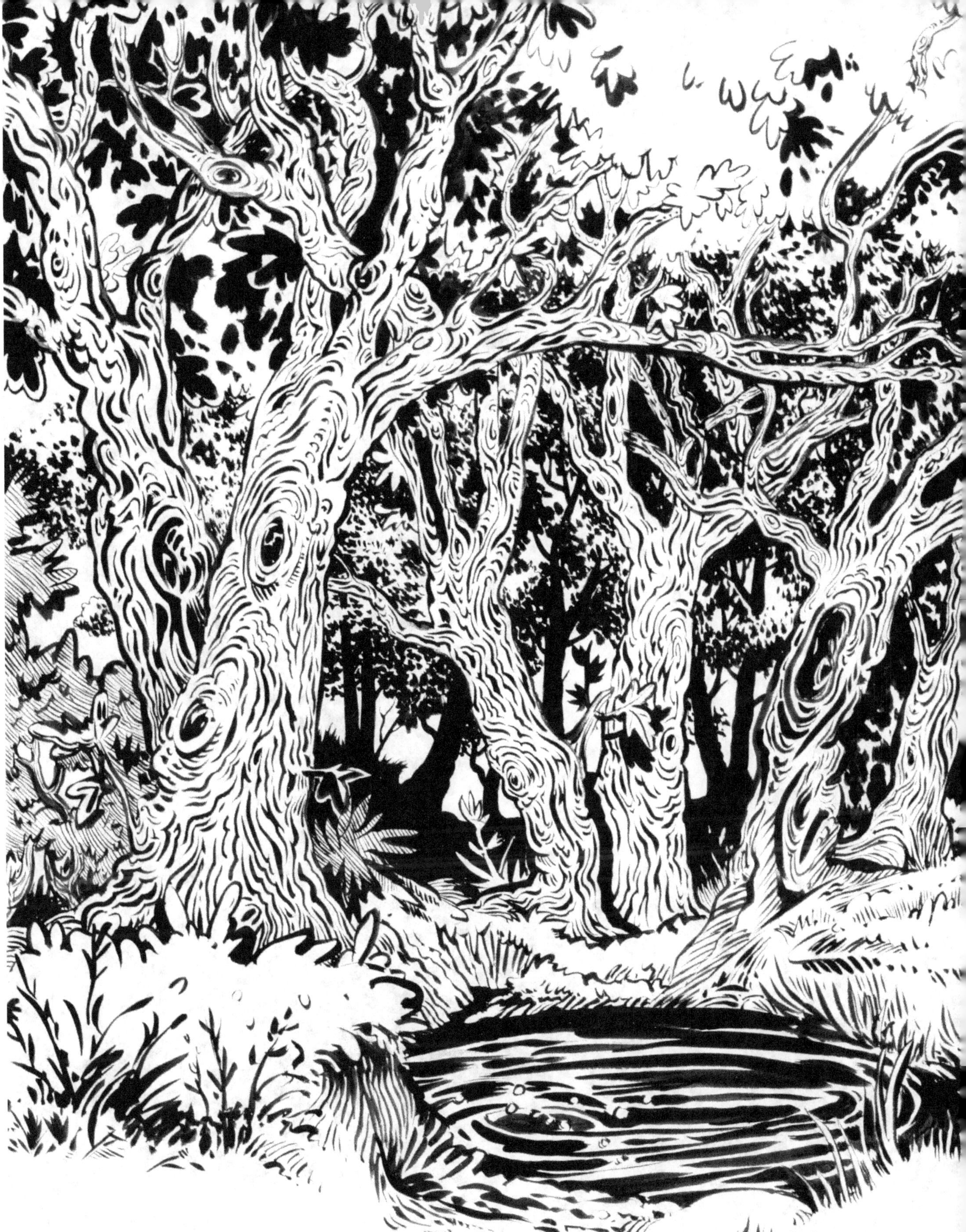

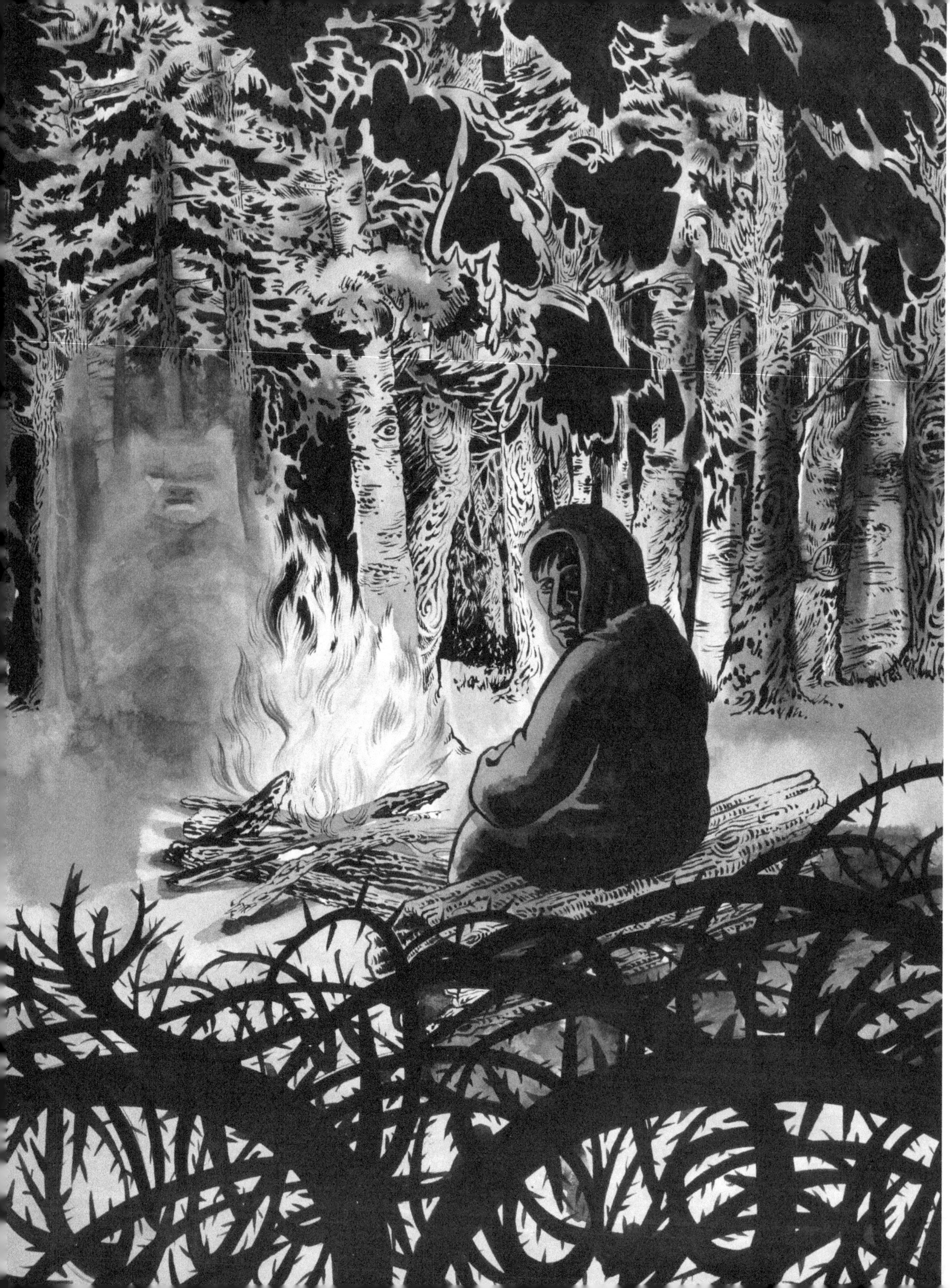

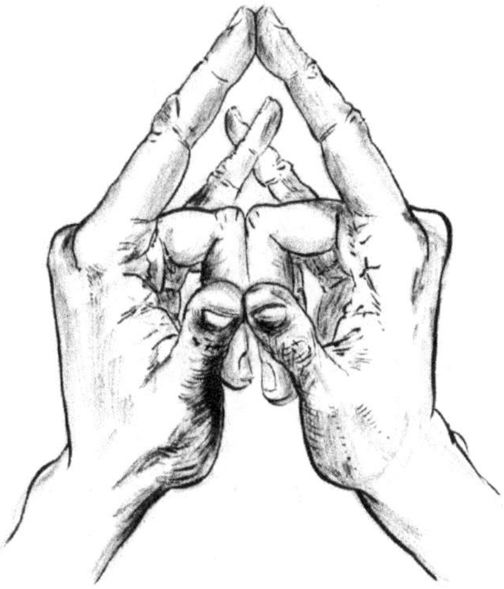

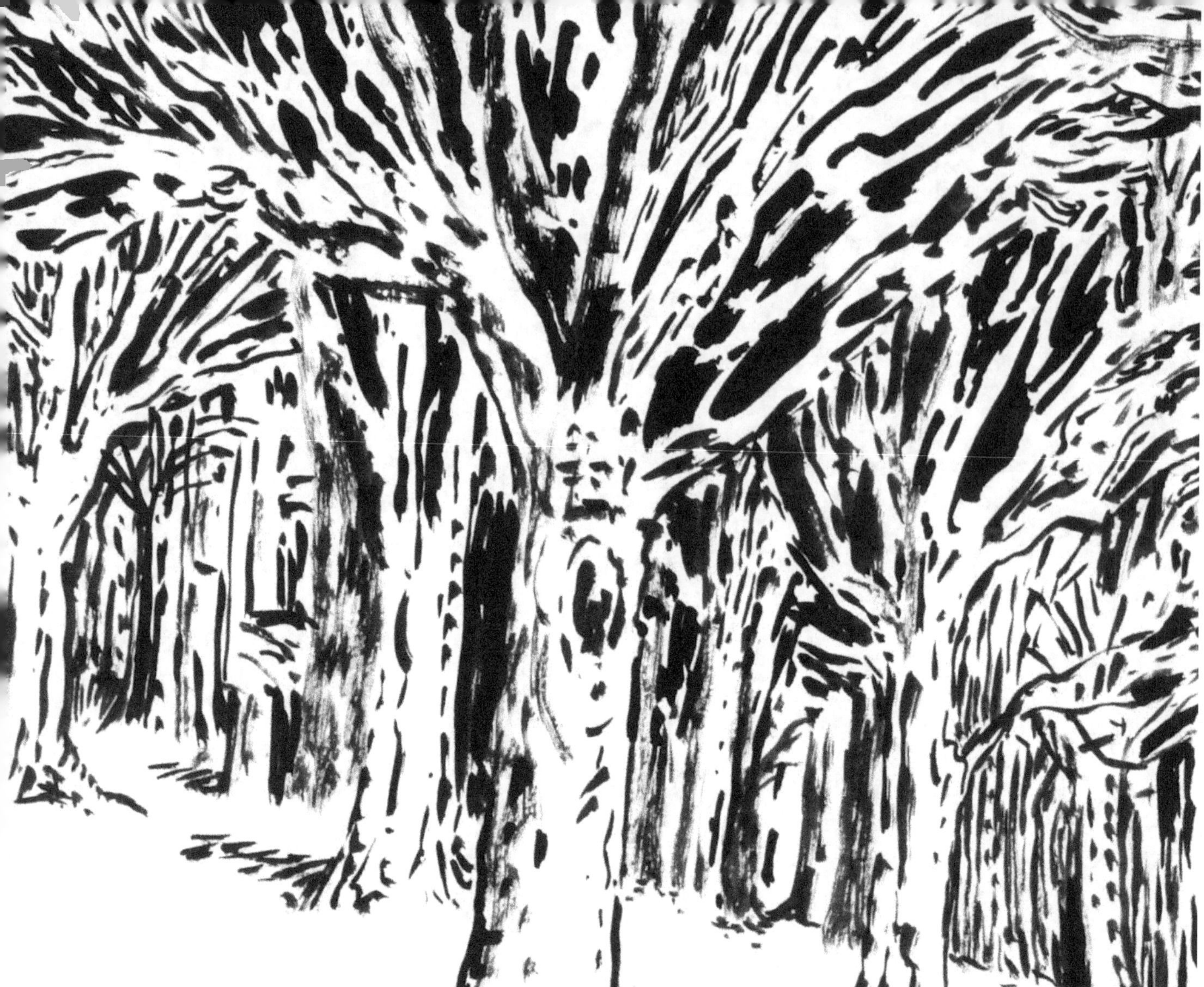

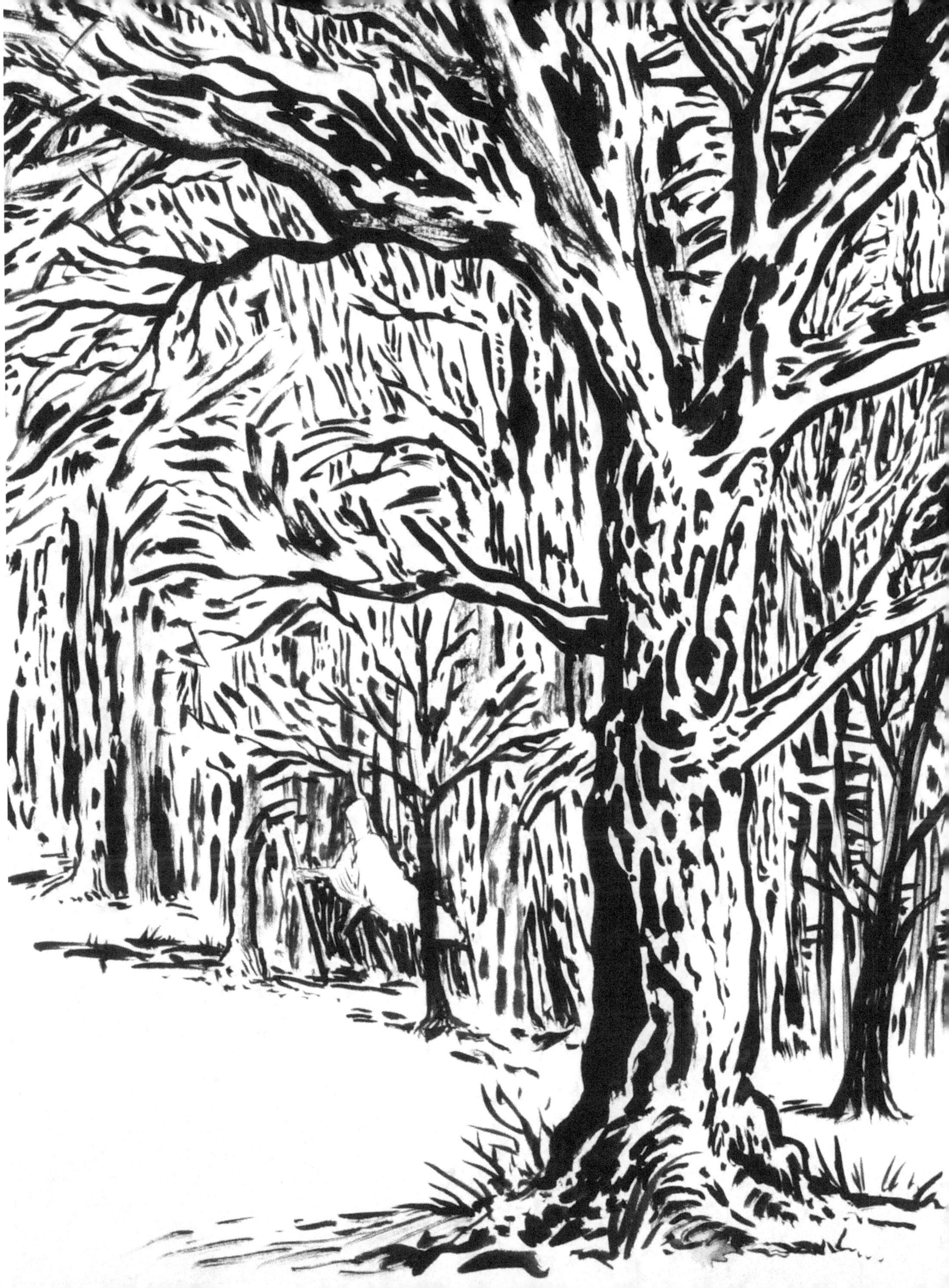

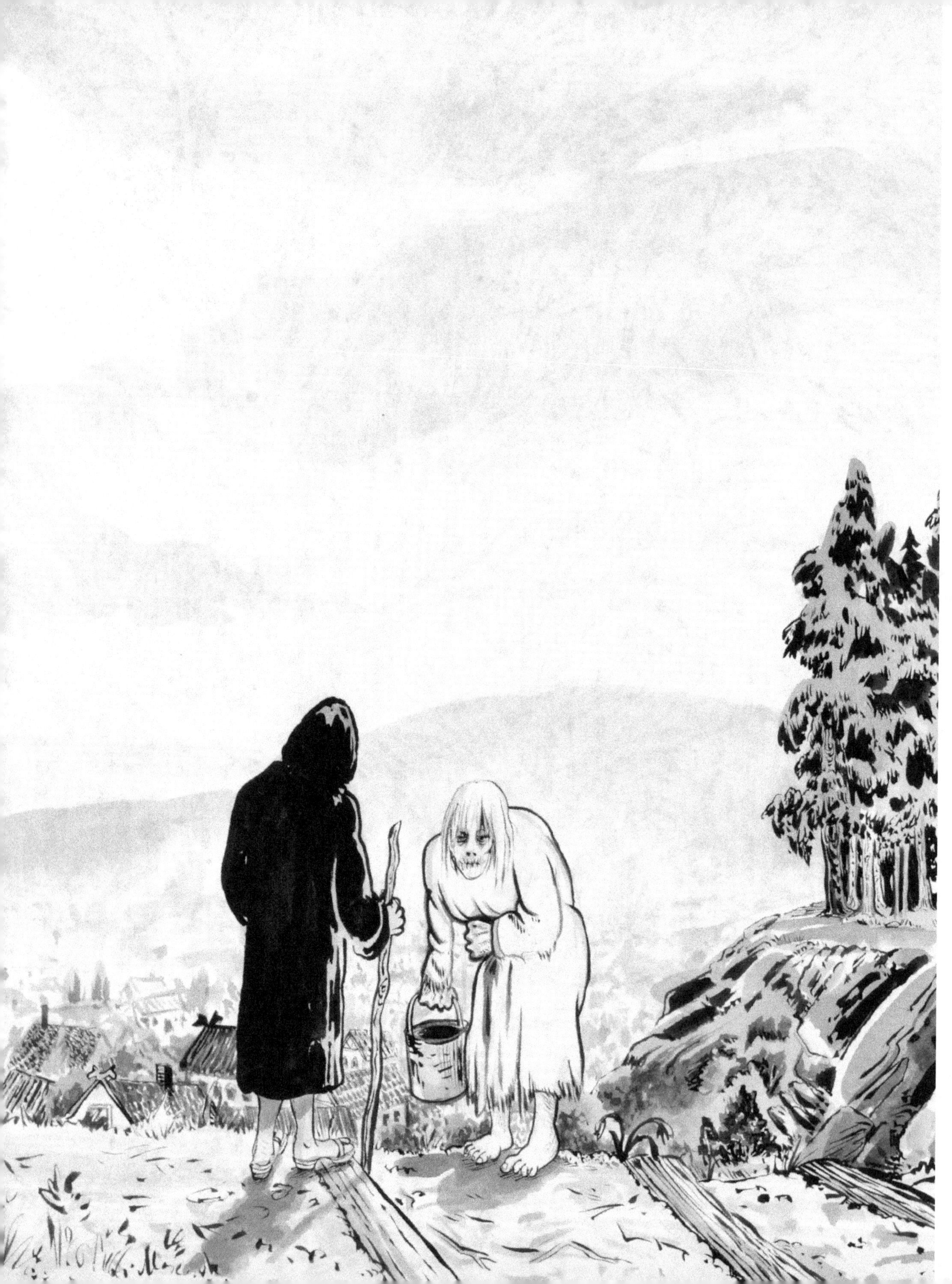

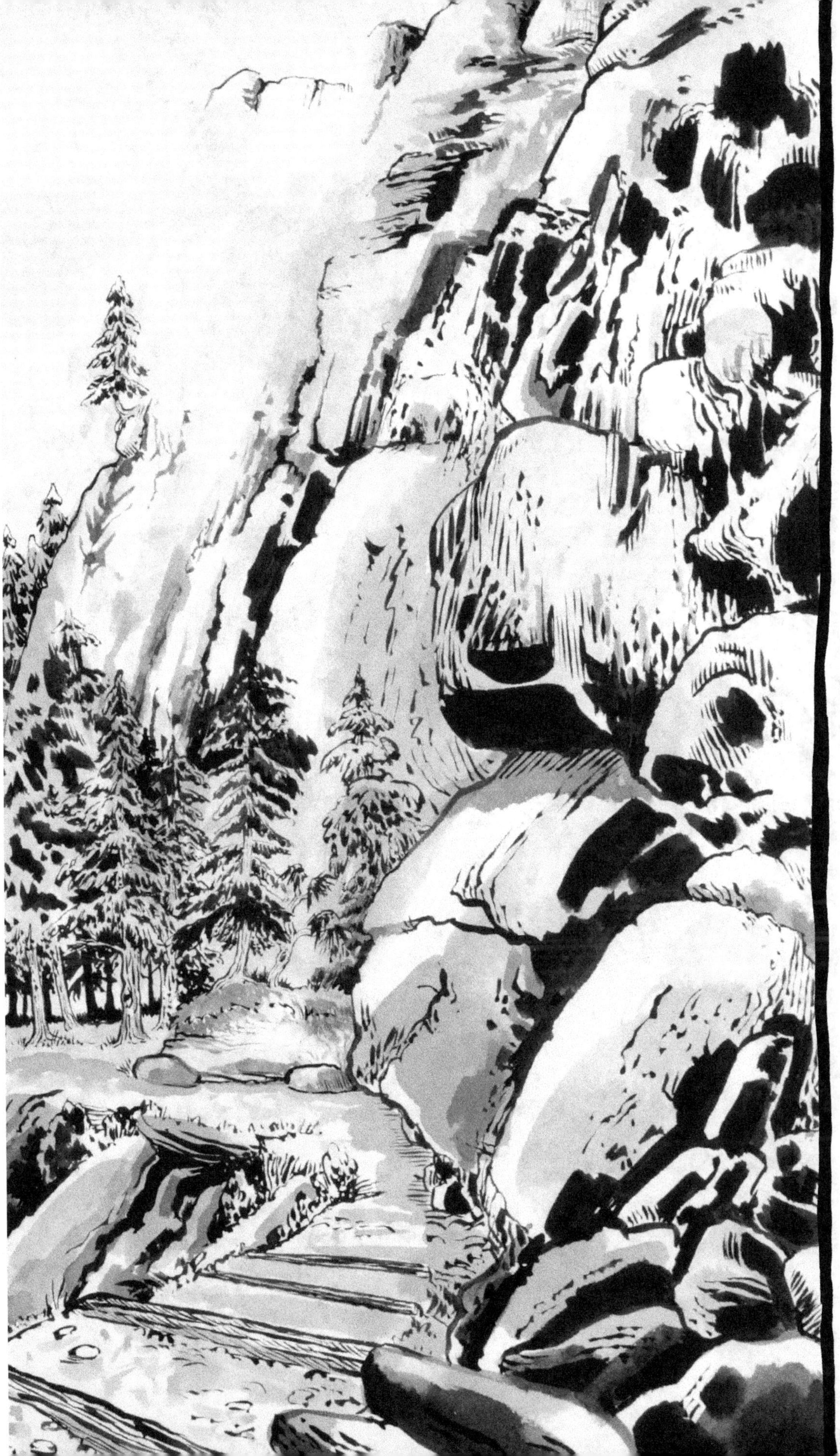

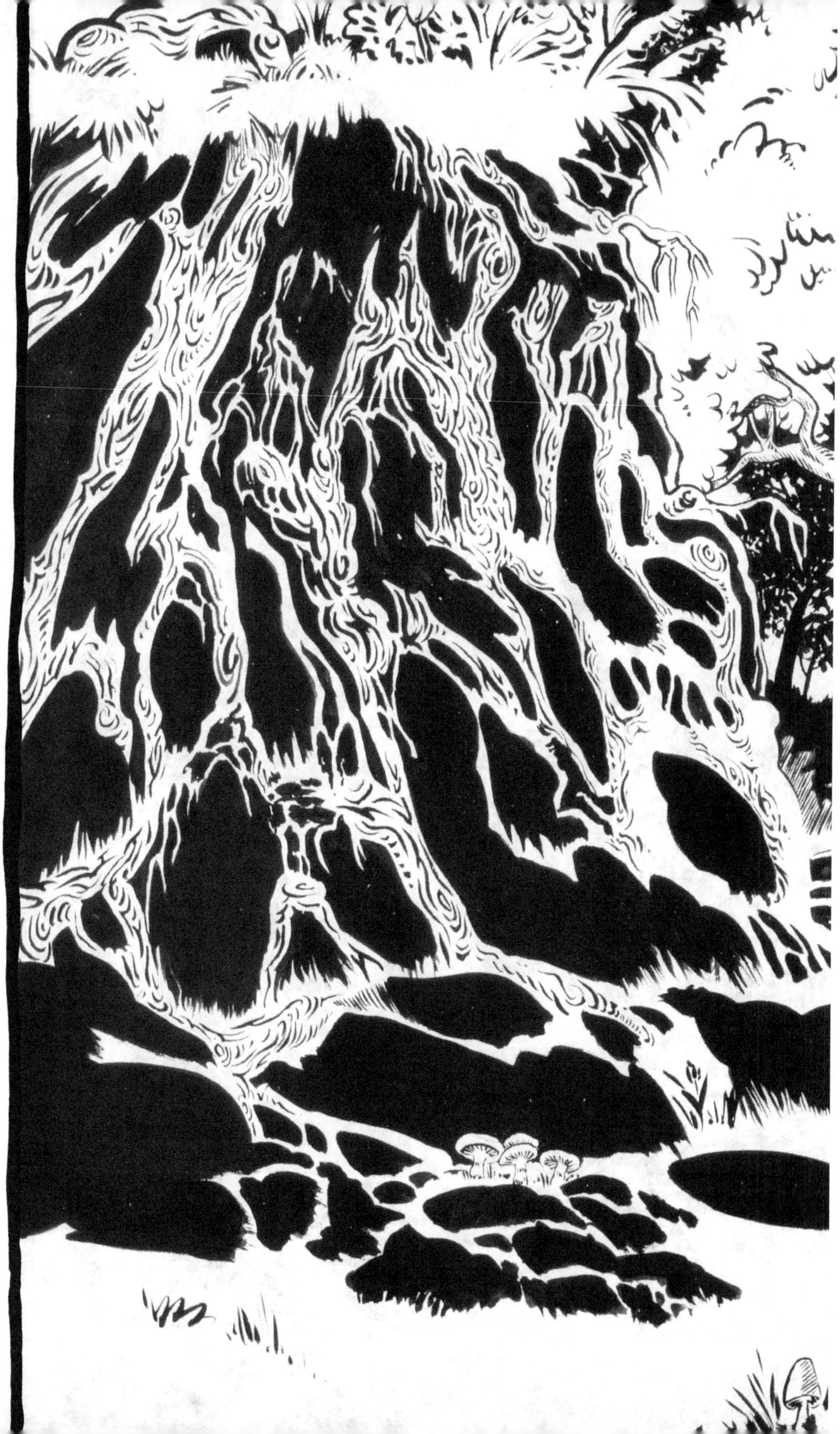

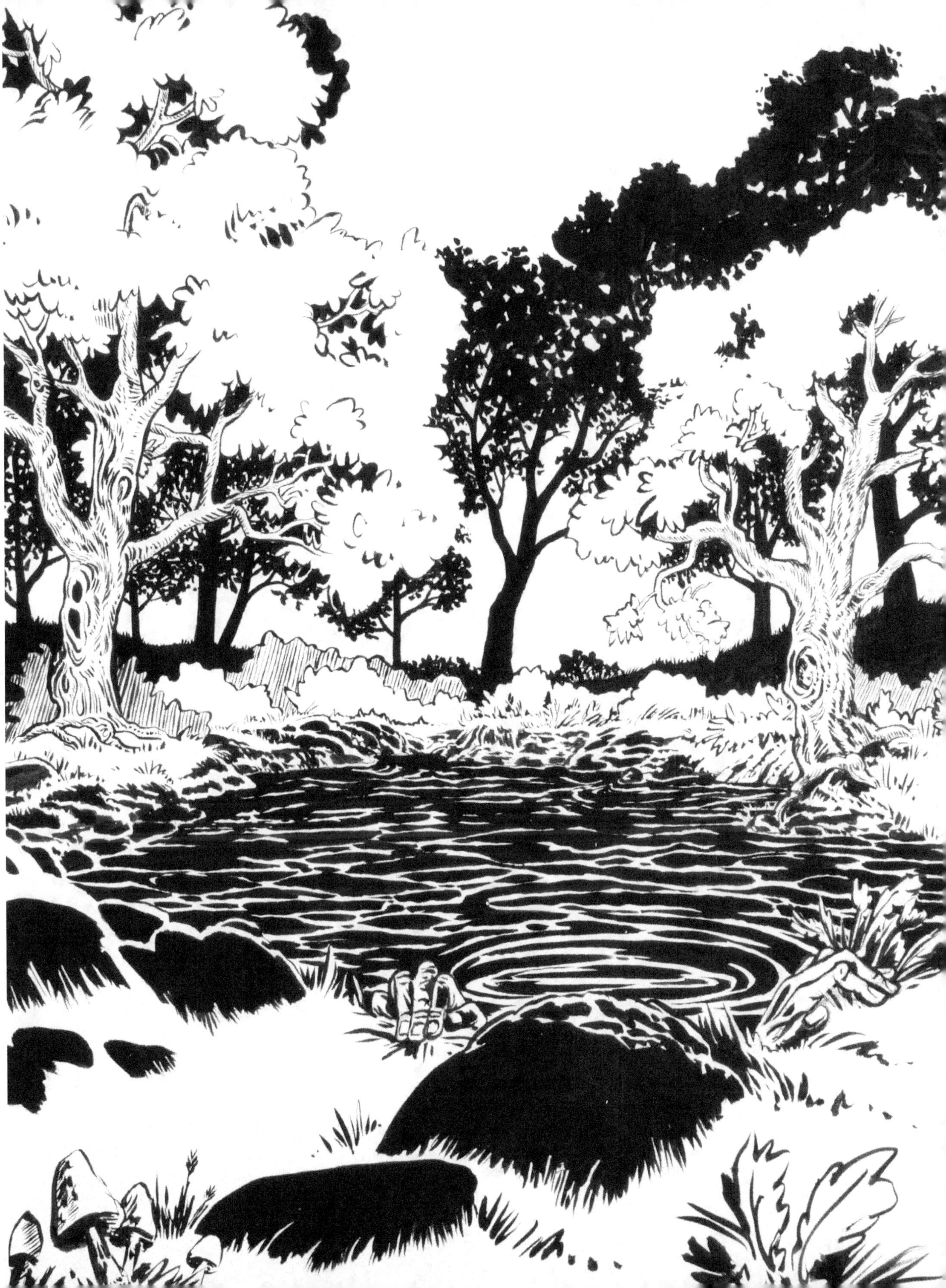

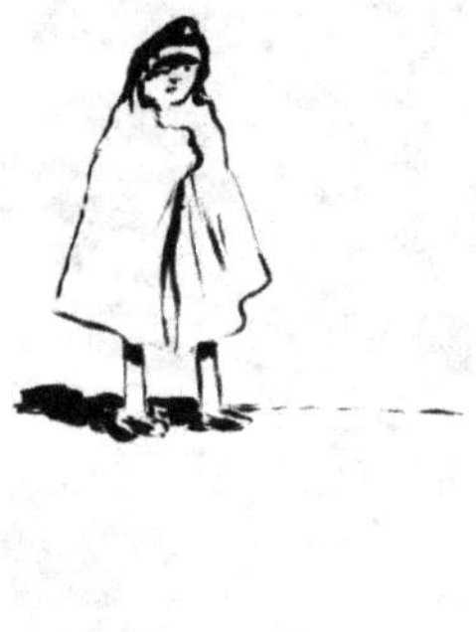

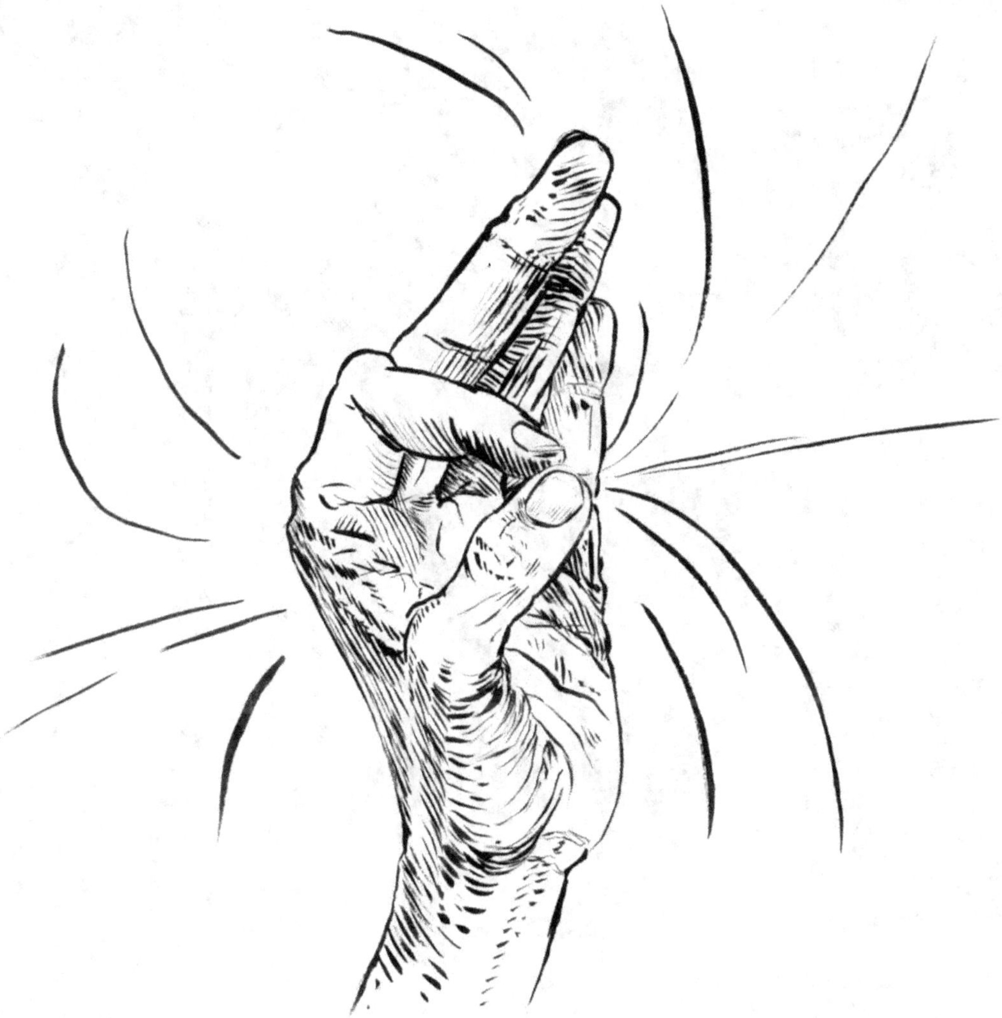

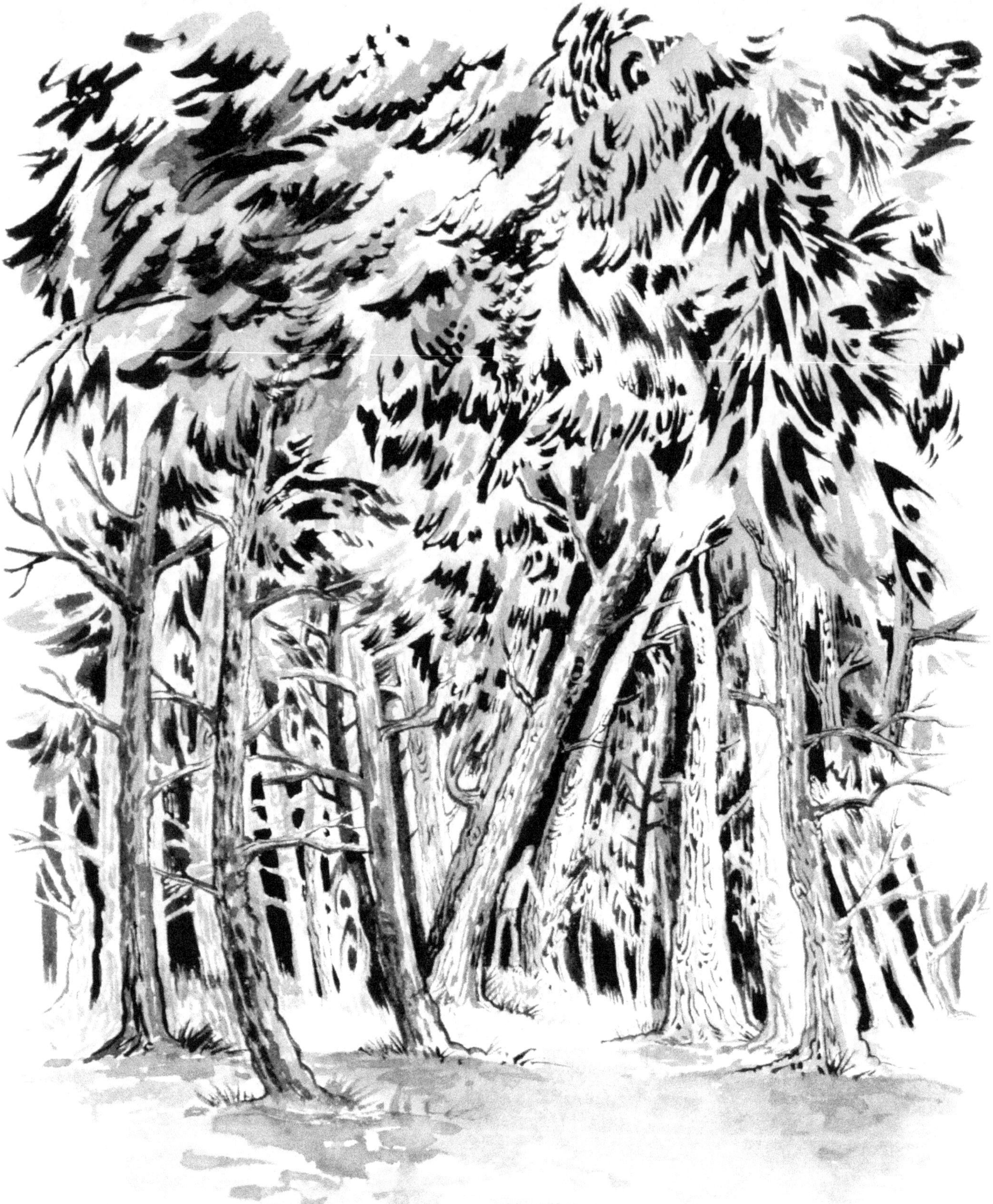

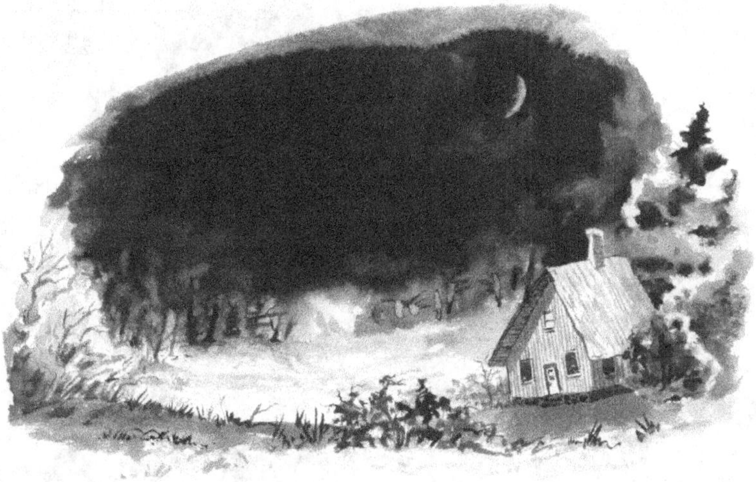

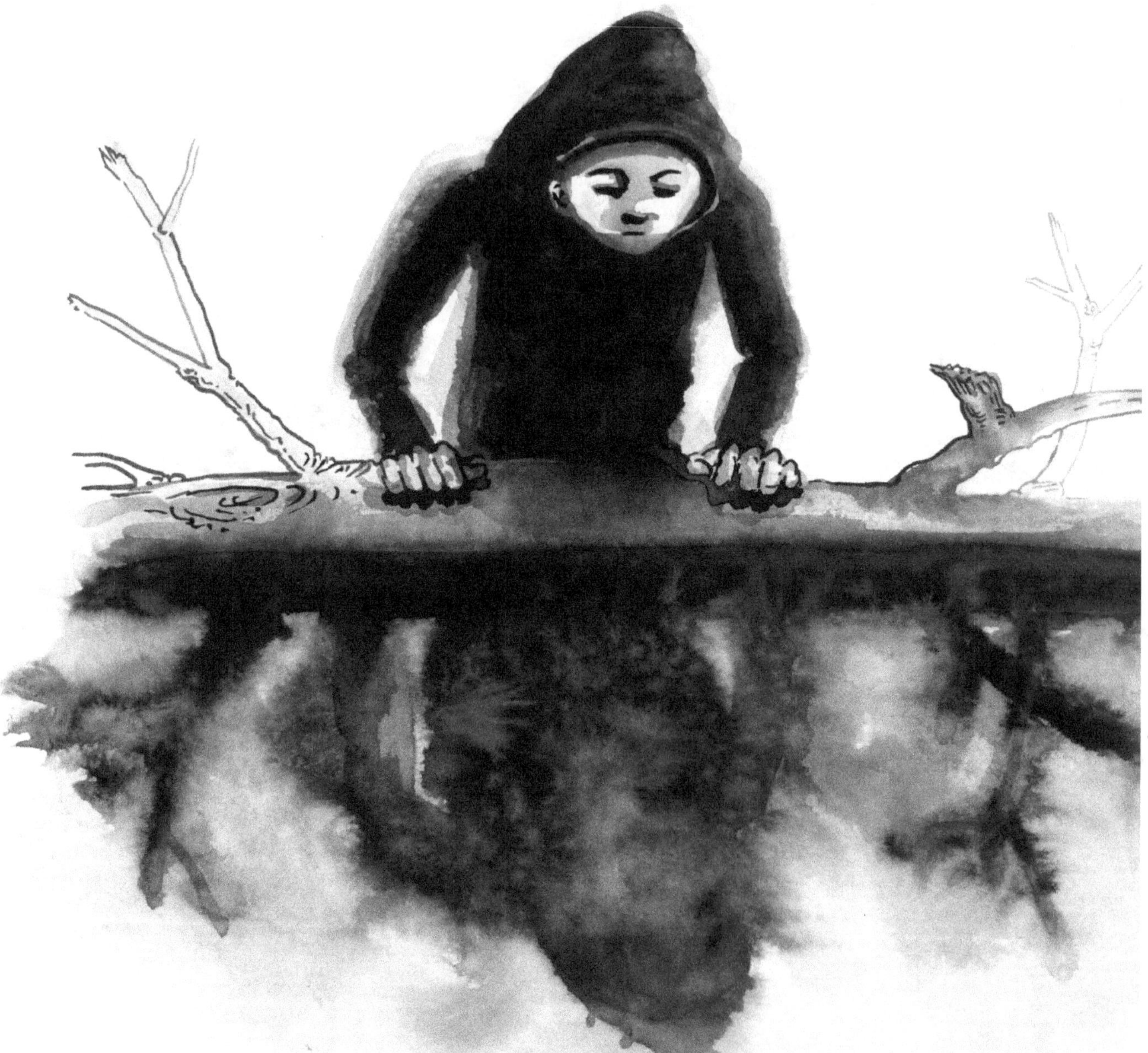

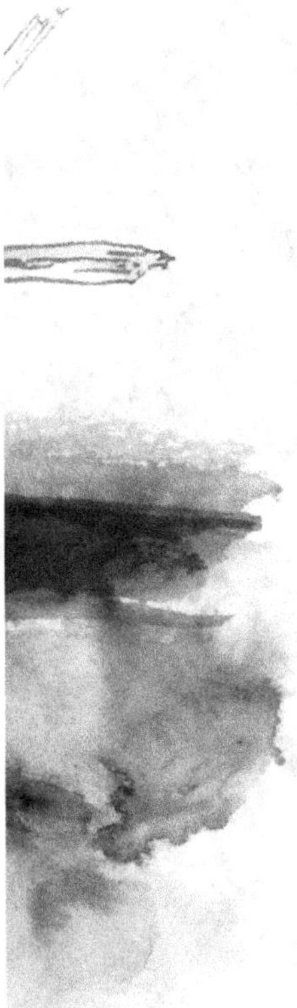

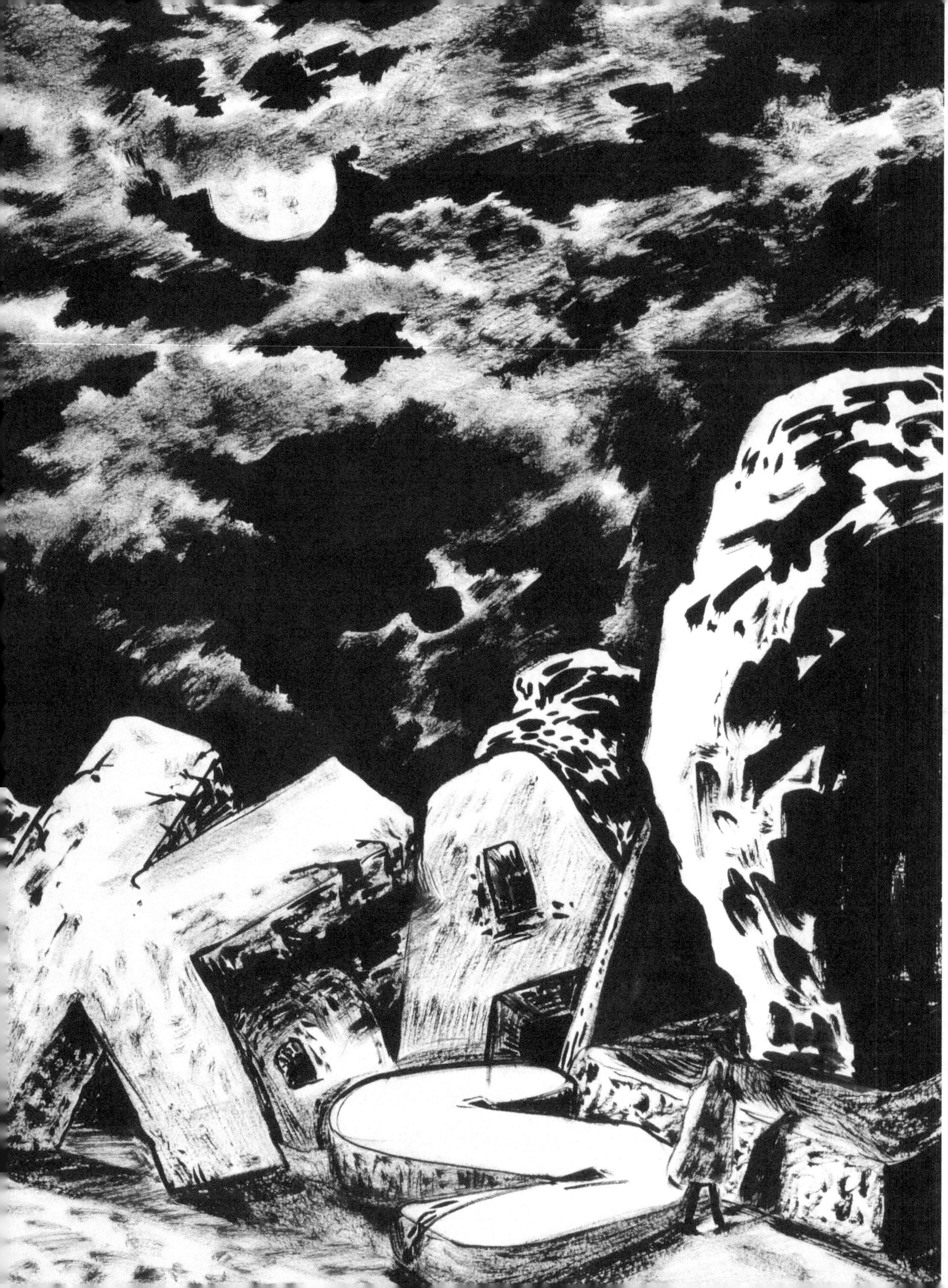

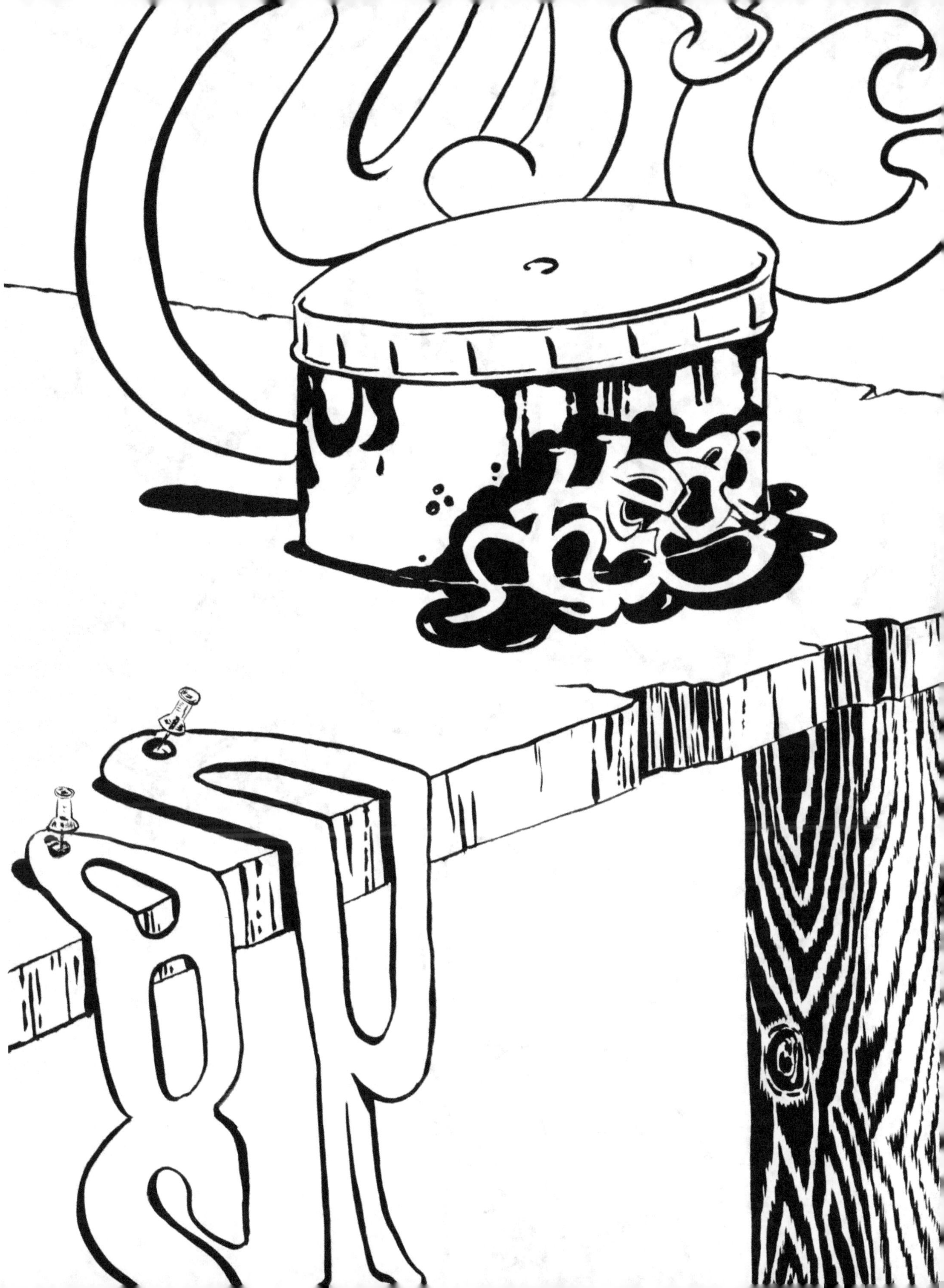

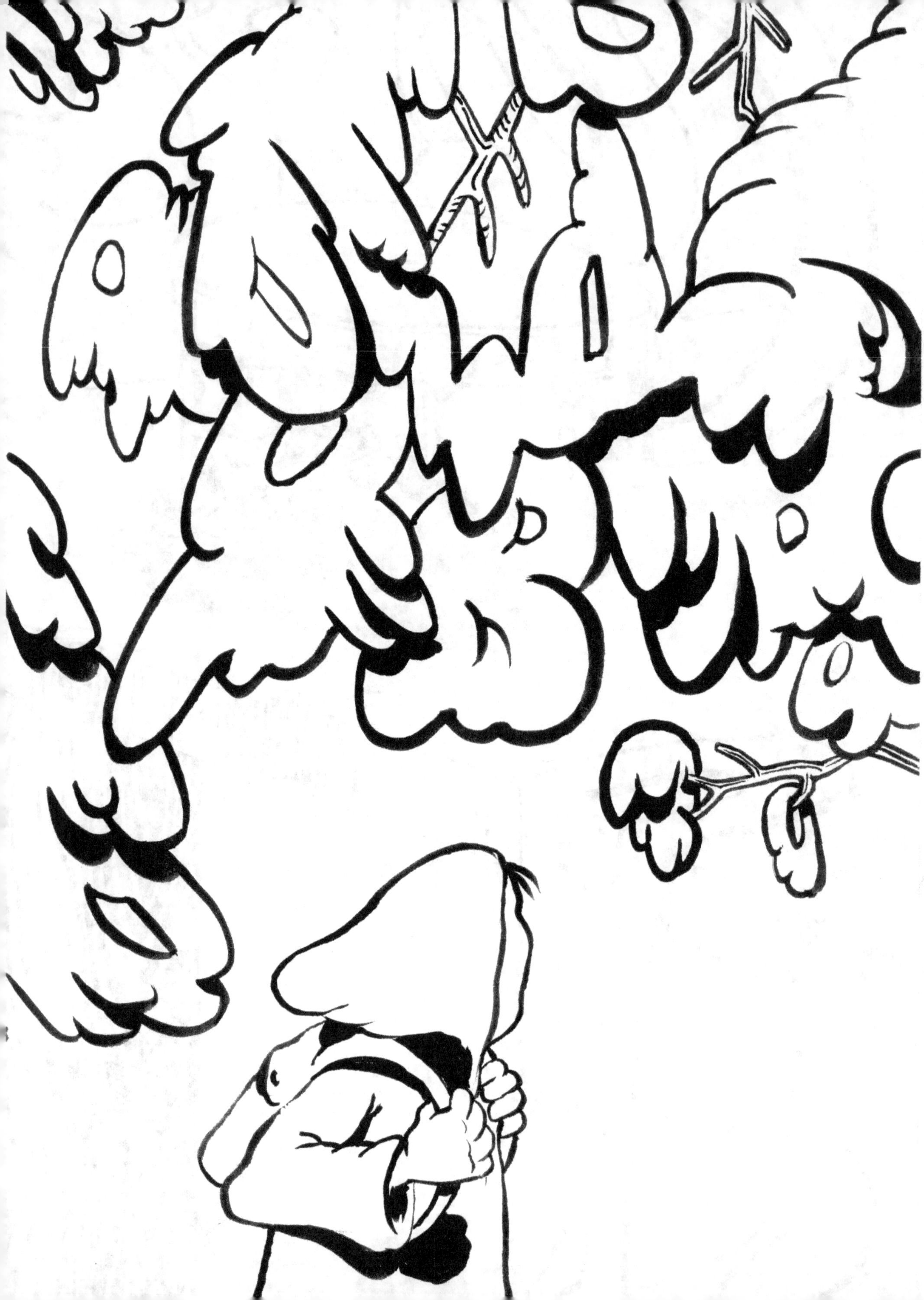

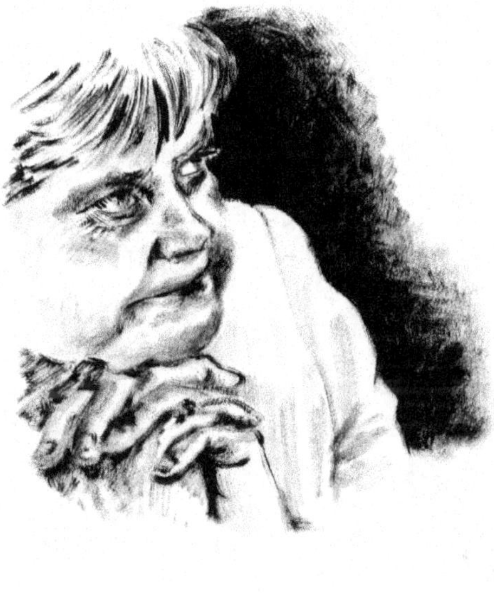

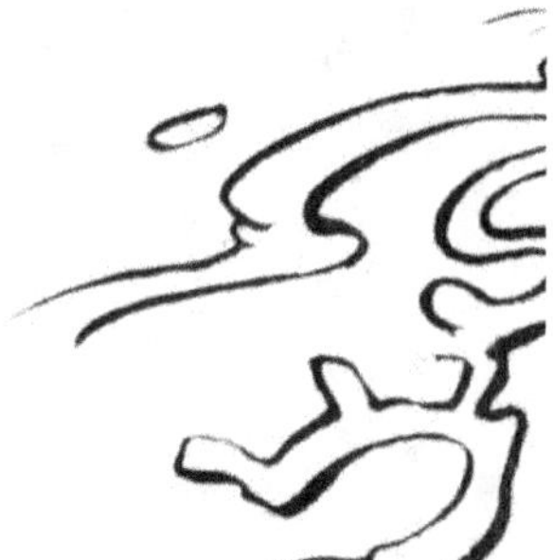

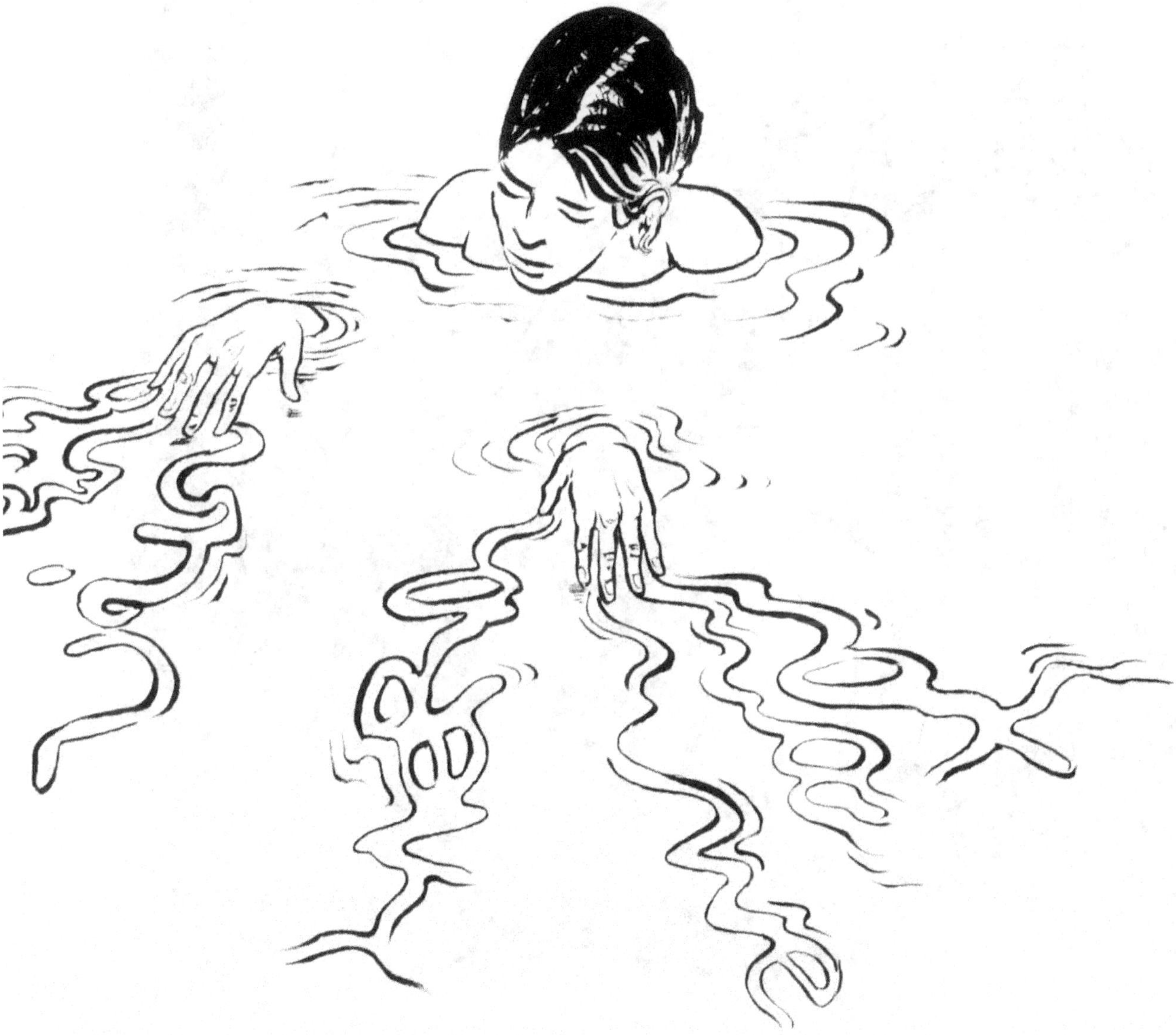

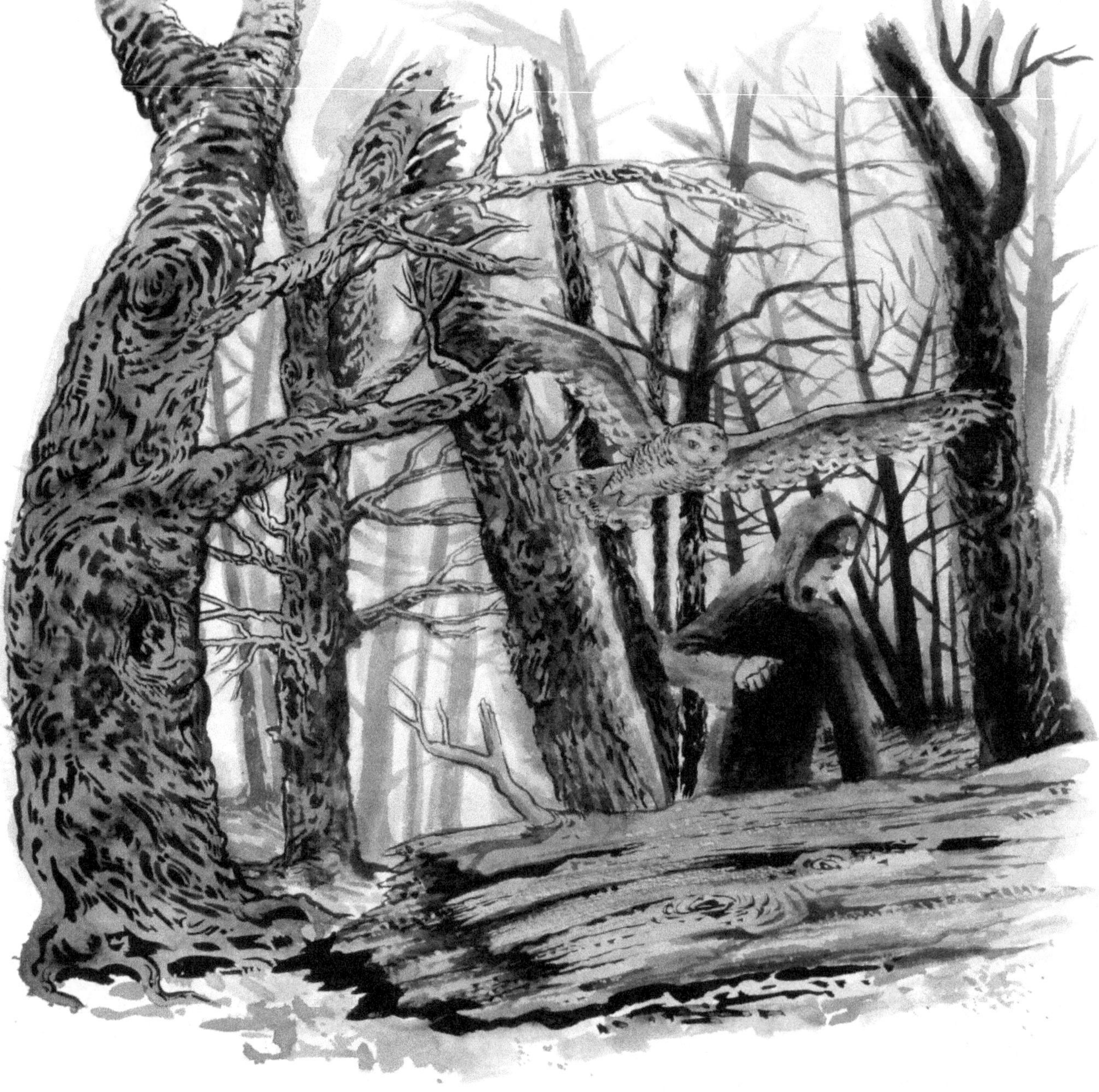

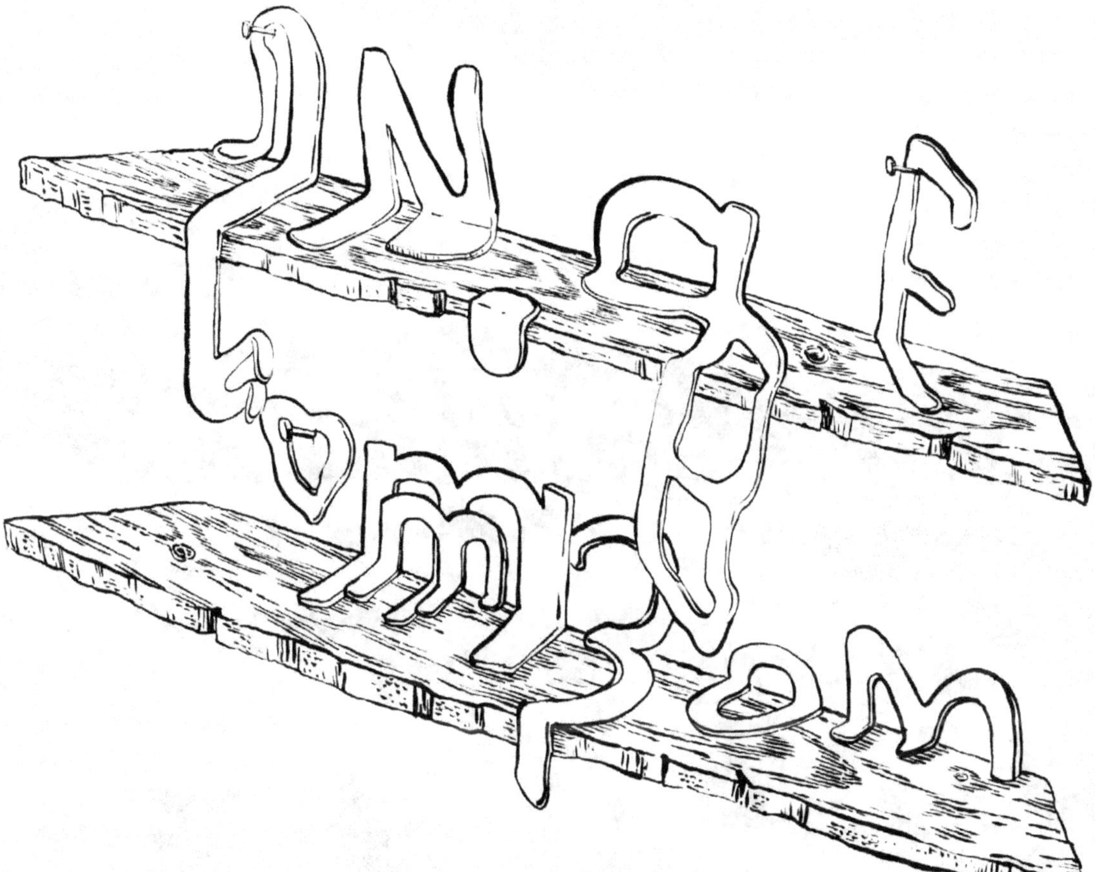

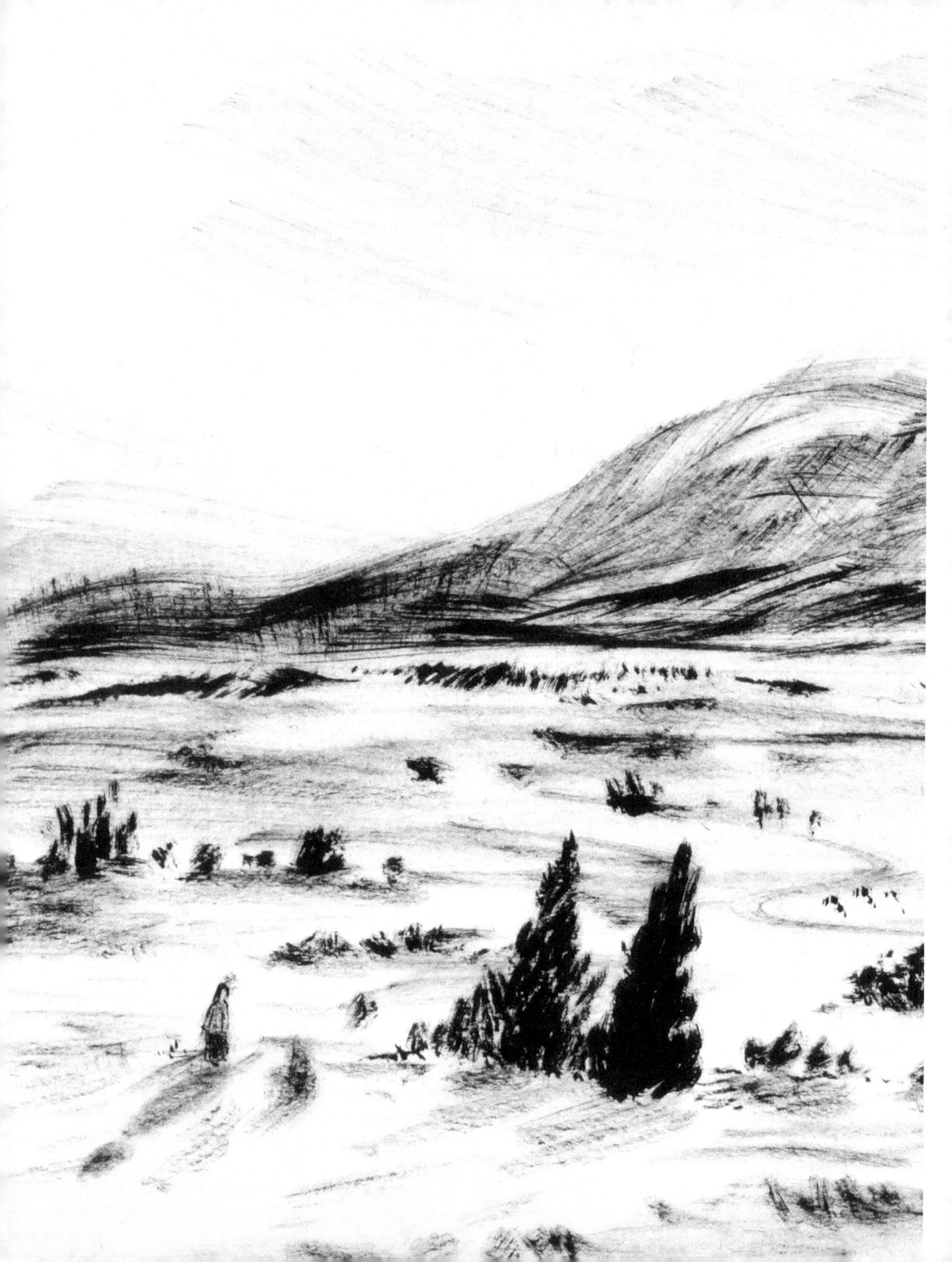

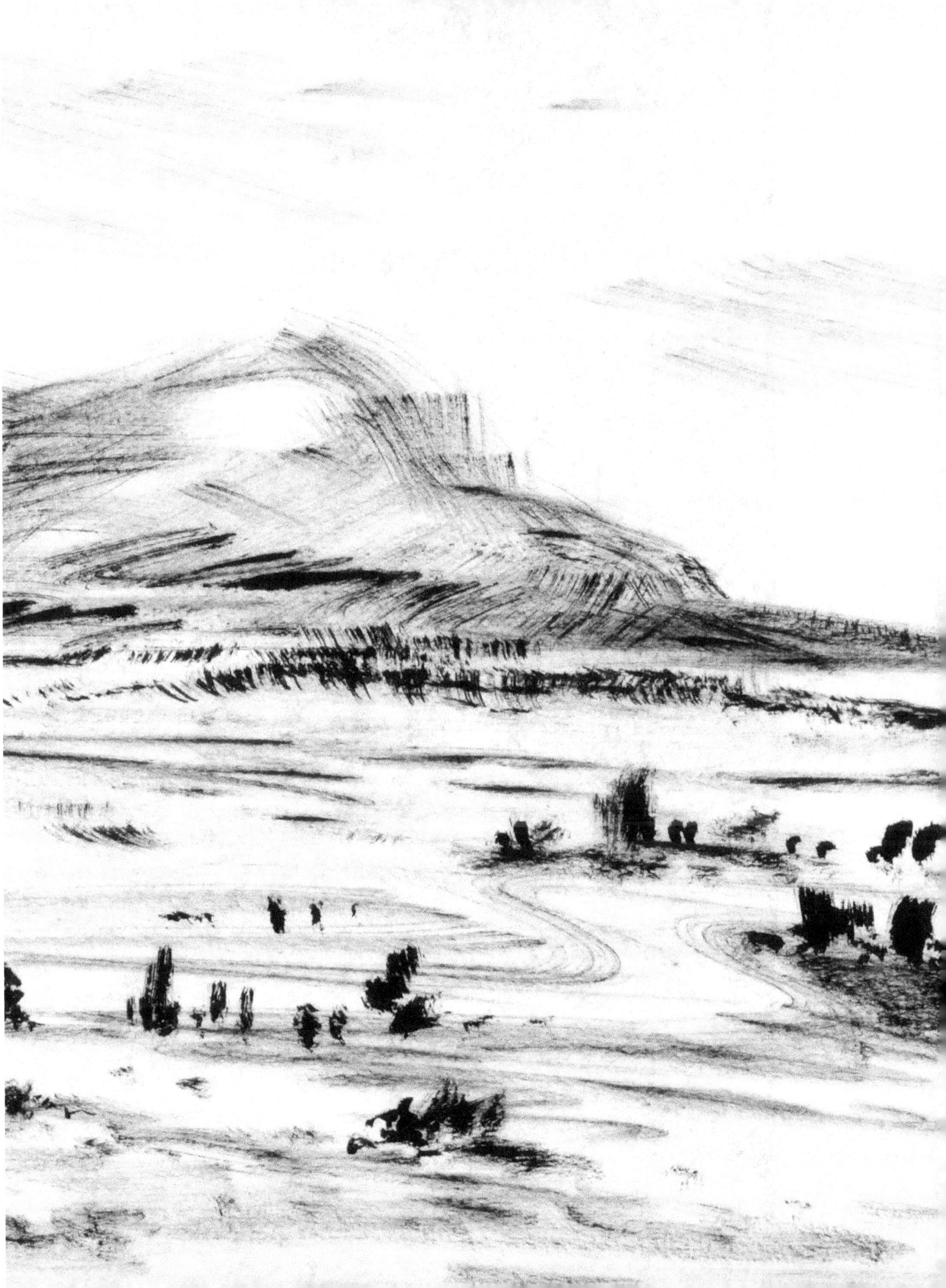

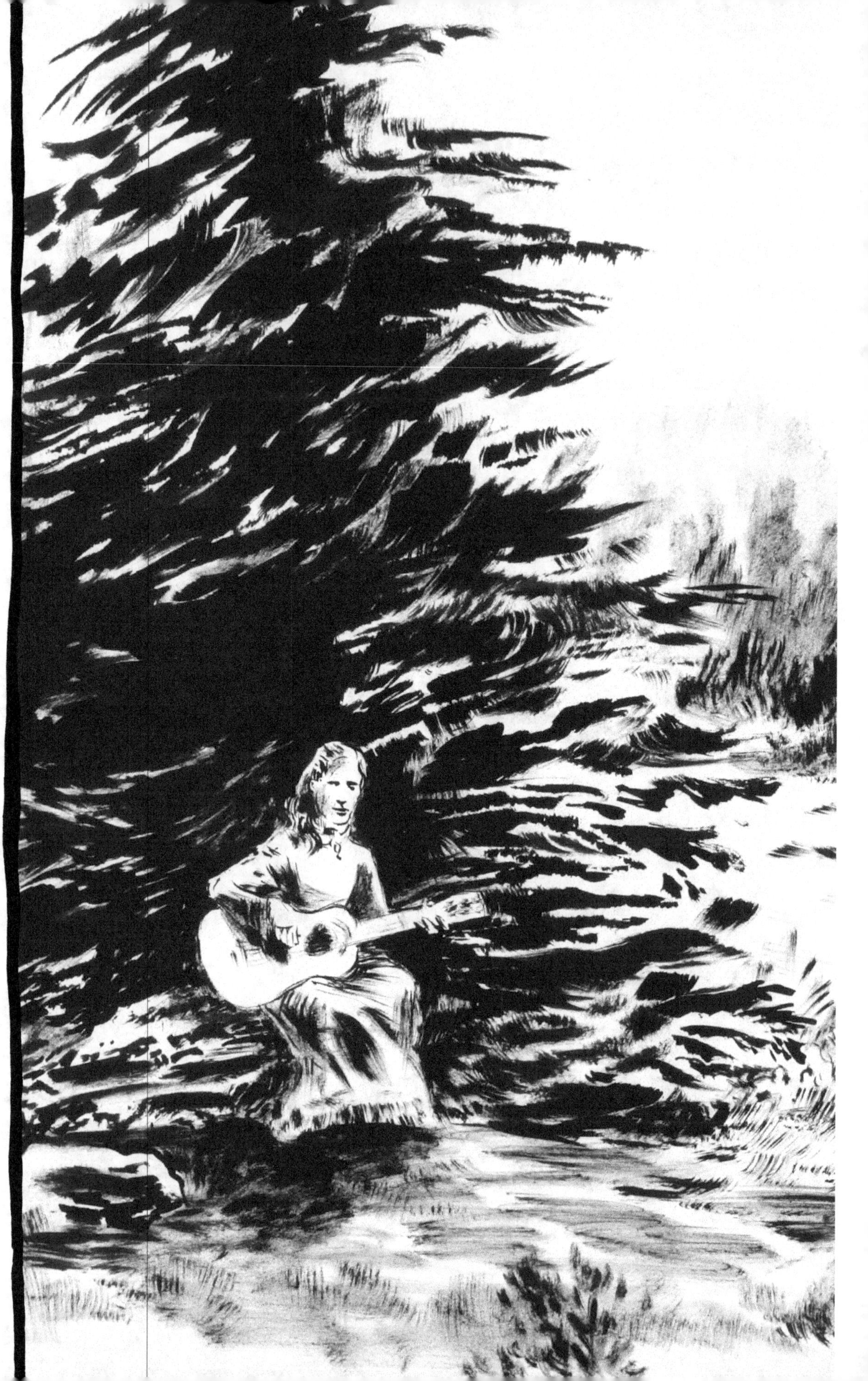

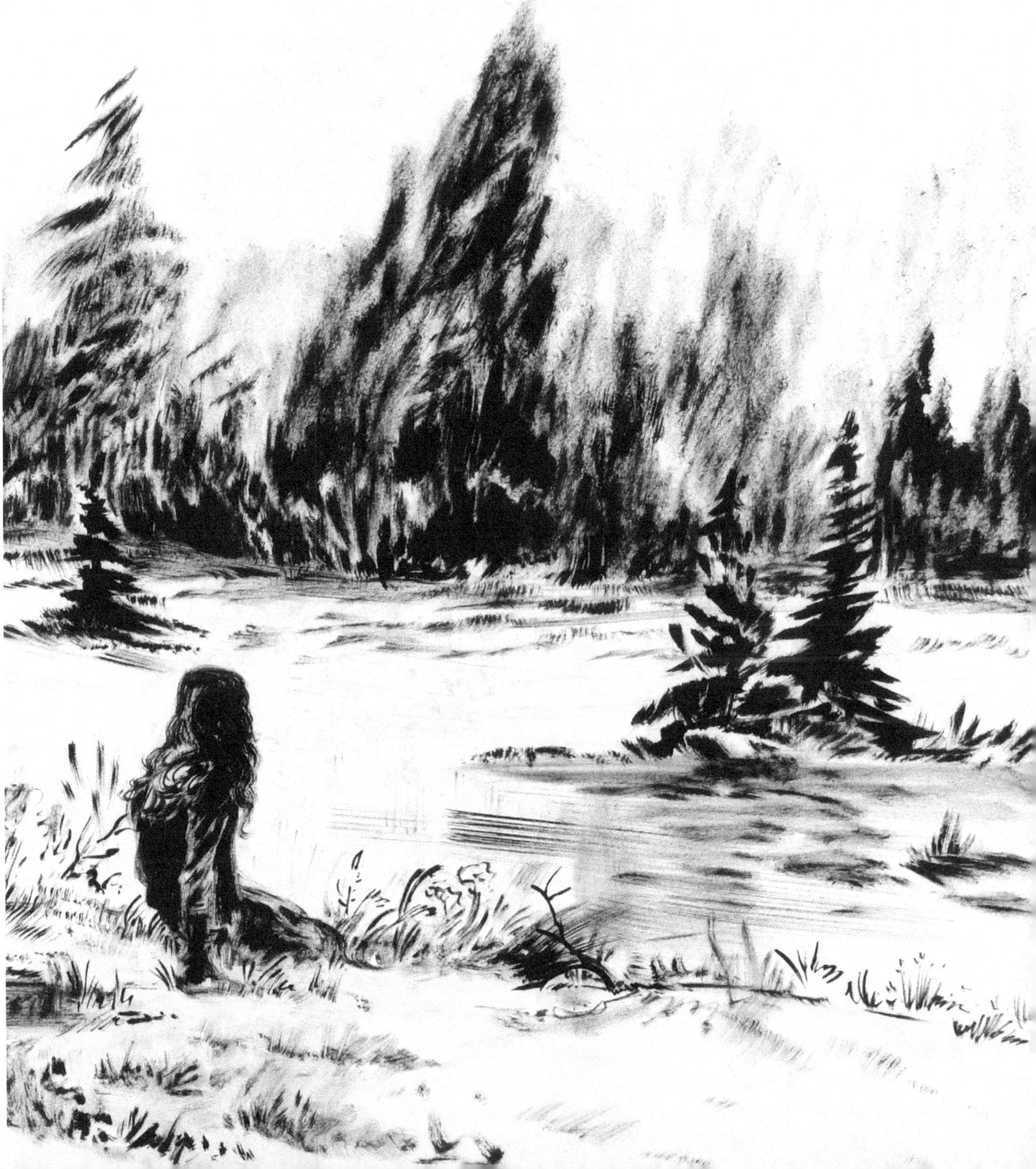

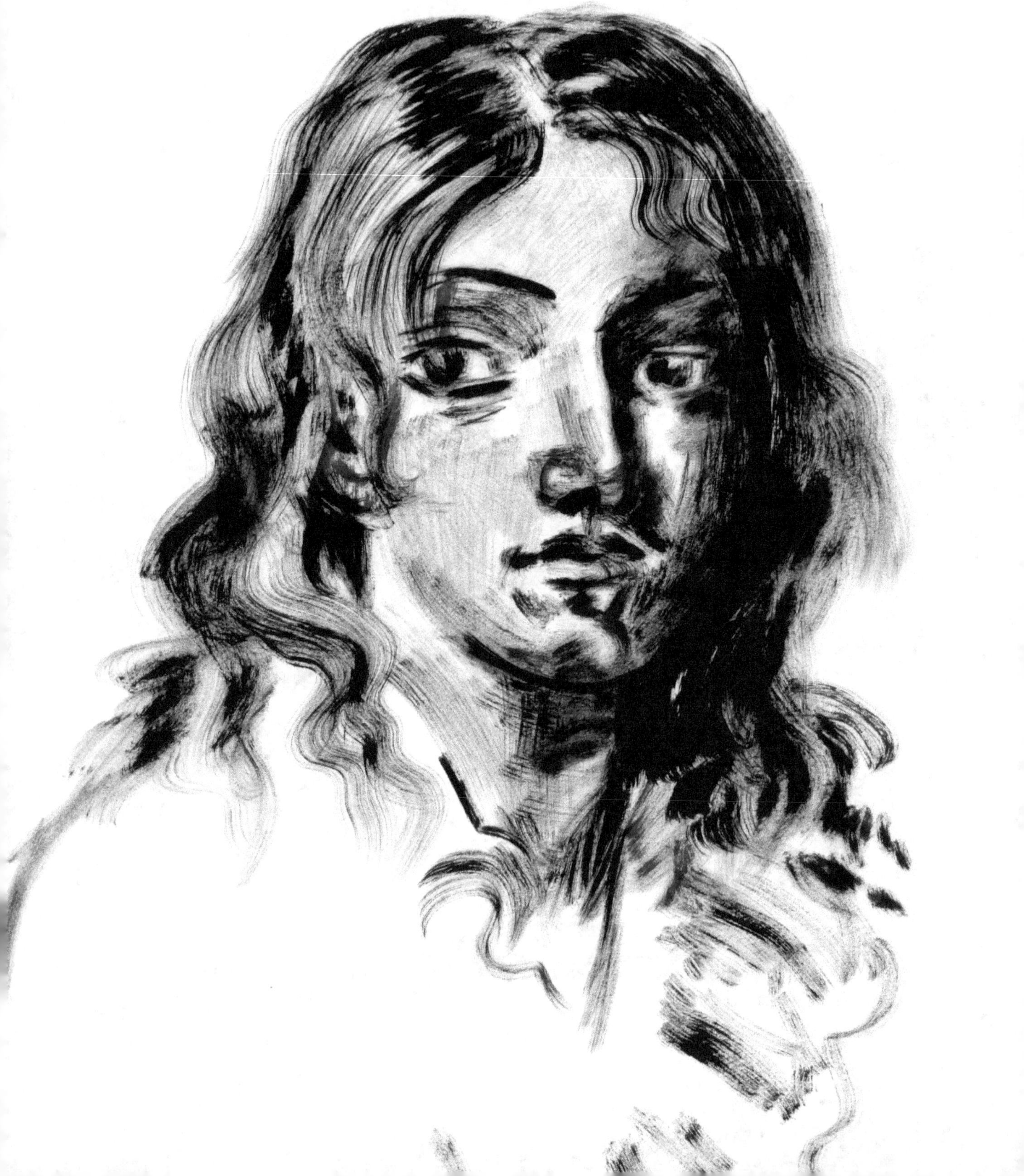

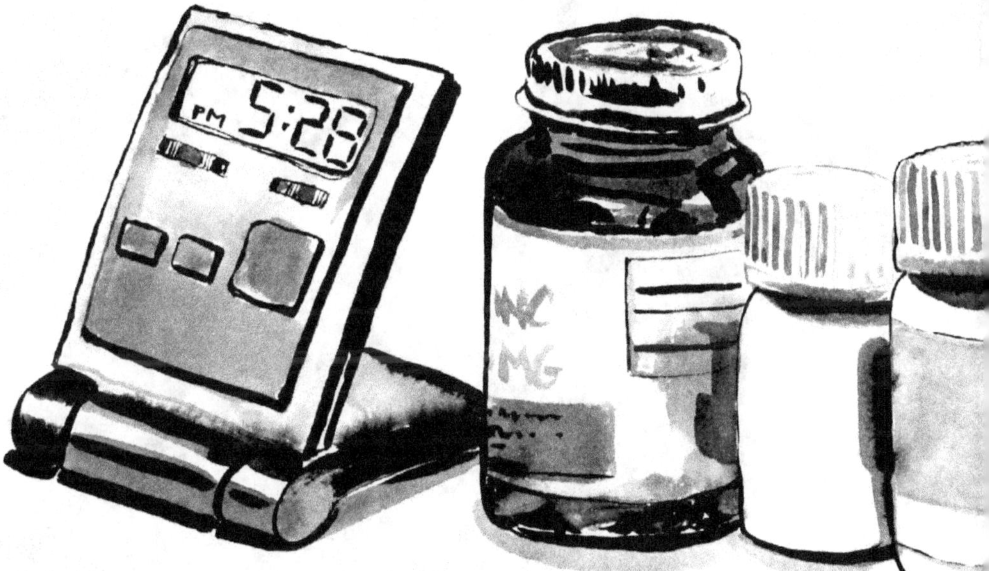
PM 5:28

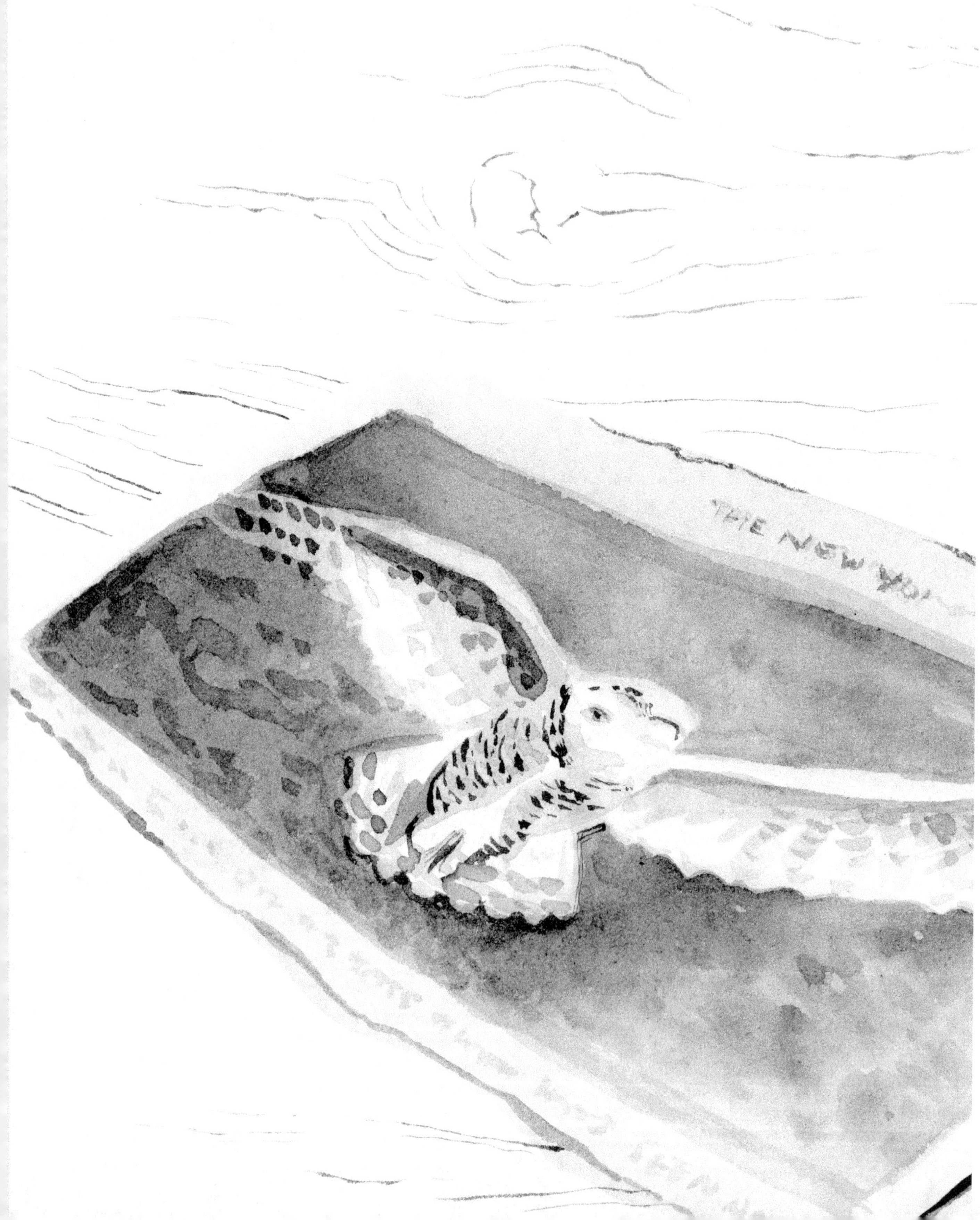
THE NEW YO

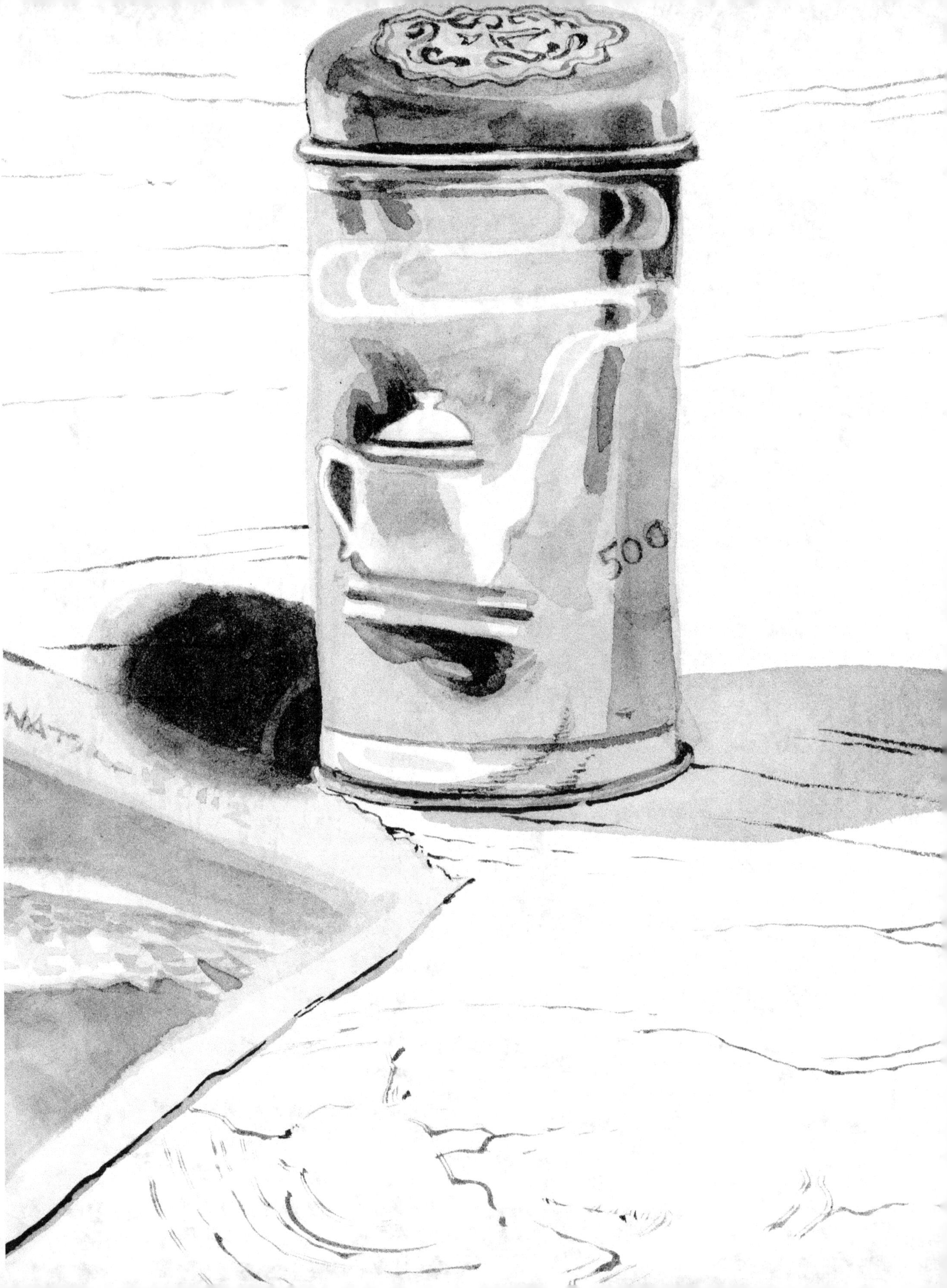
500

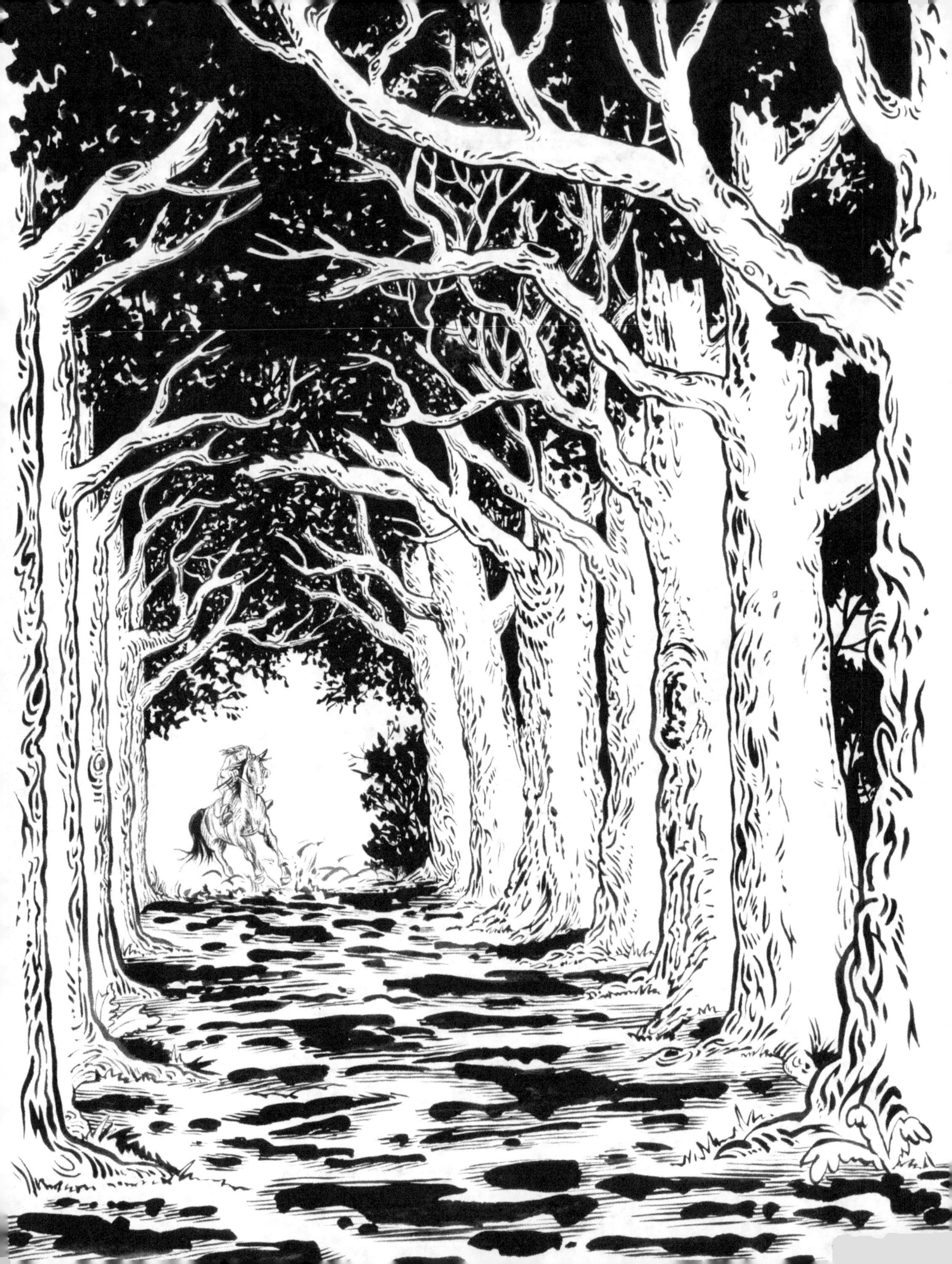

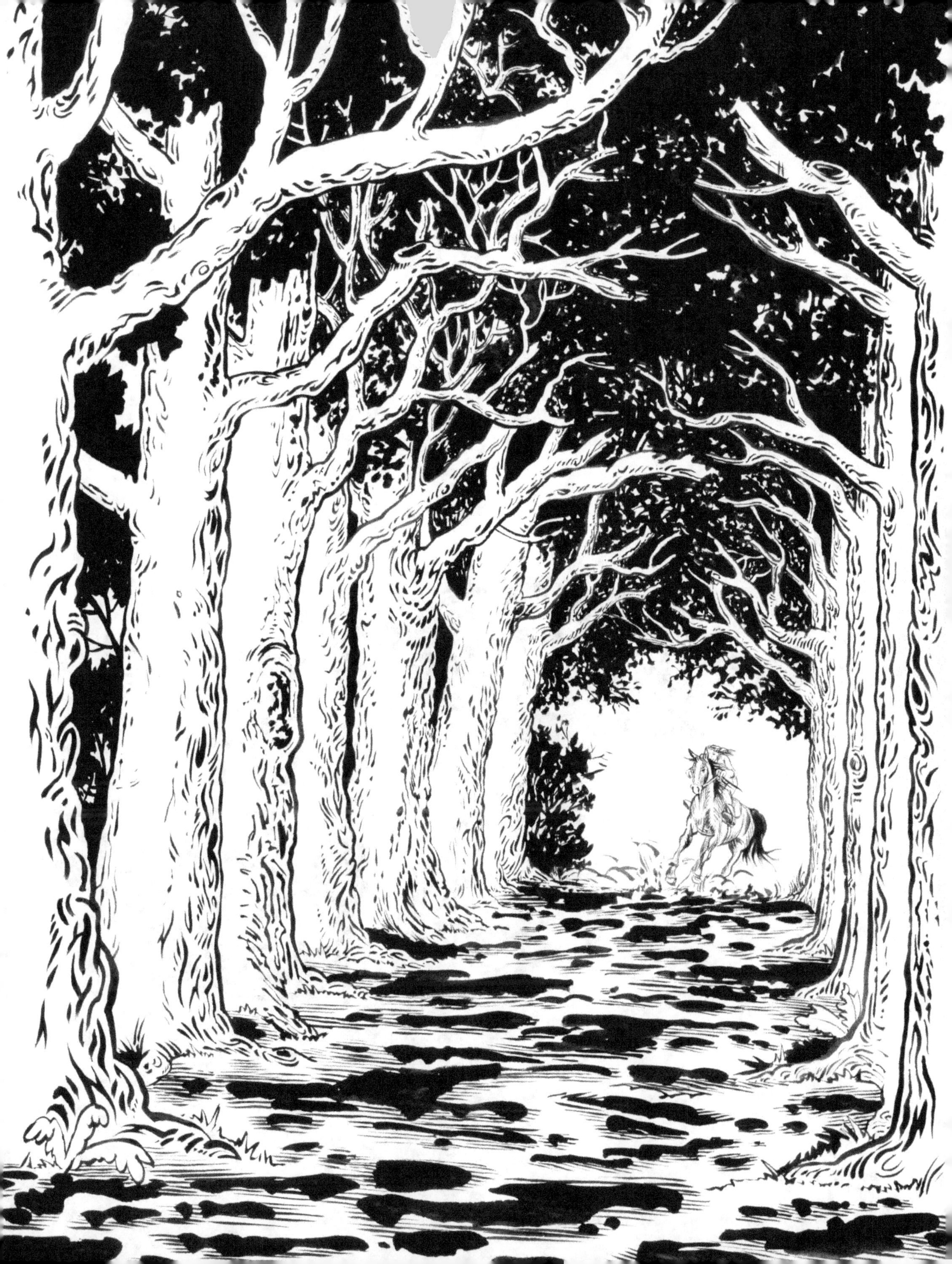

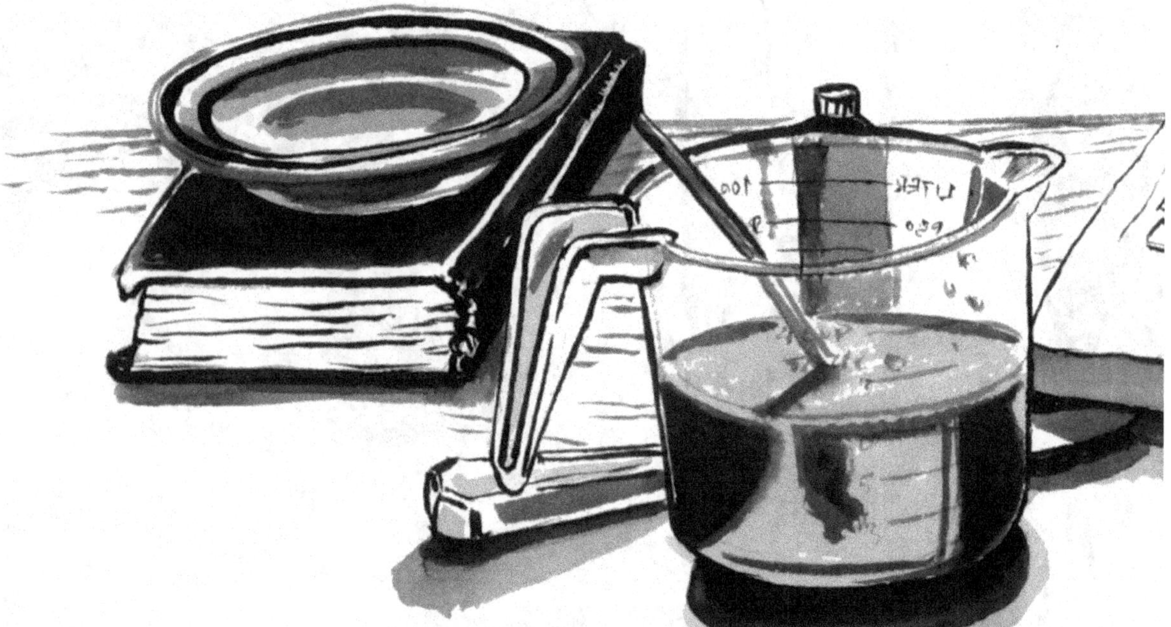

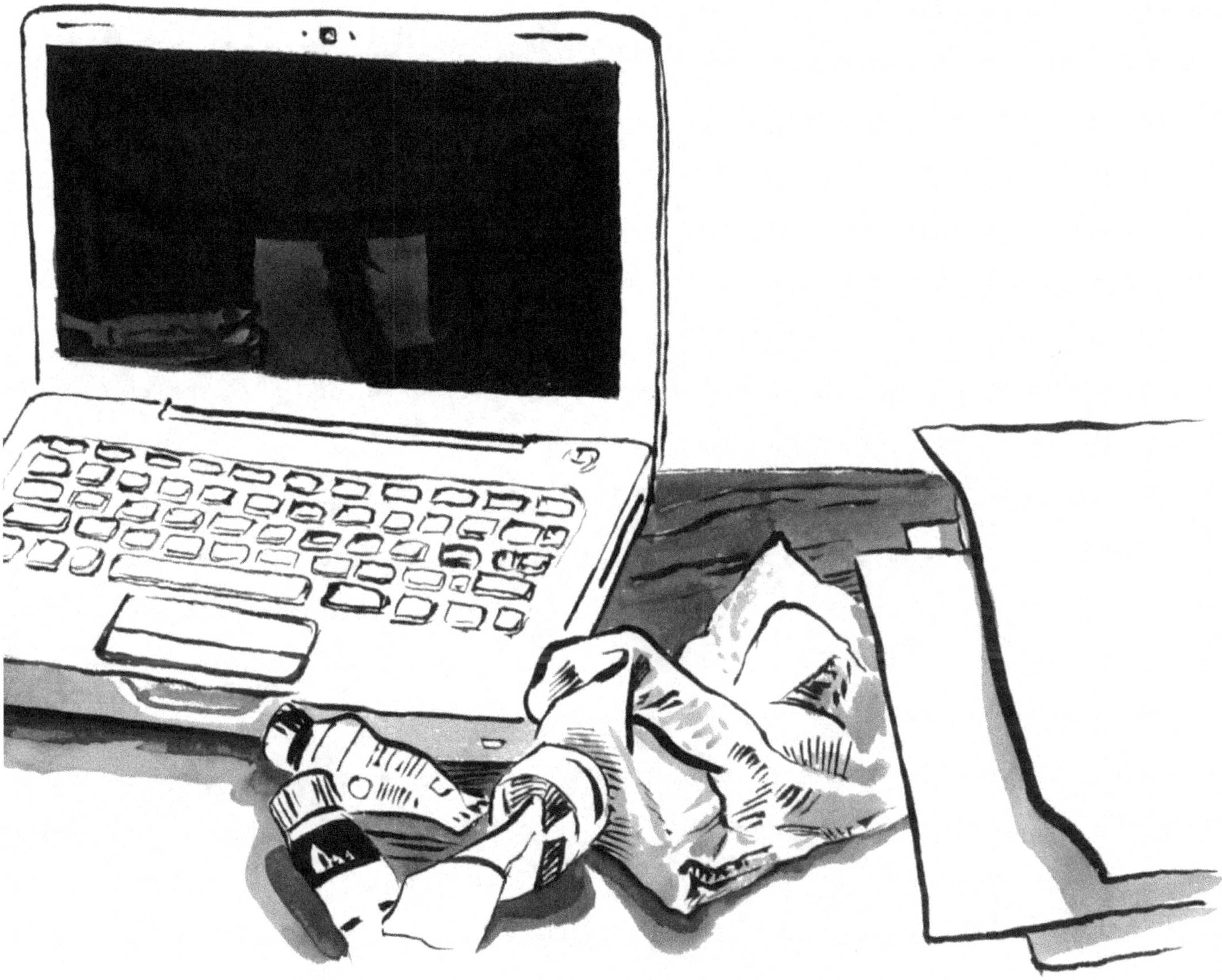

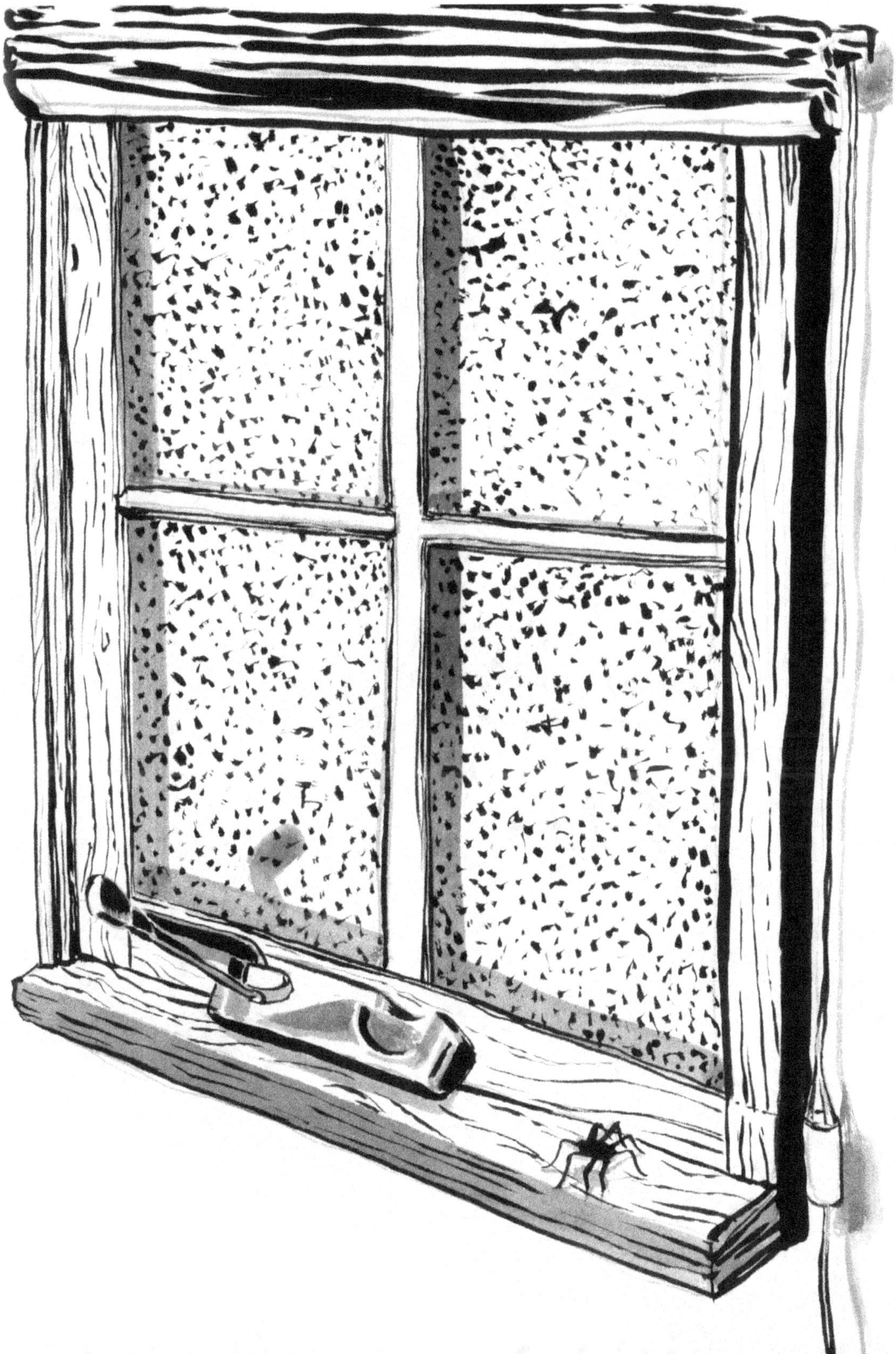

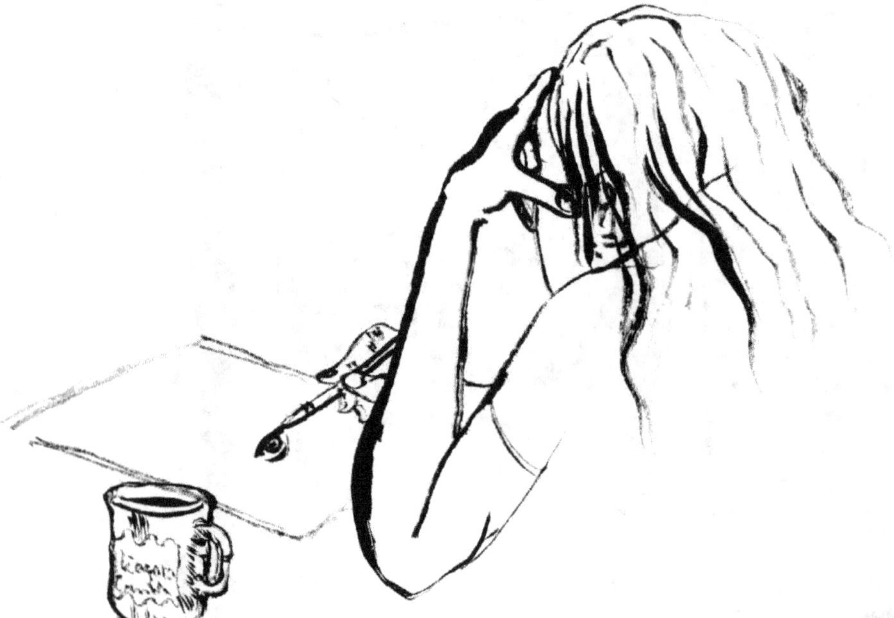

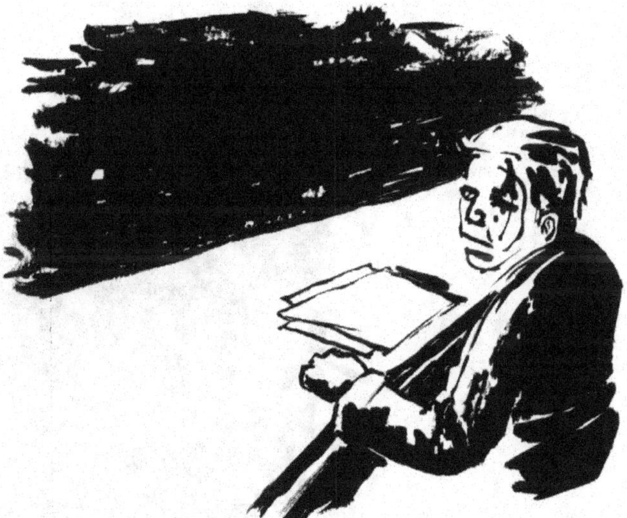

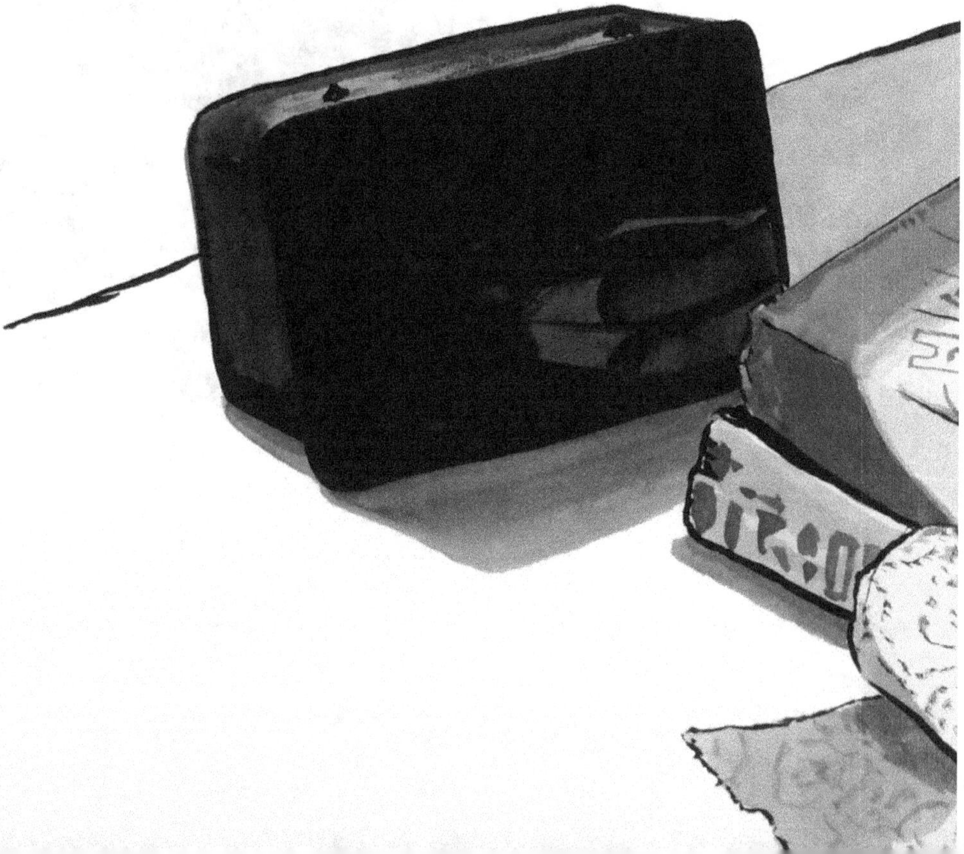

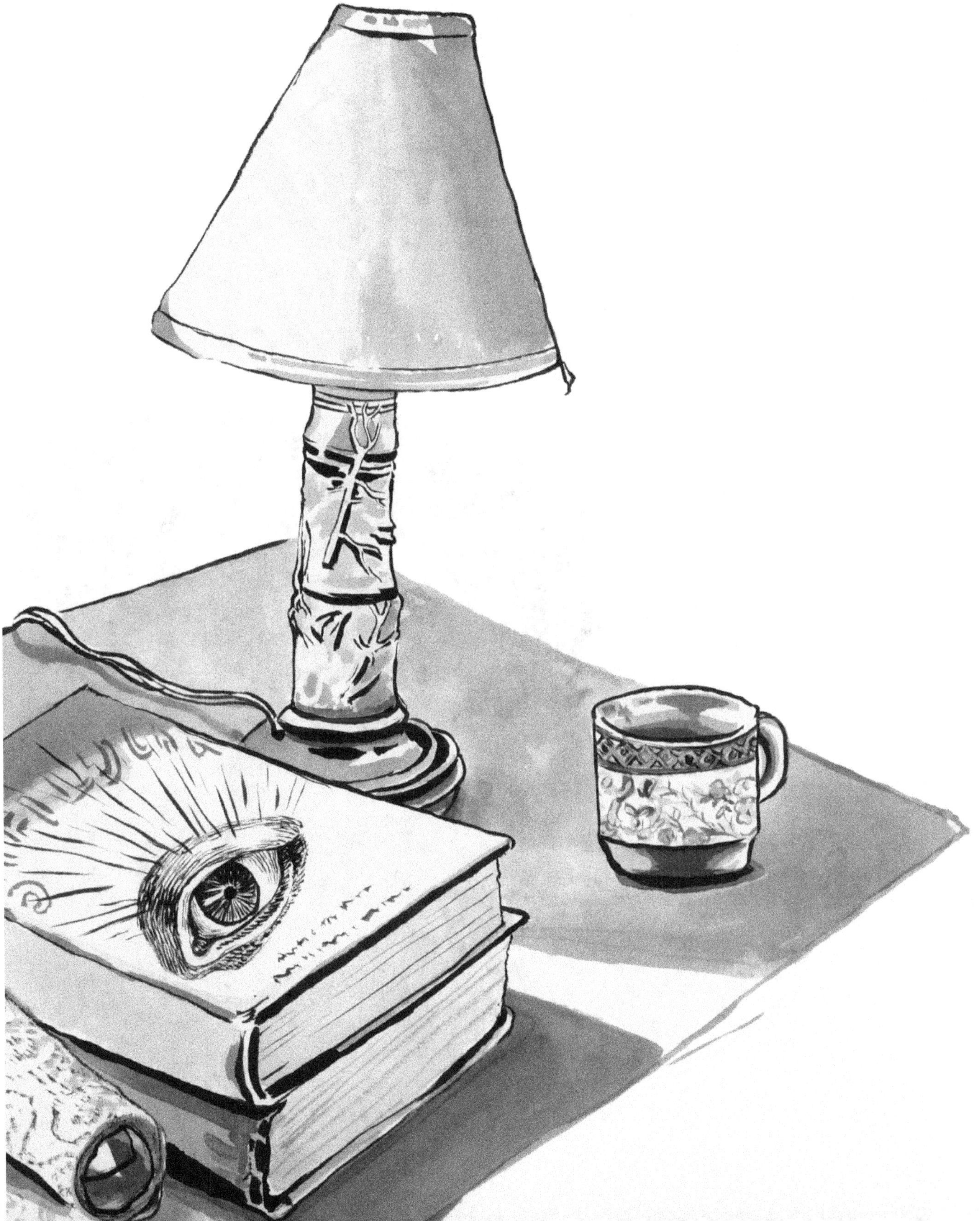

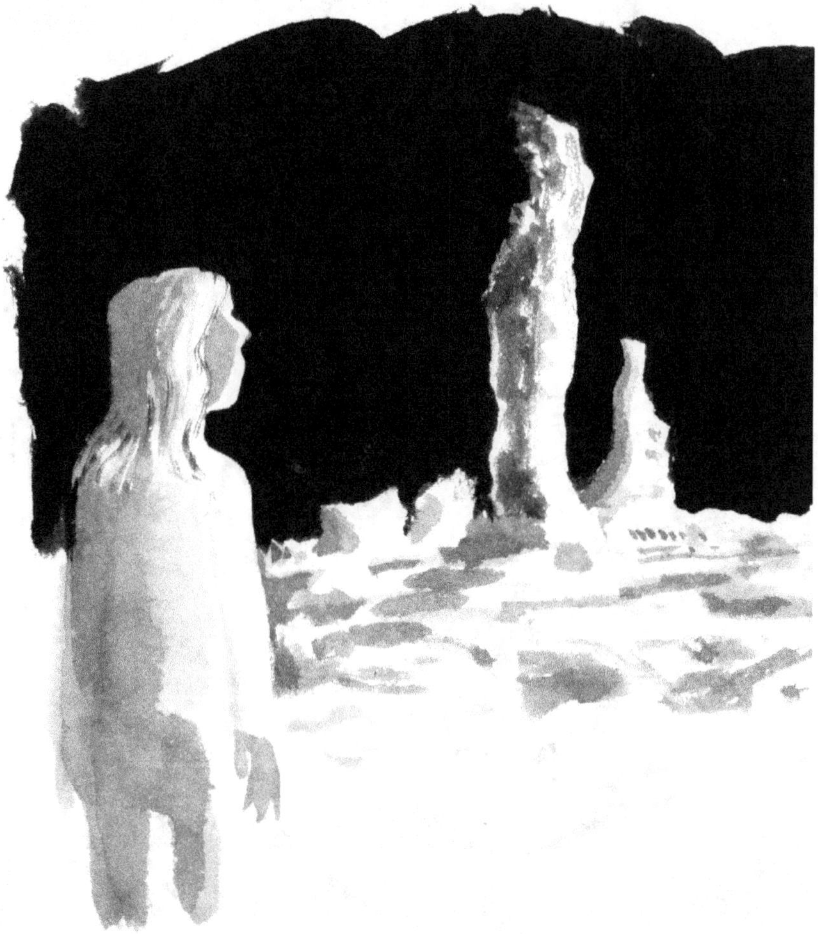

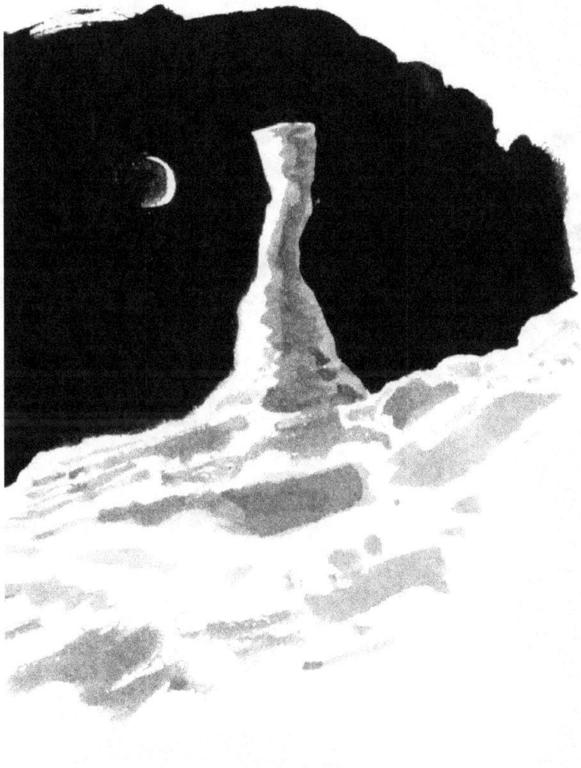

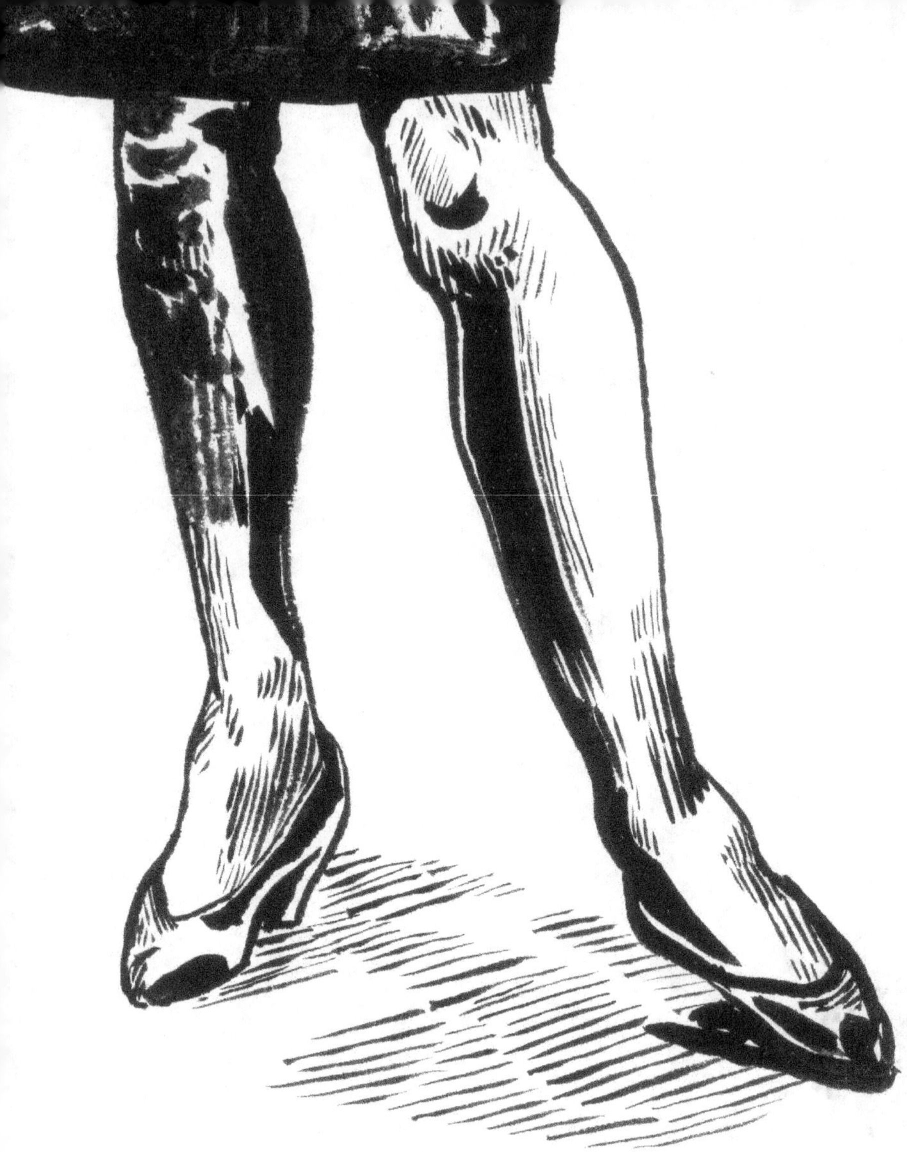

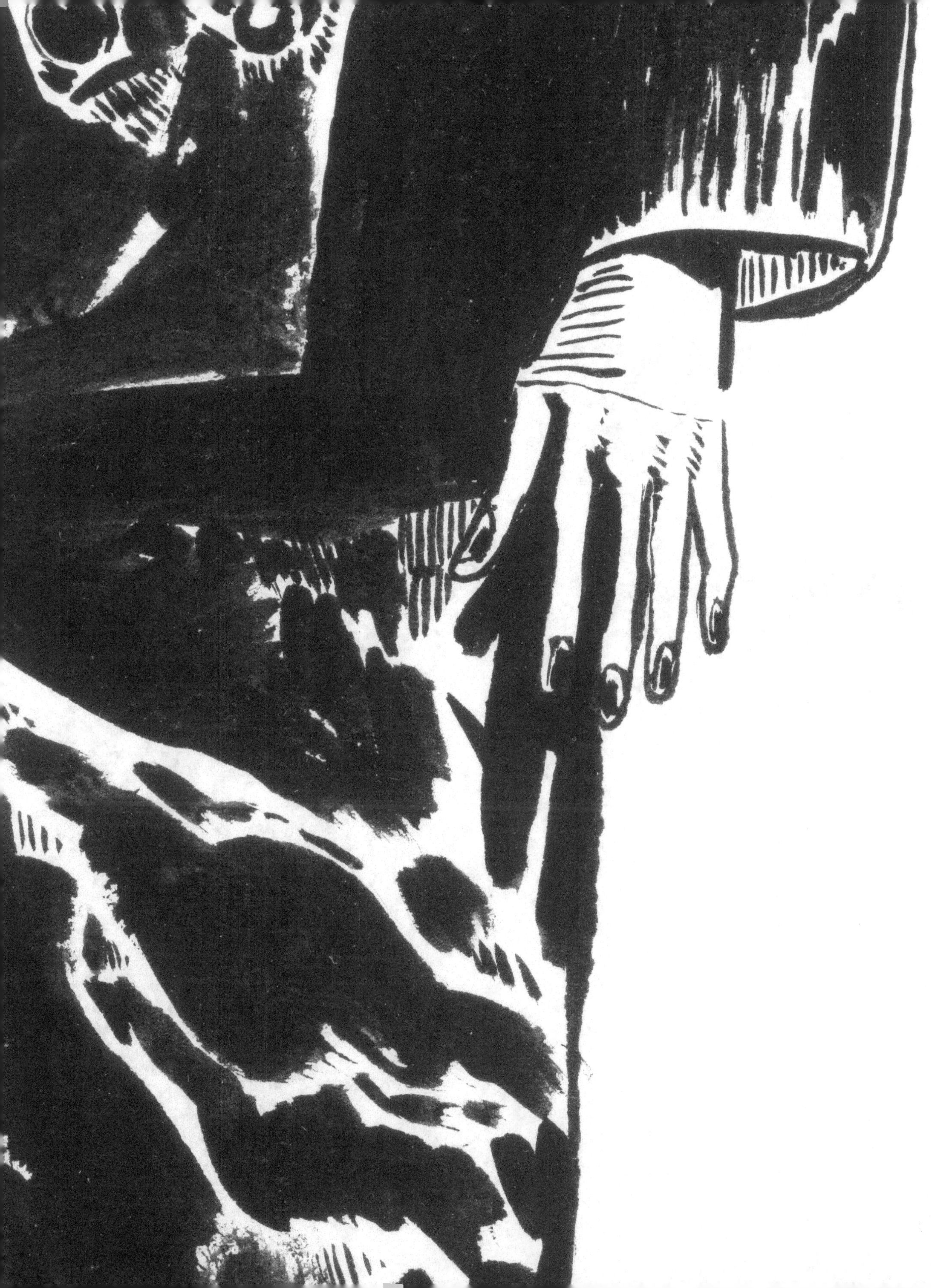

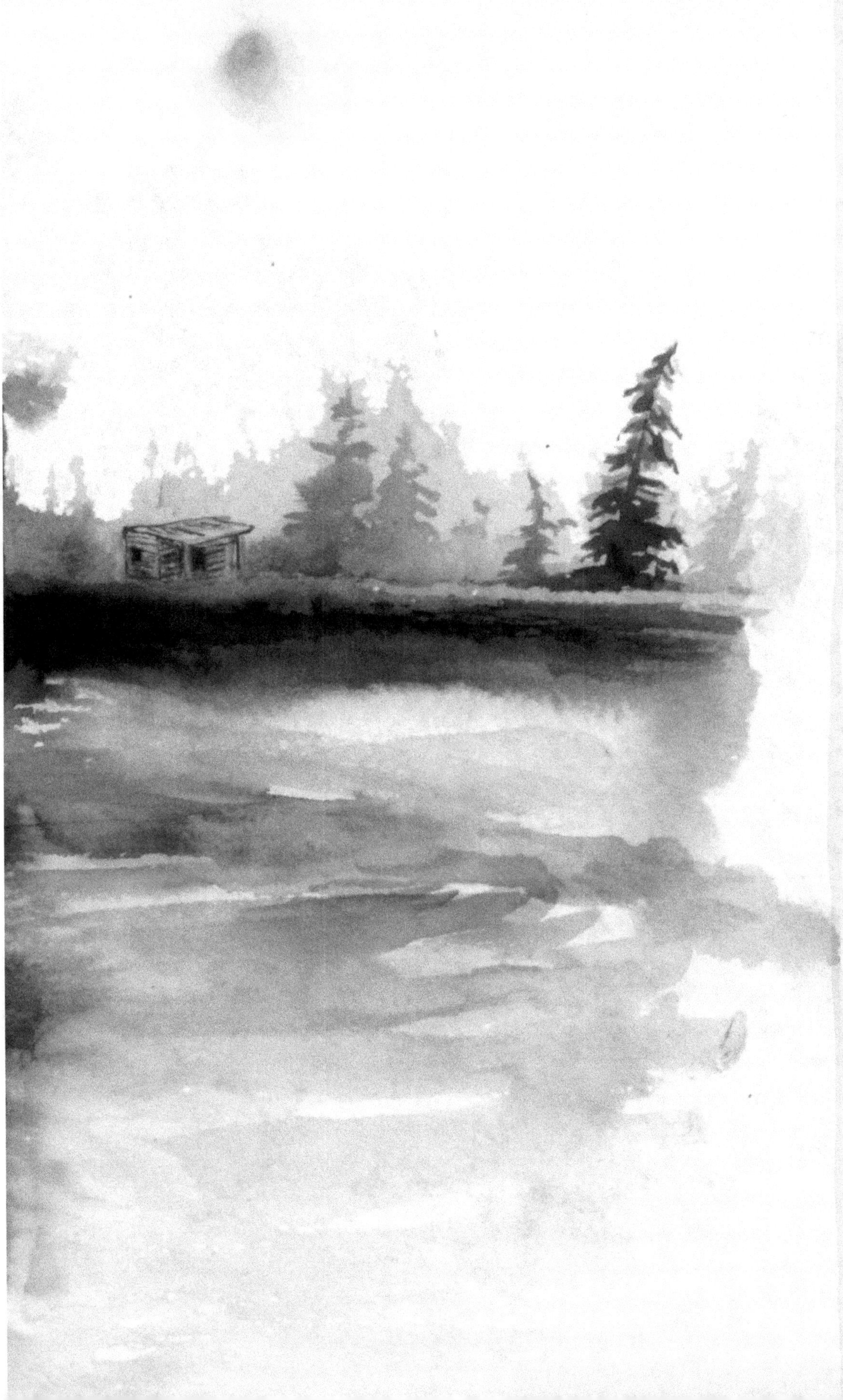

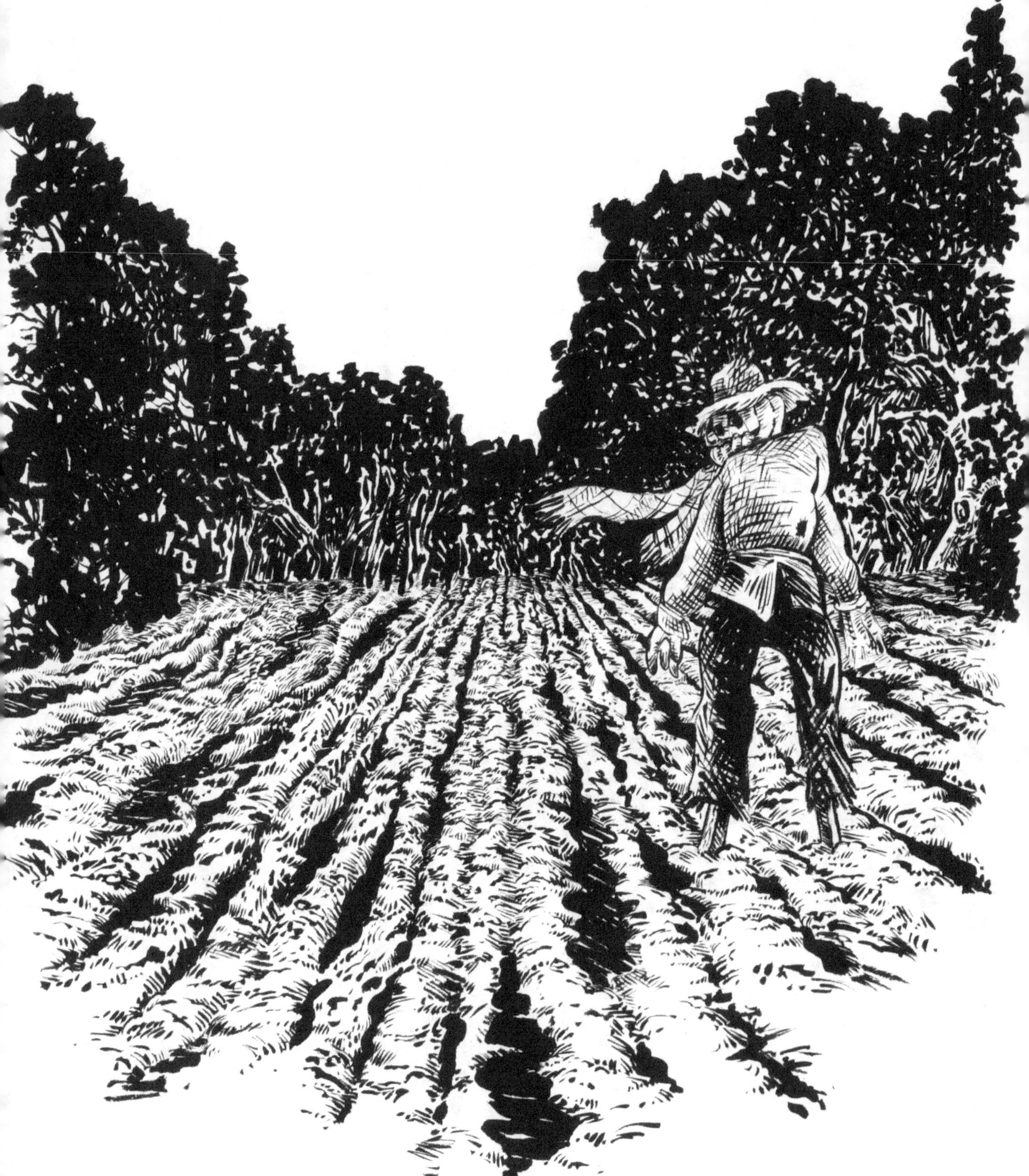

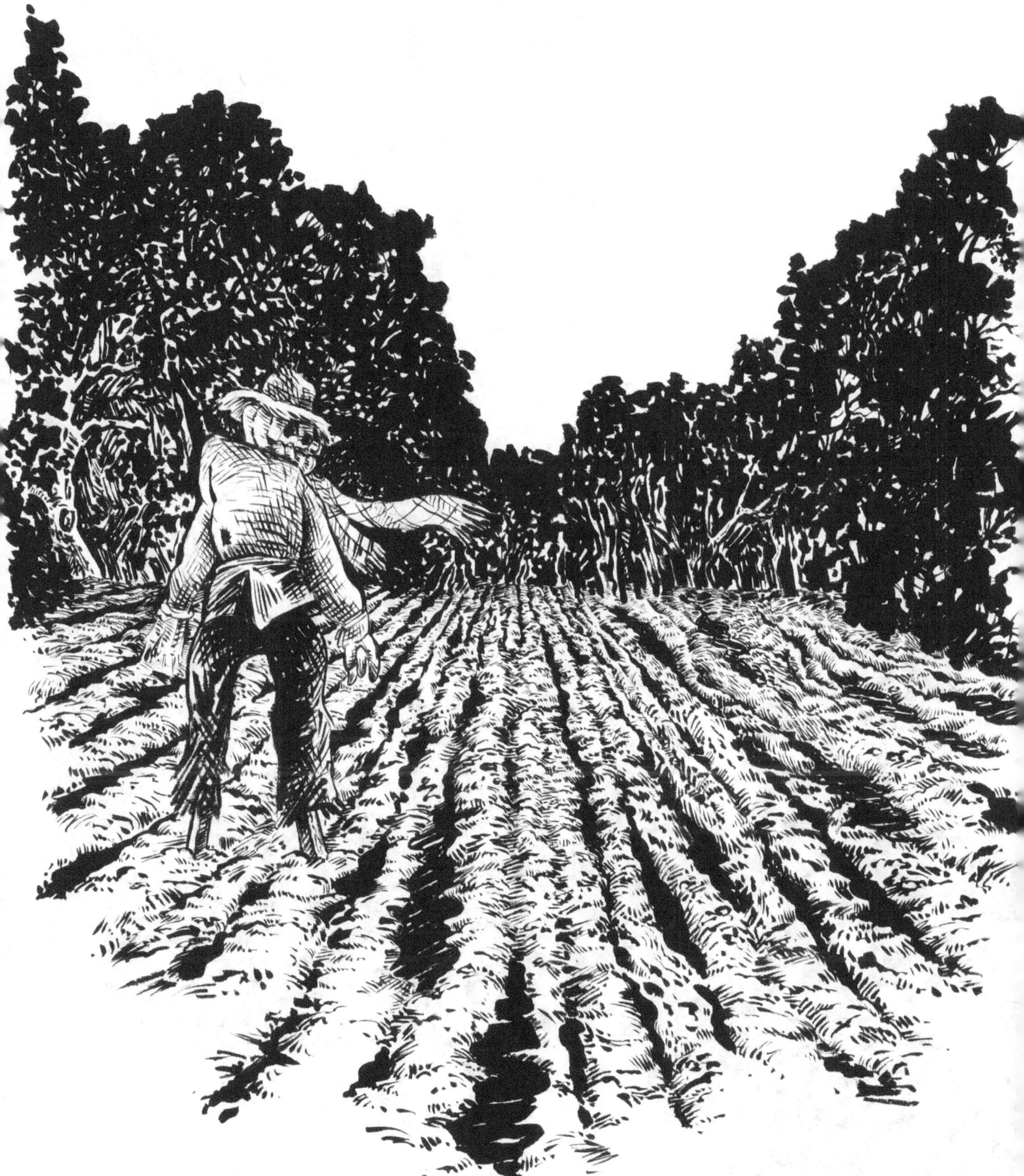

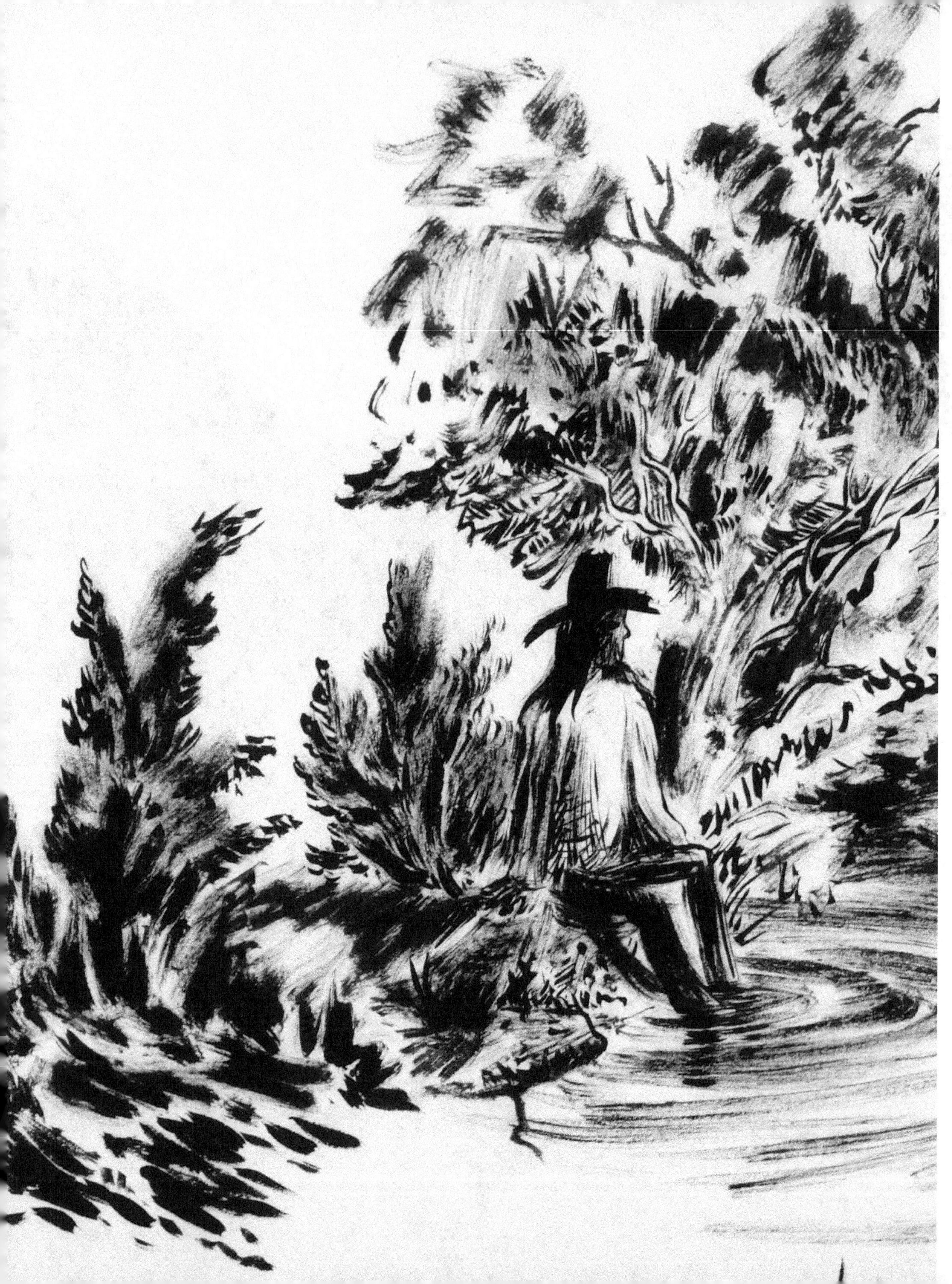

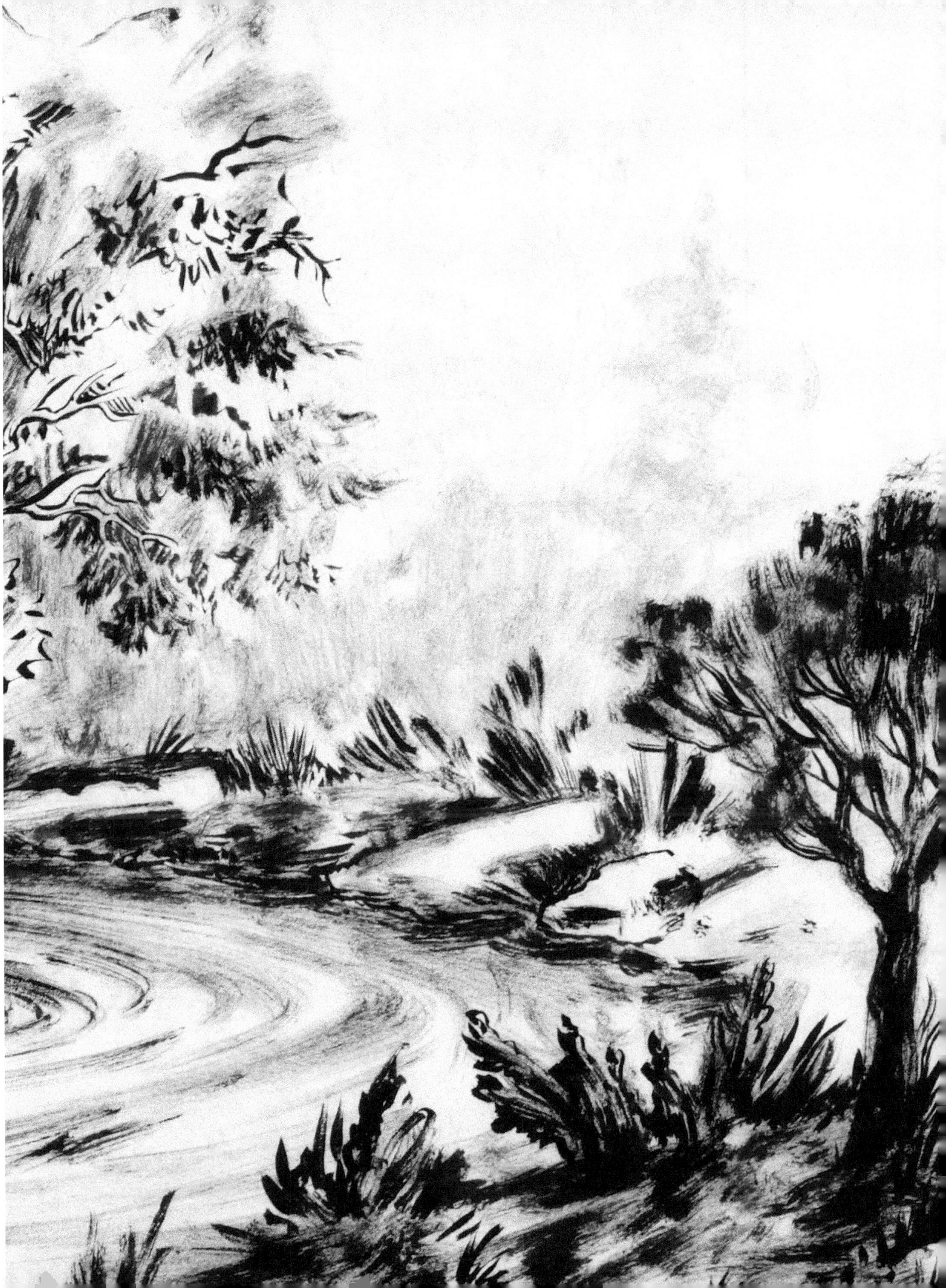

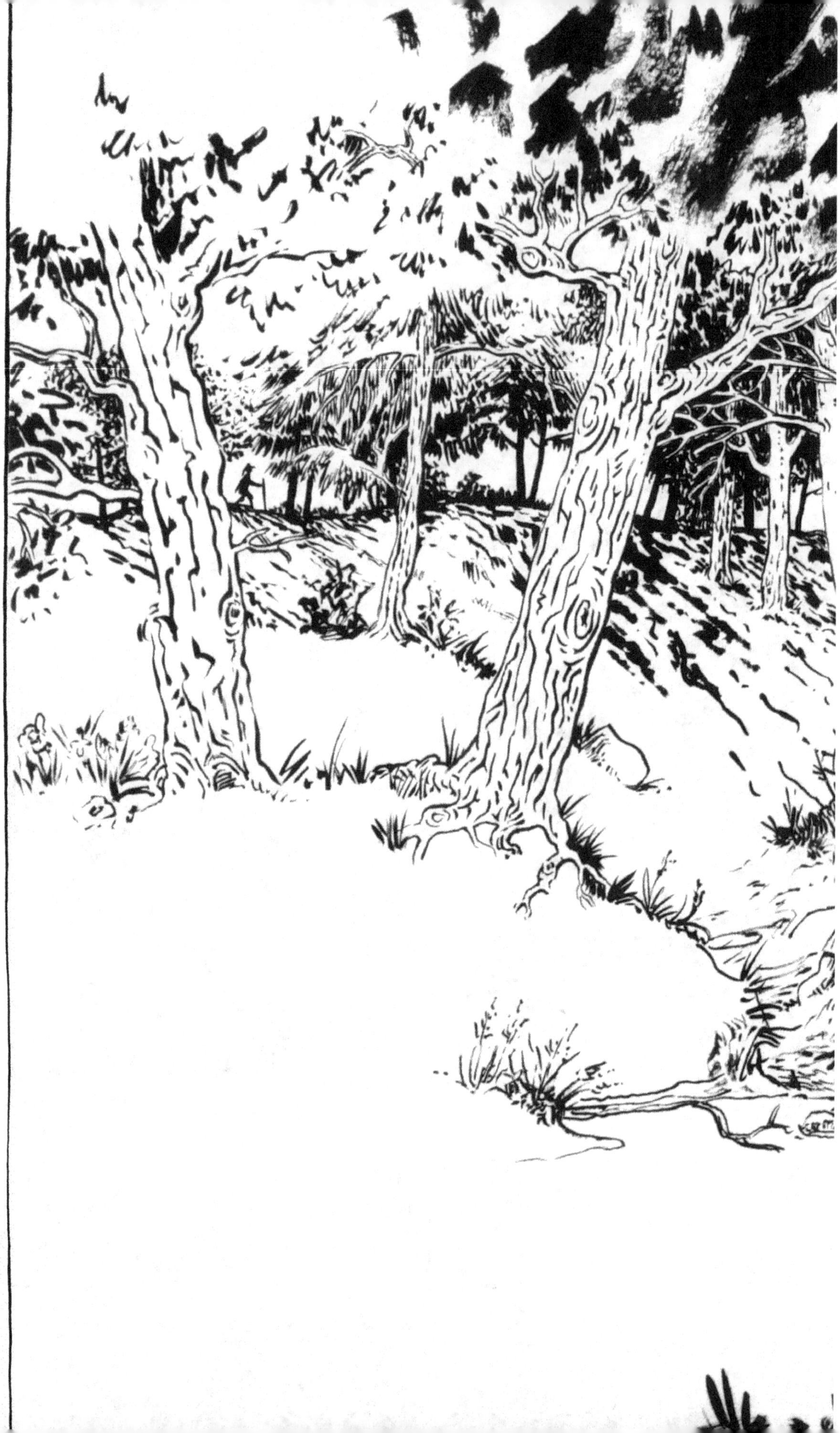

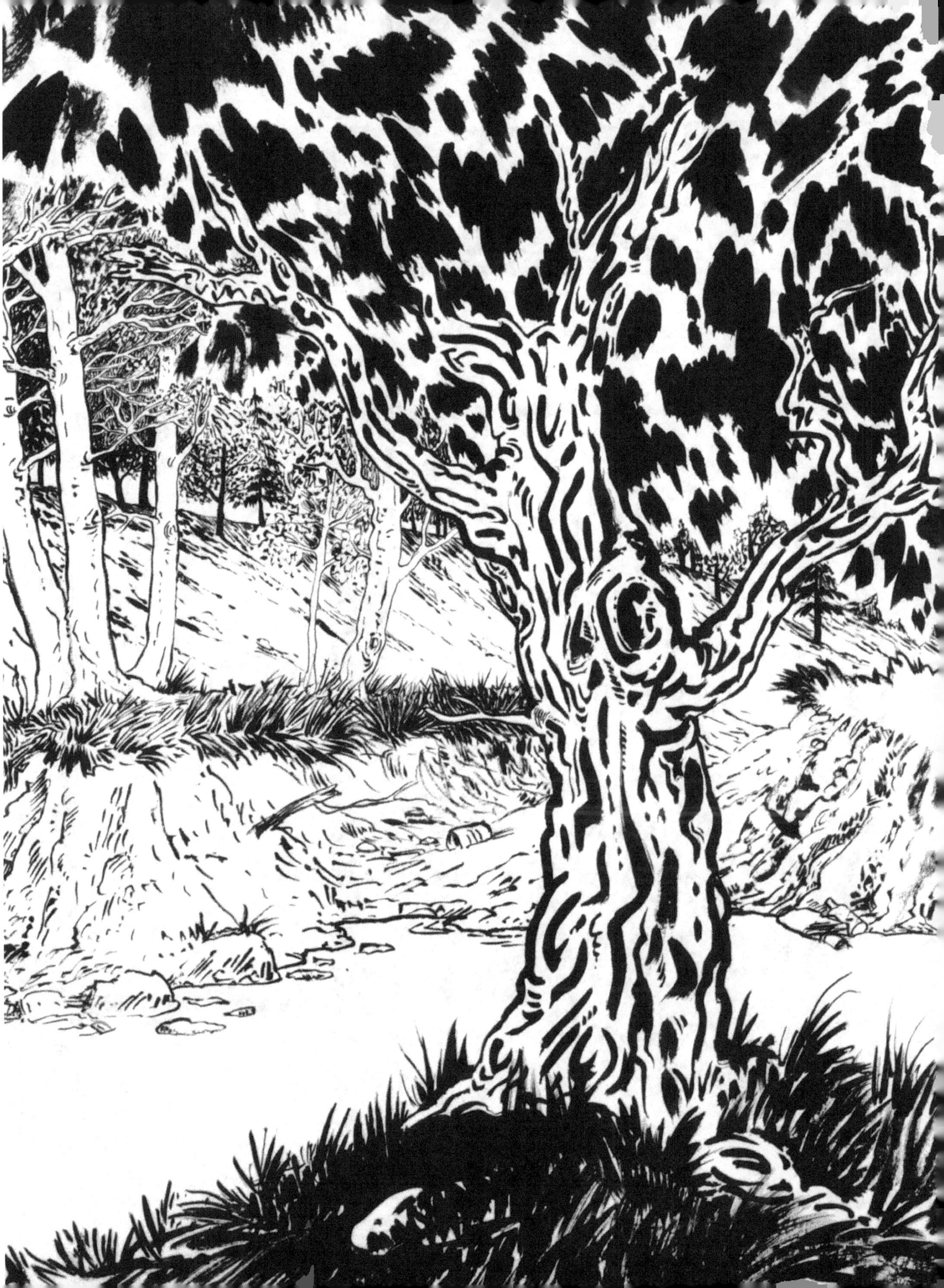

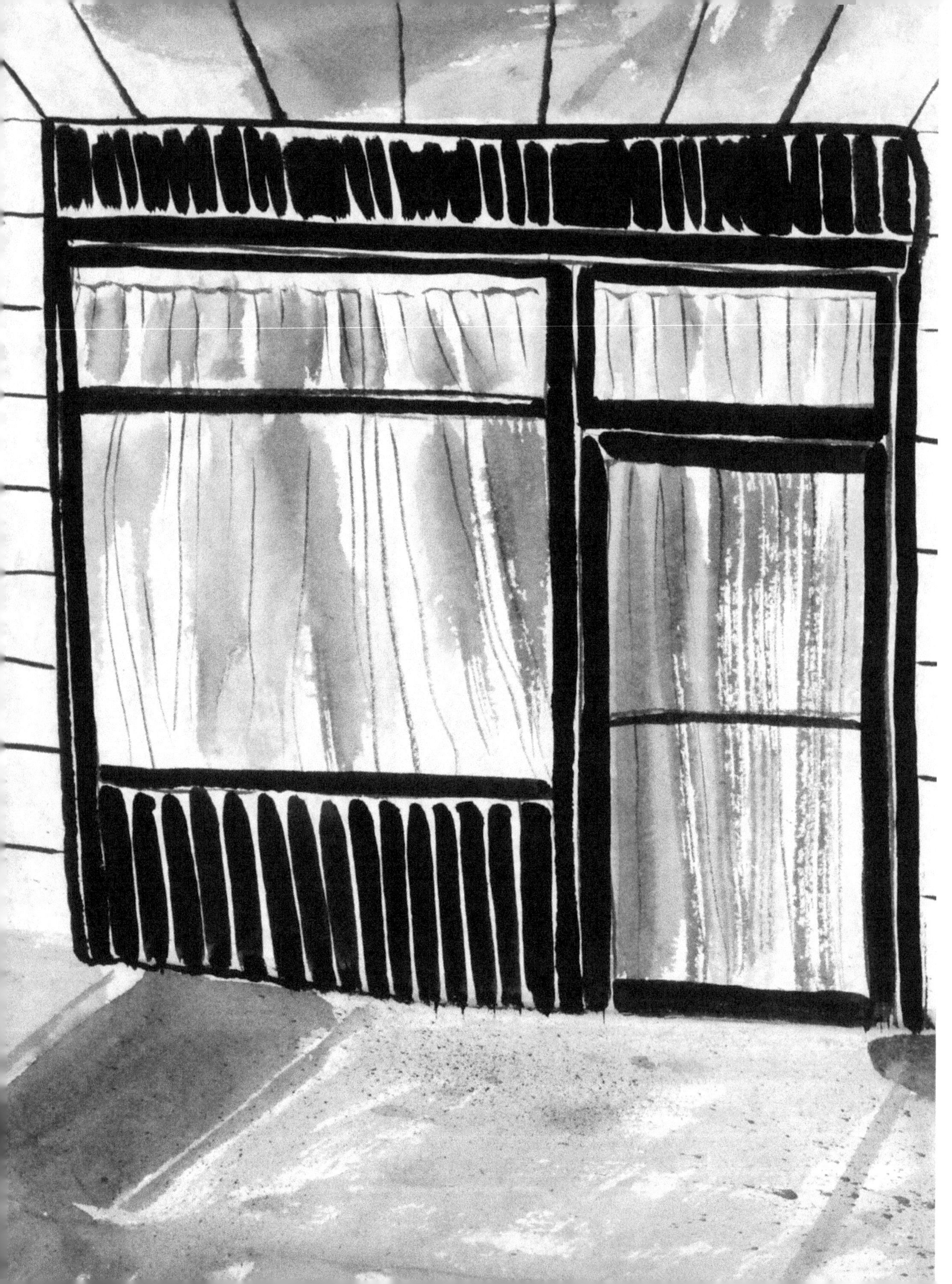

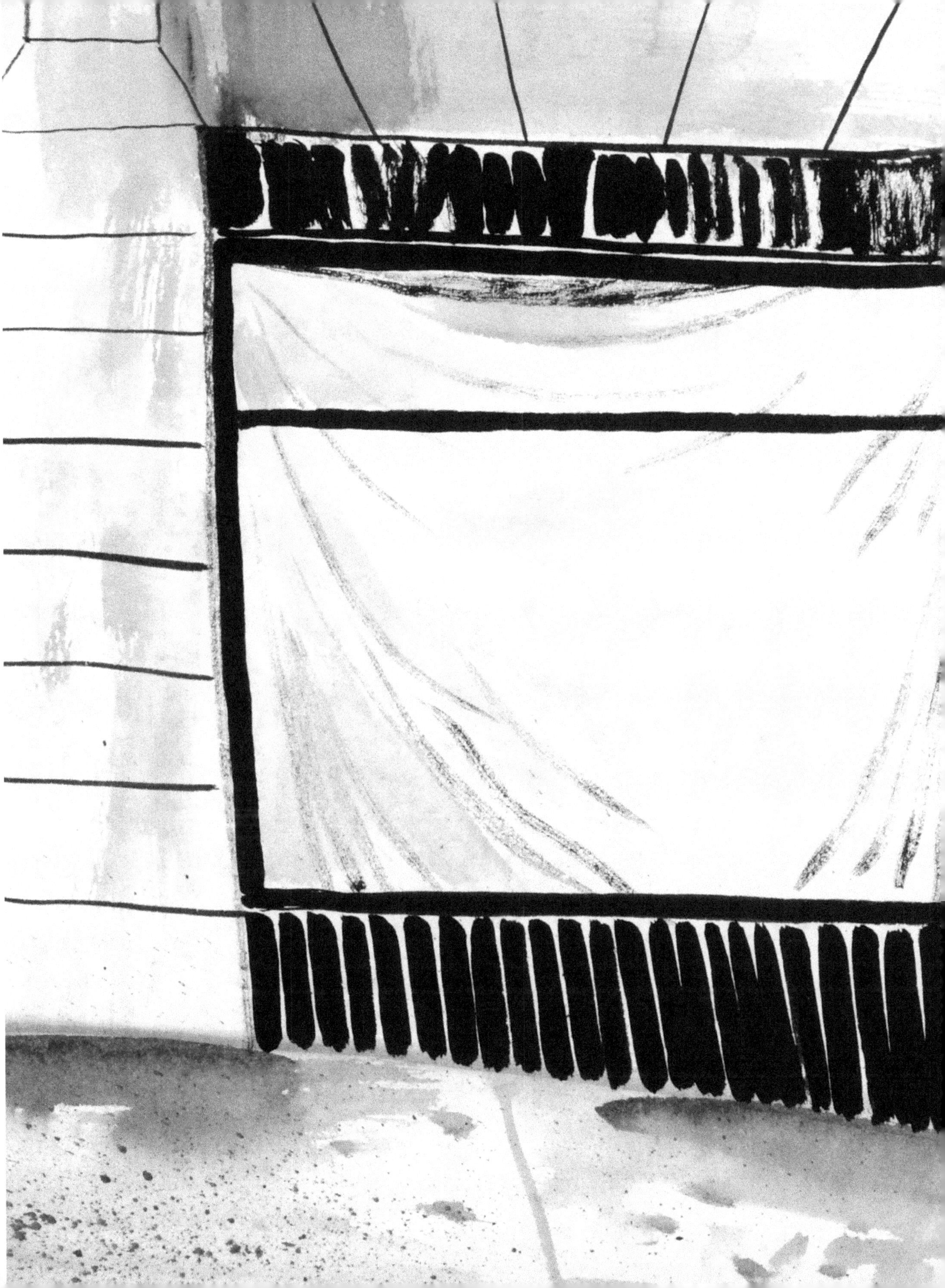

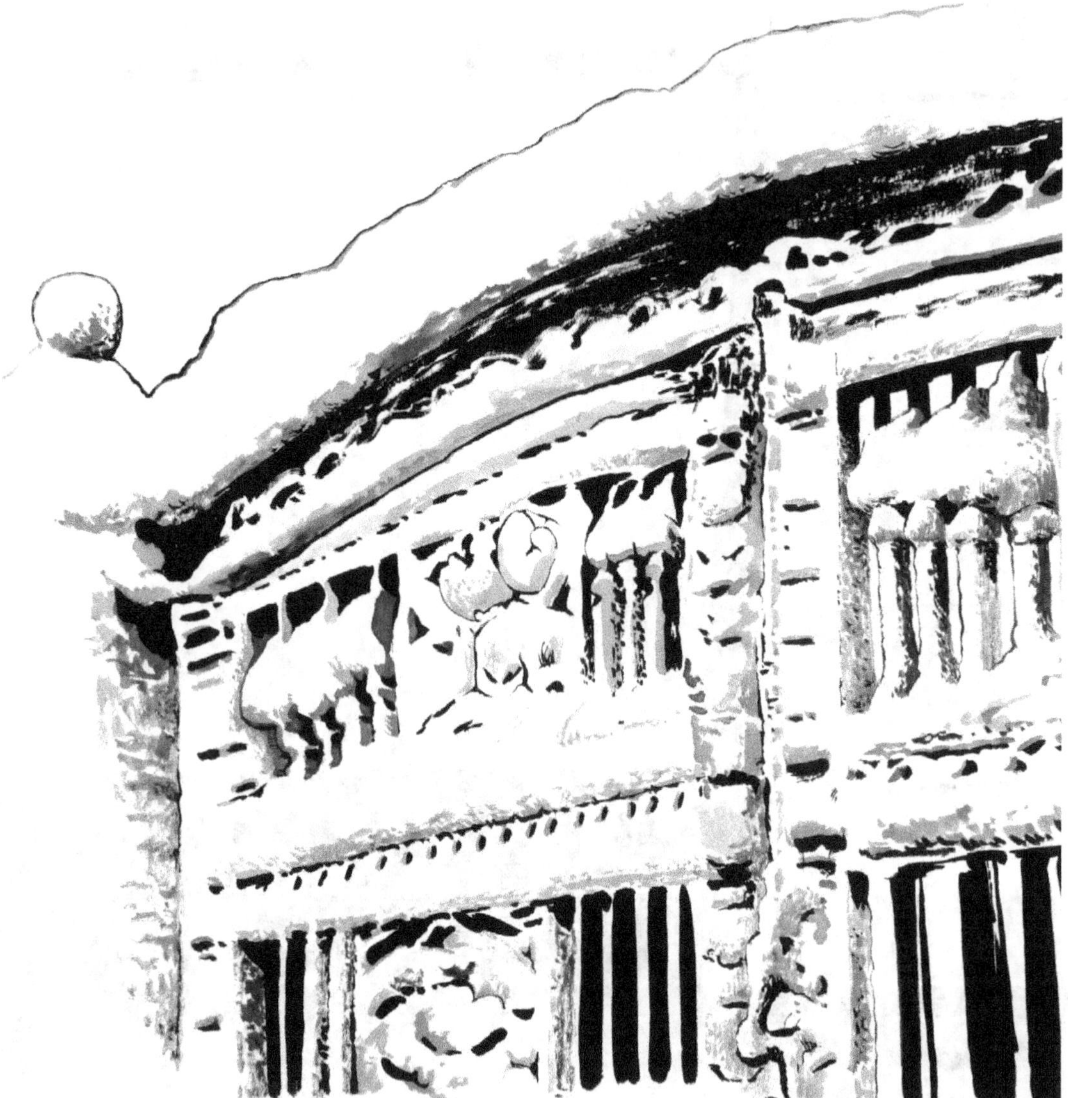

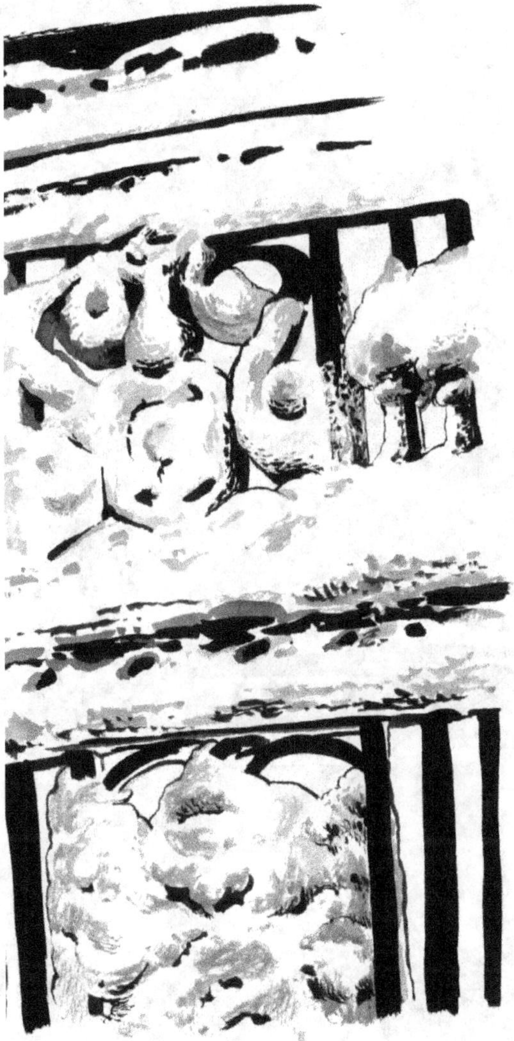

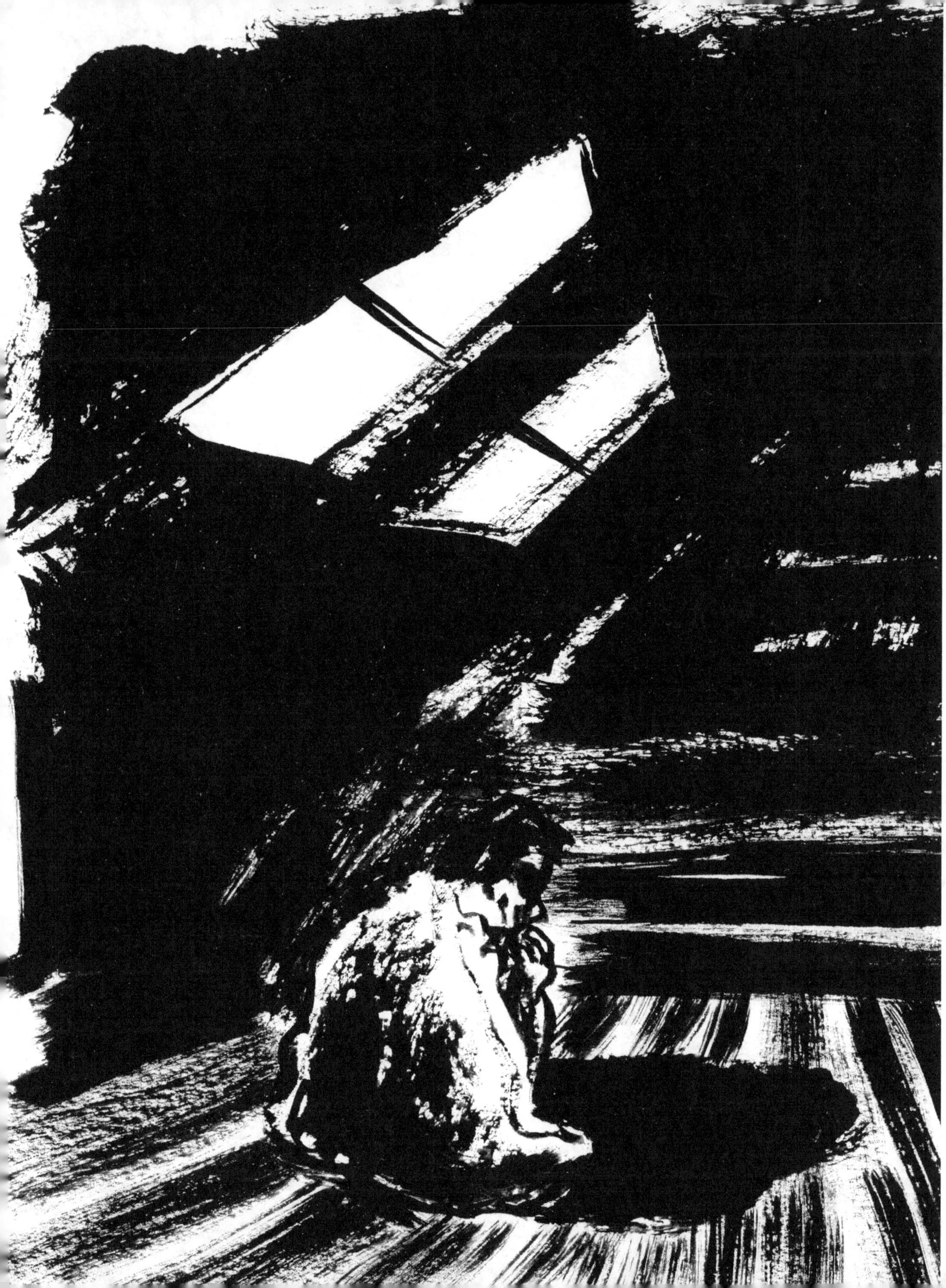

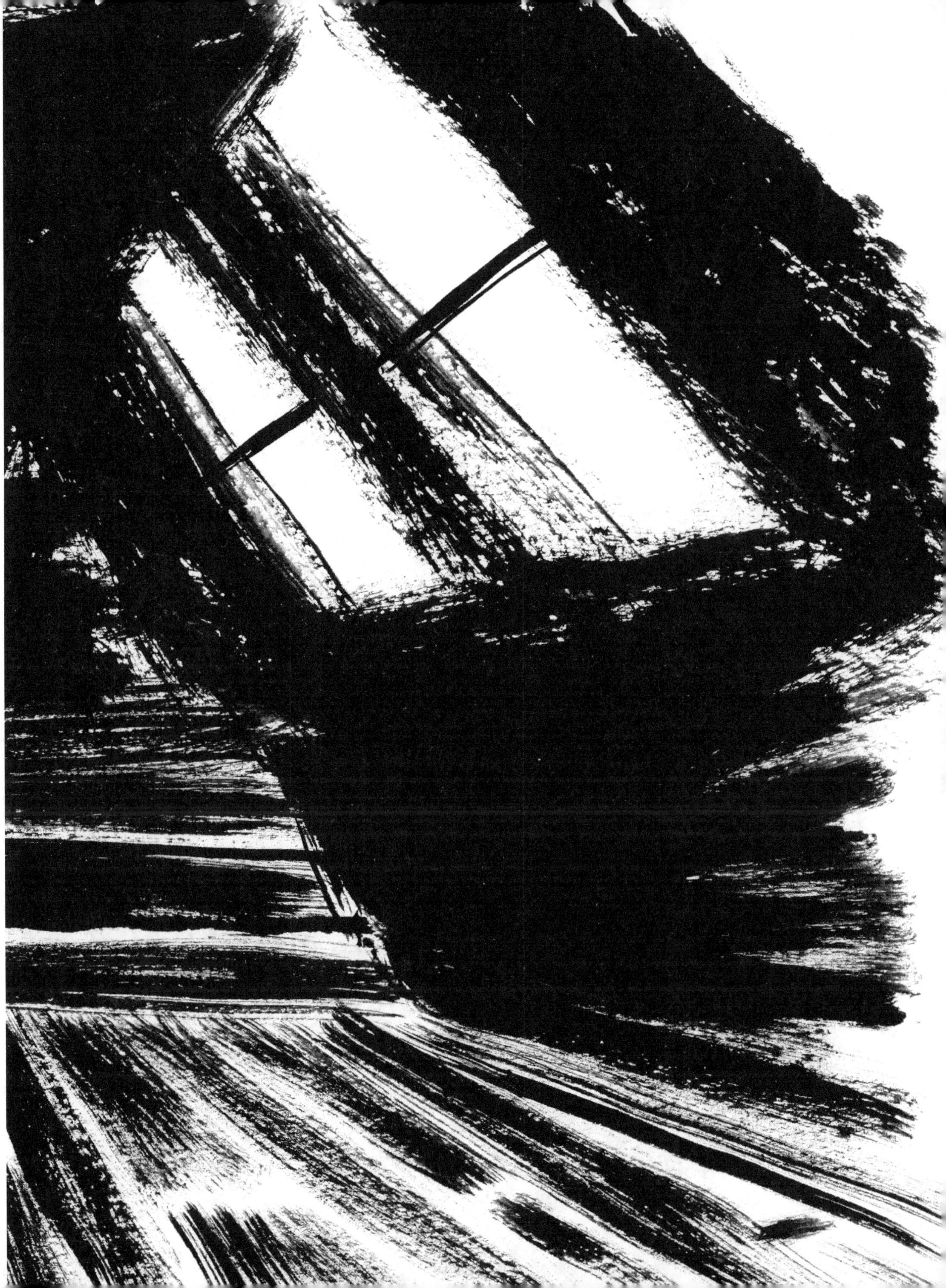

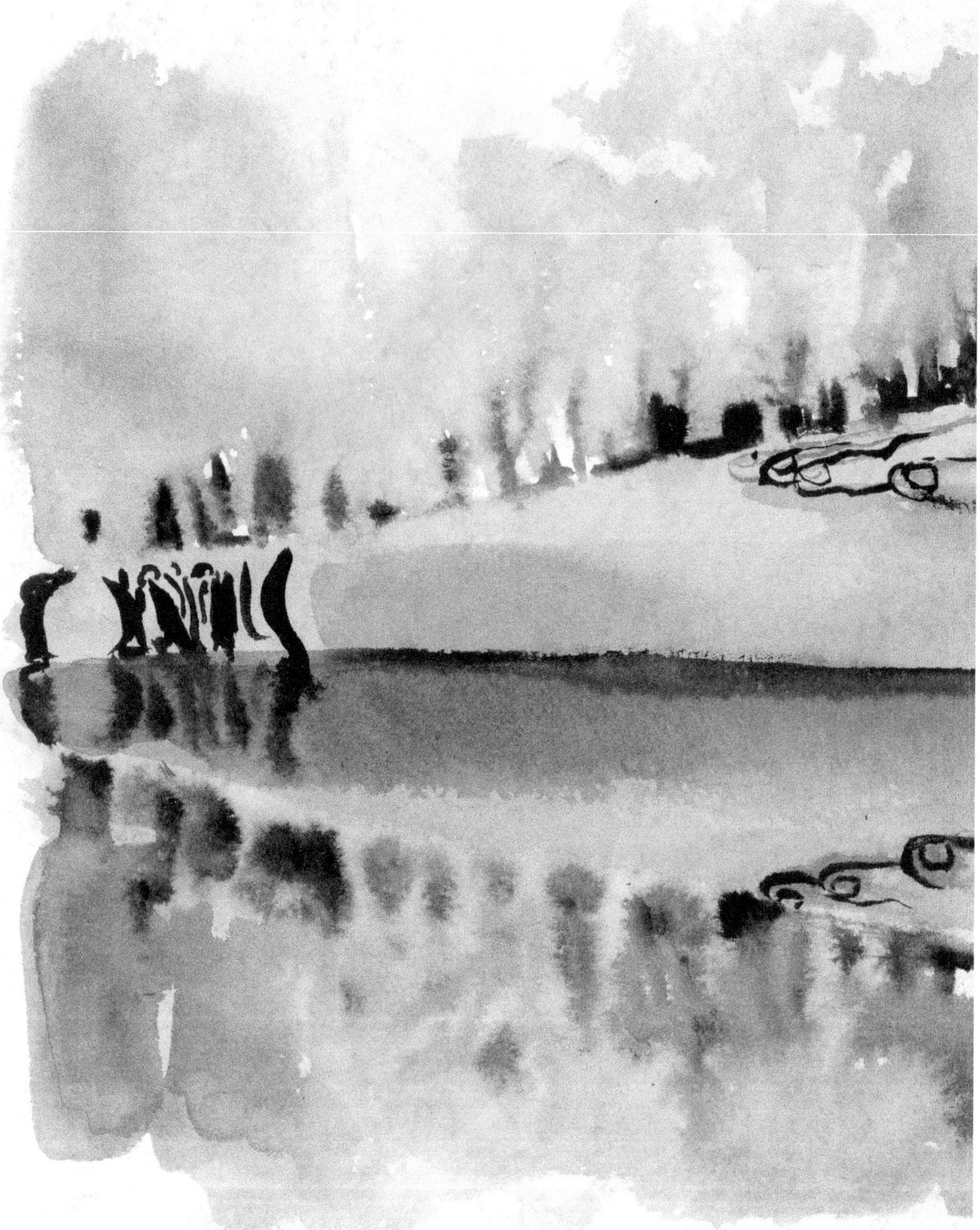

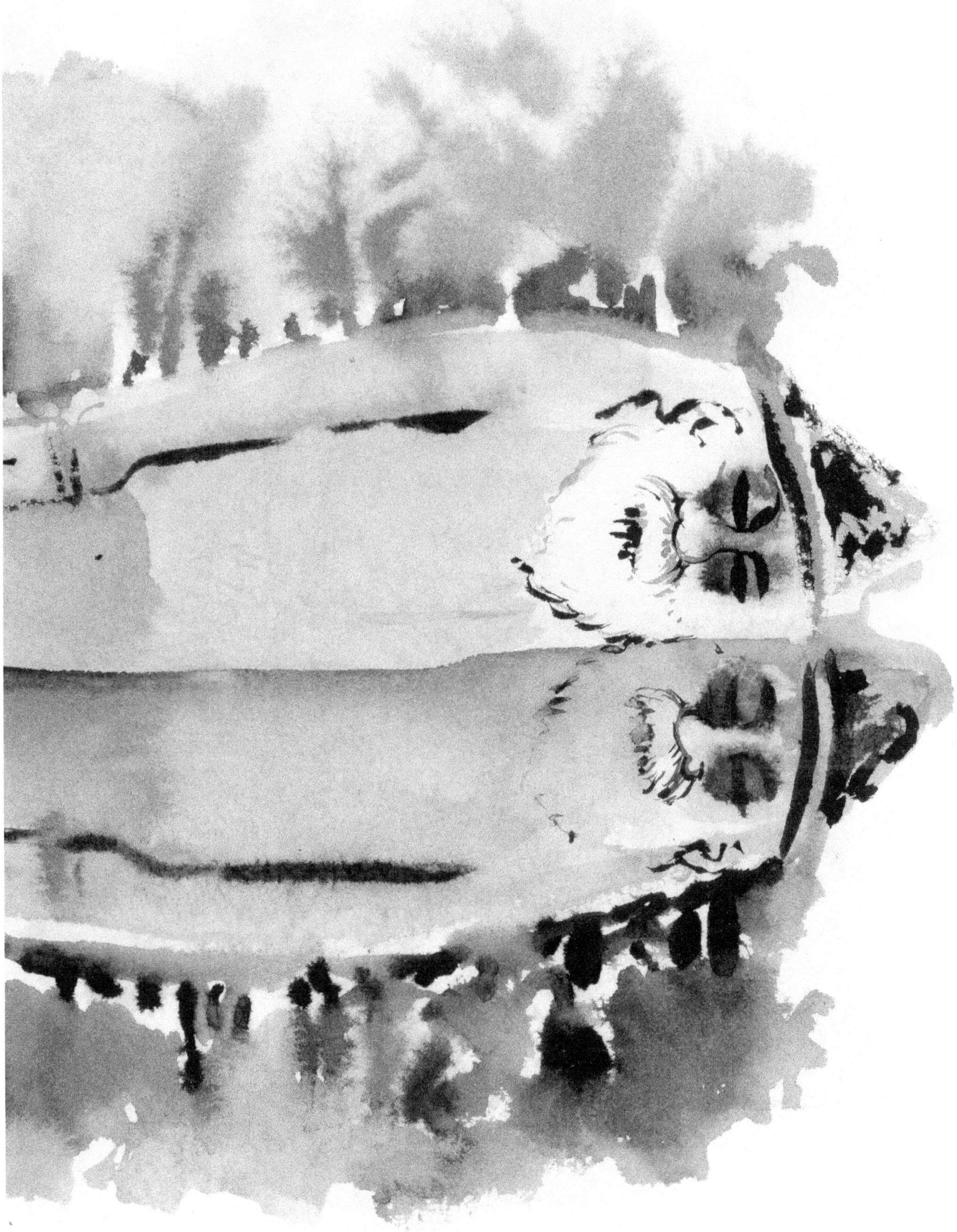

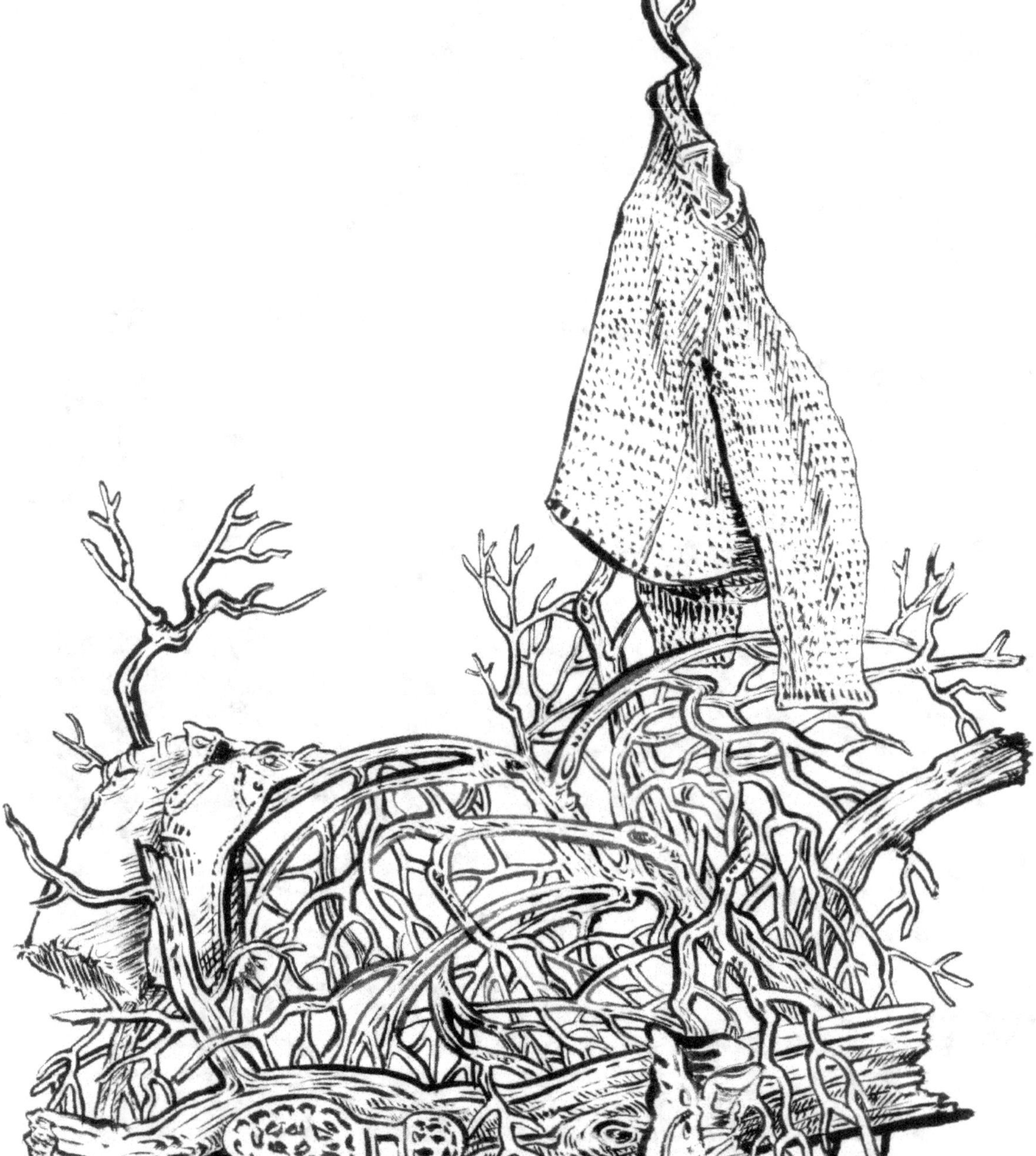

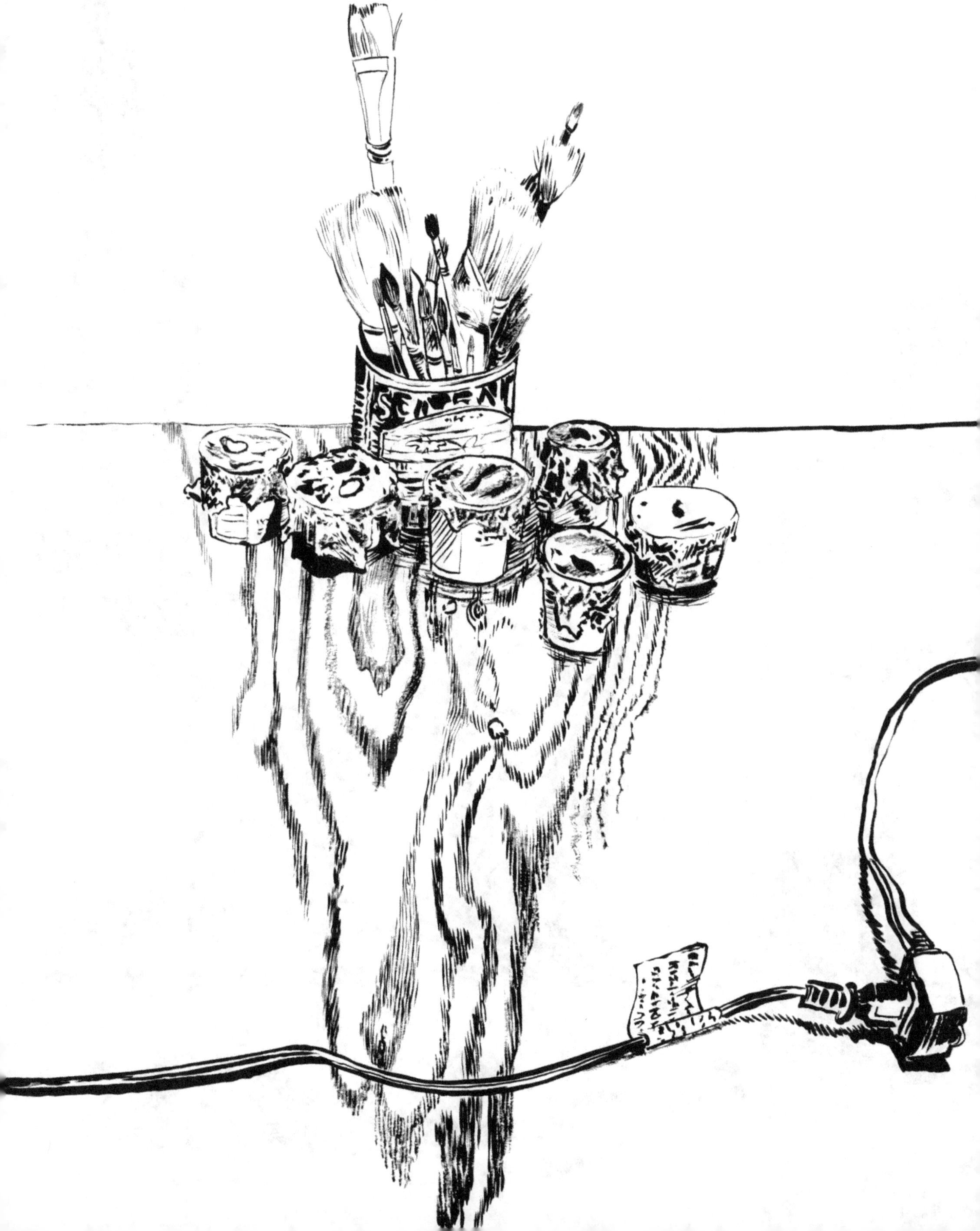

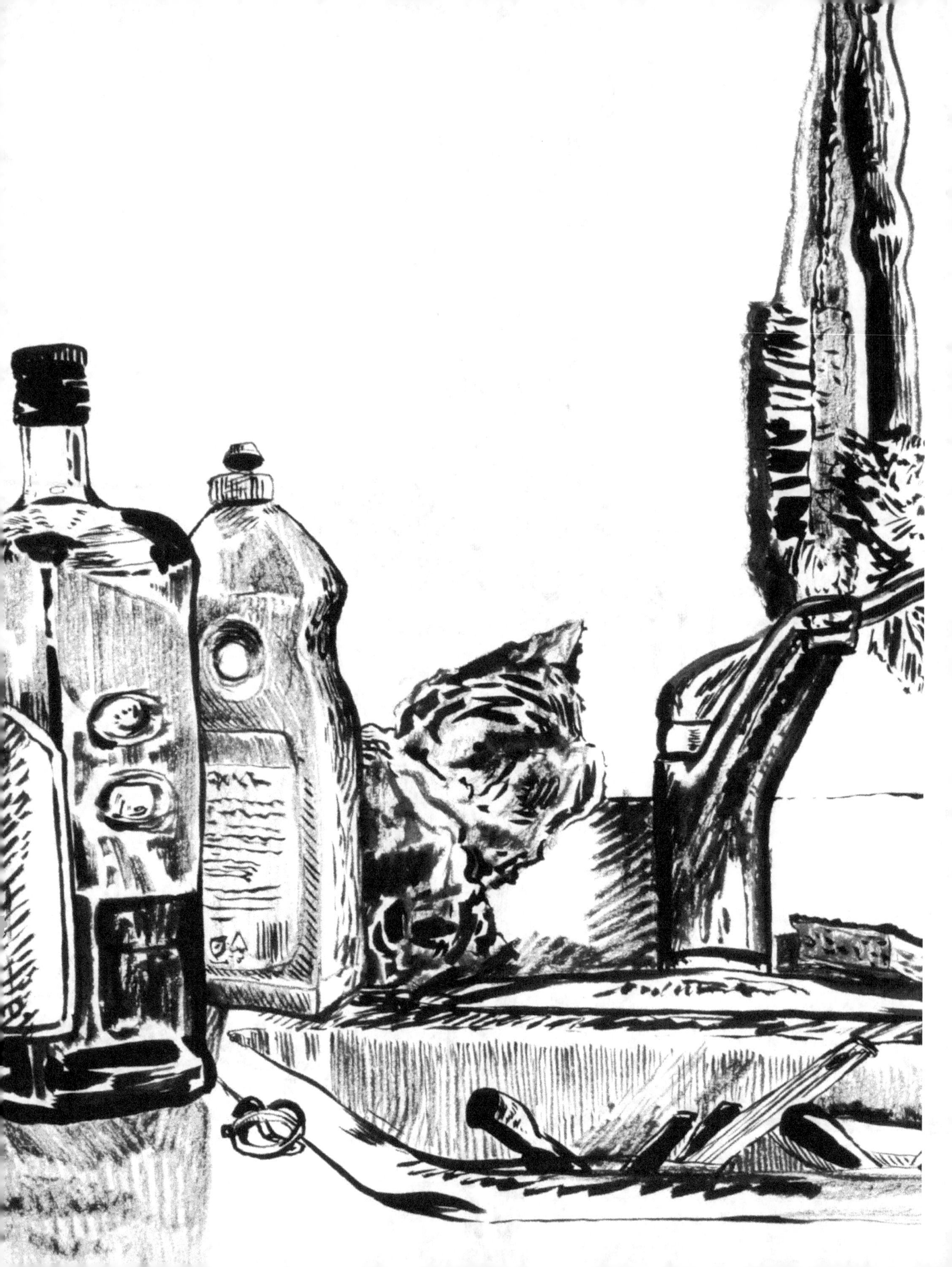

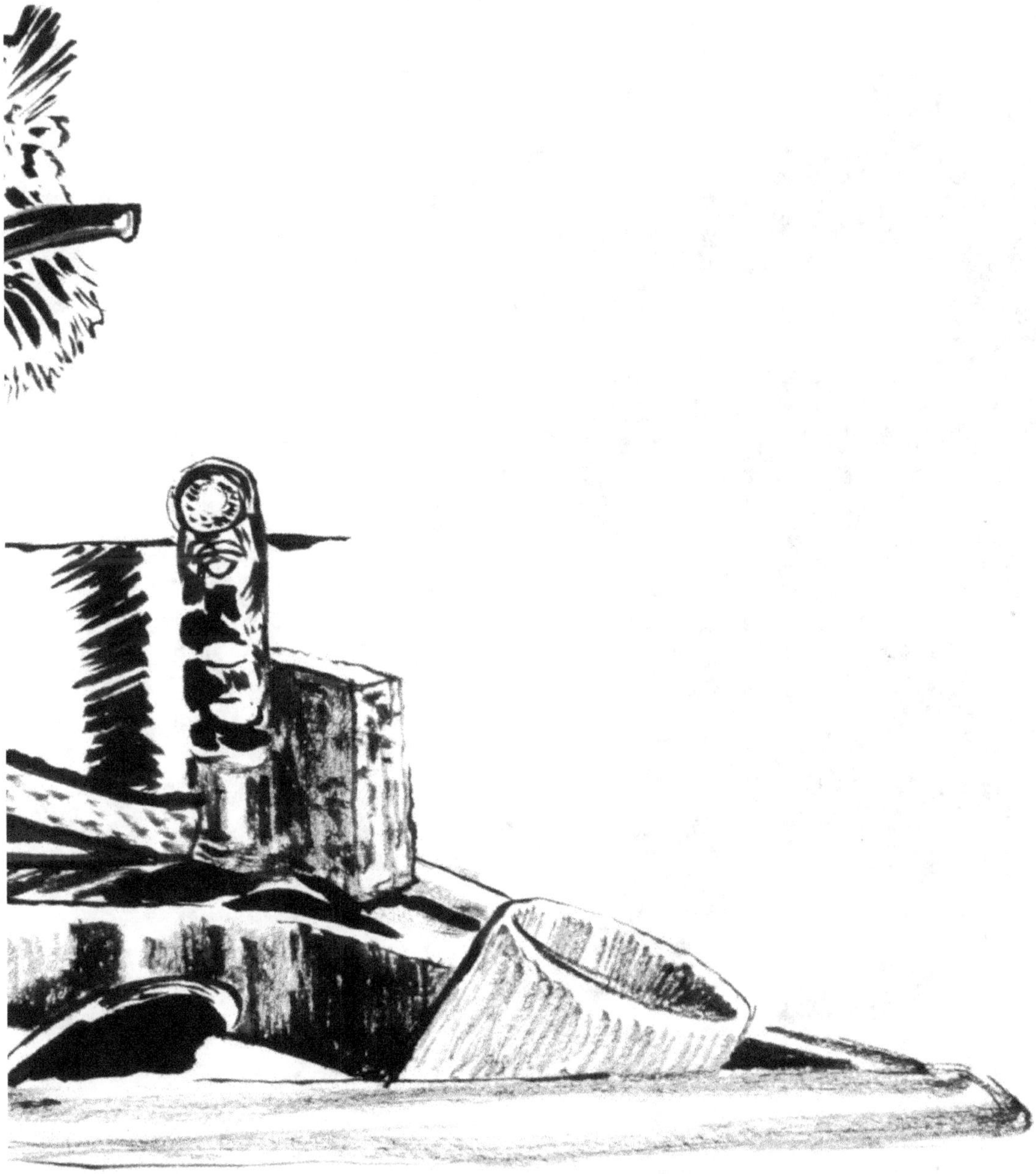

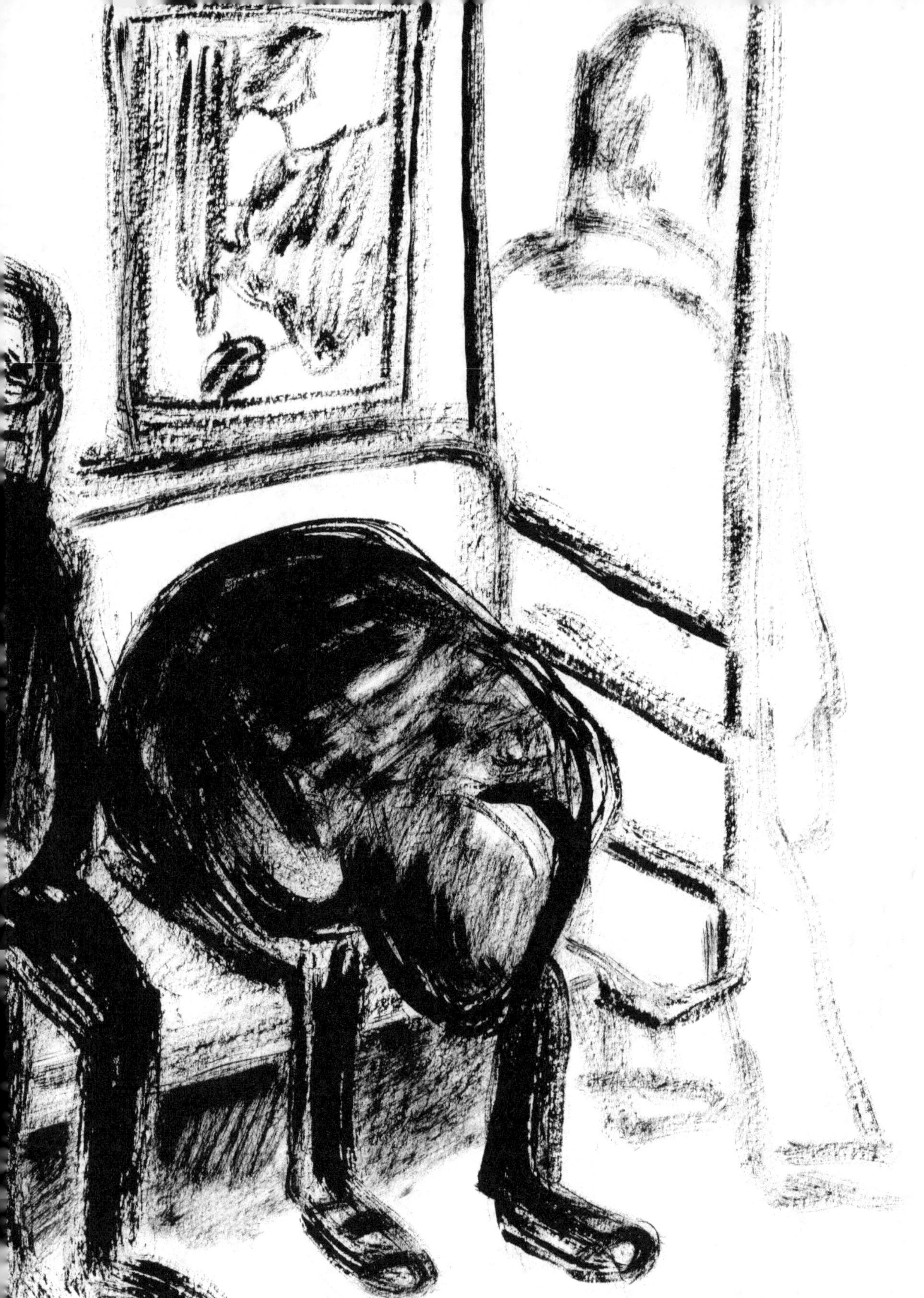

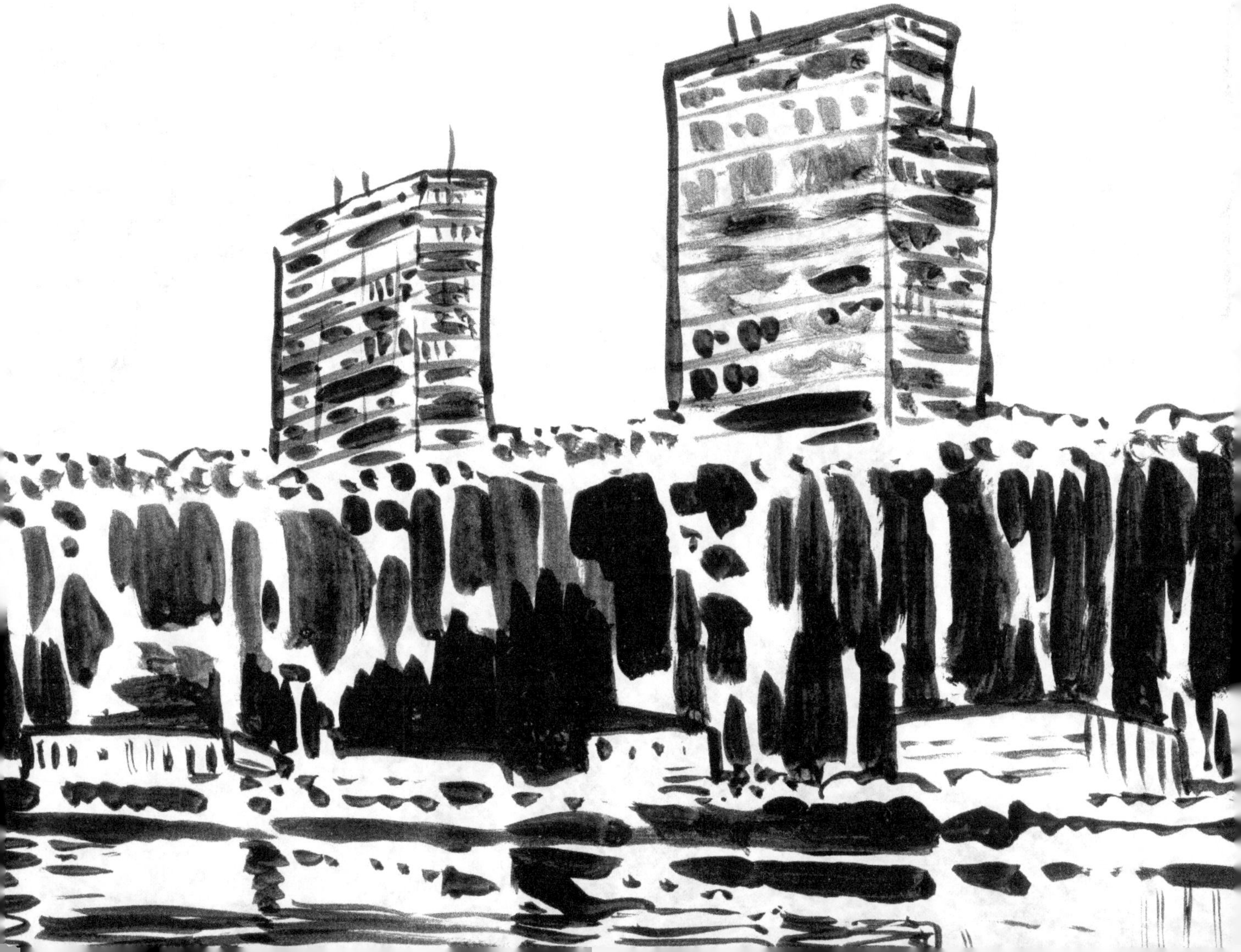

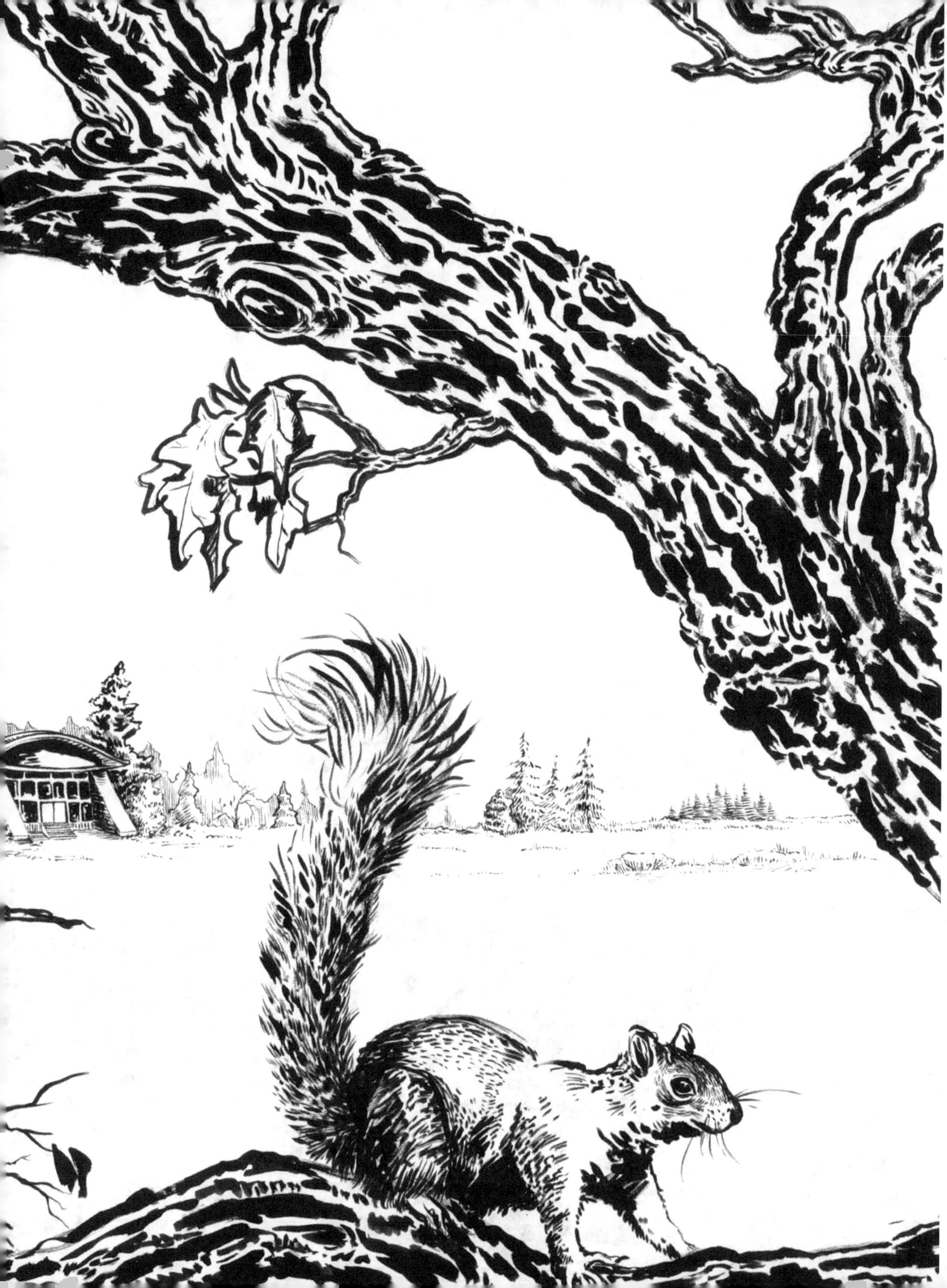

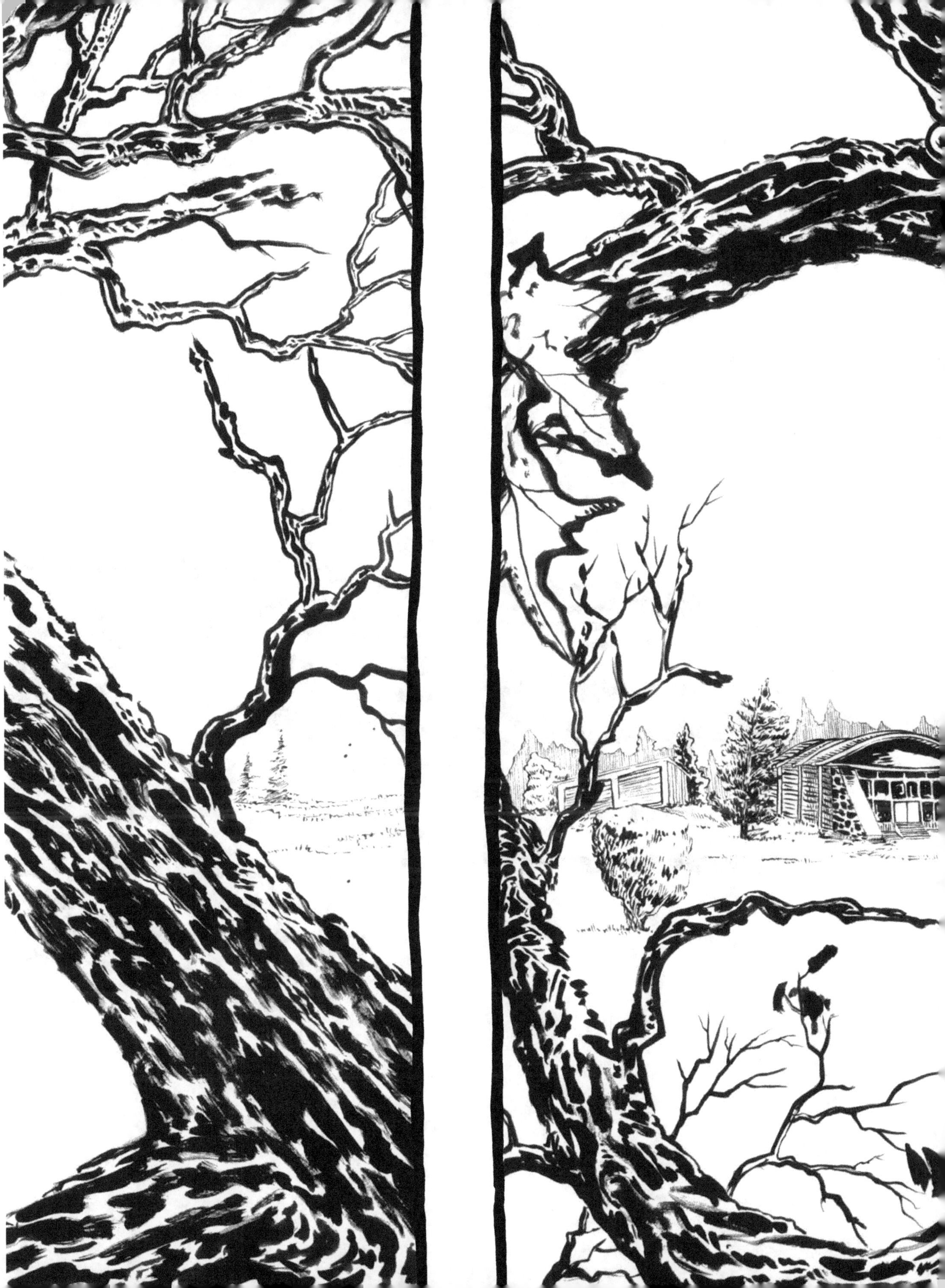

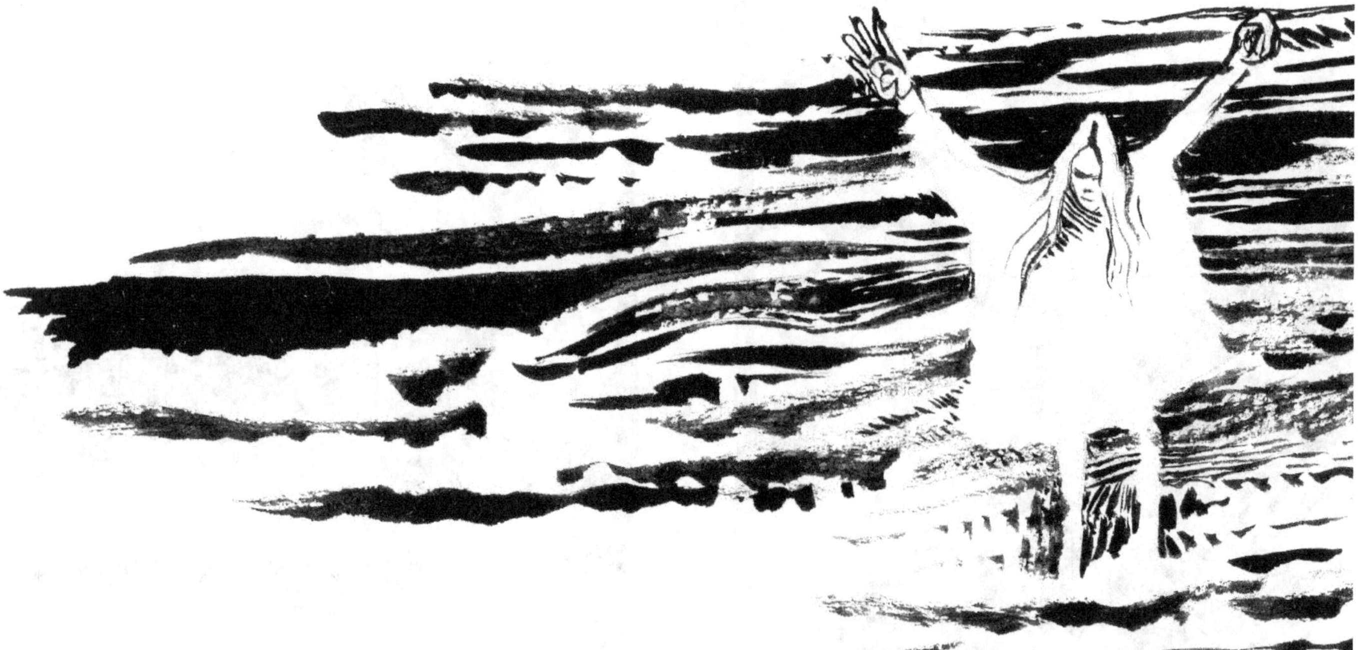

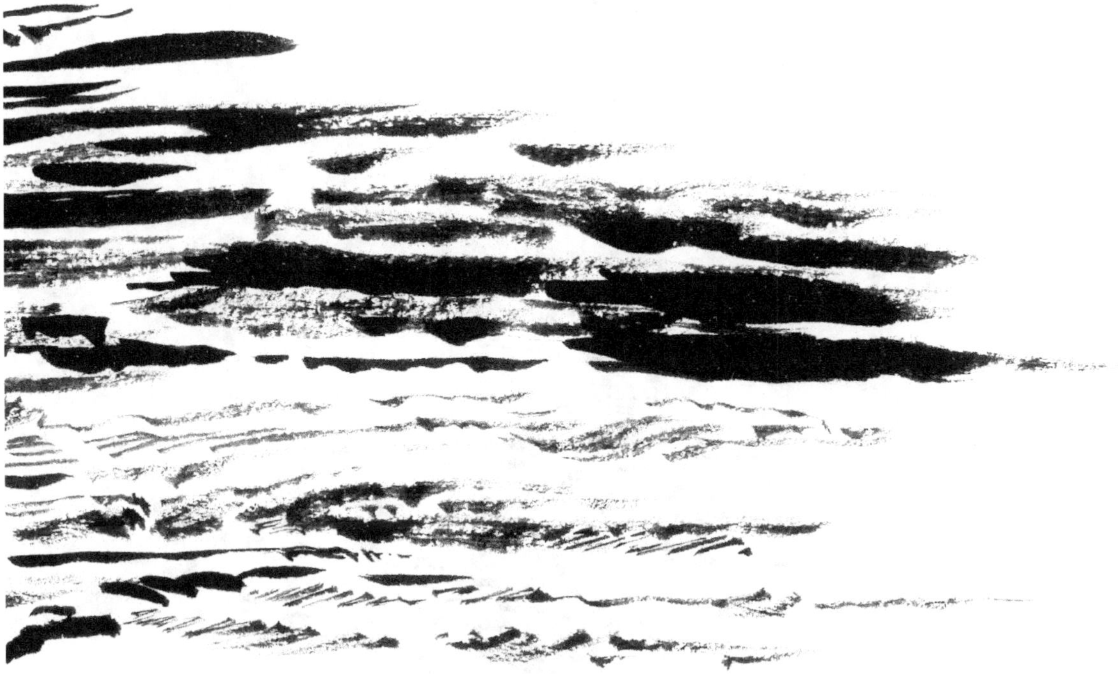

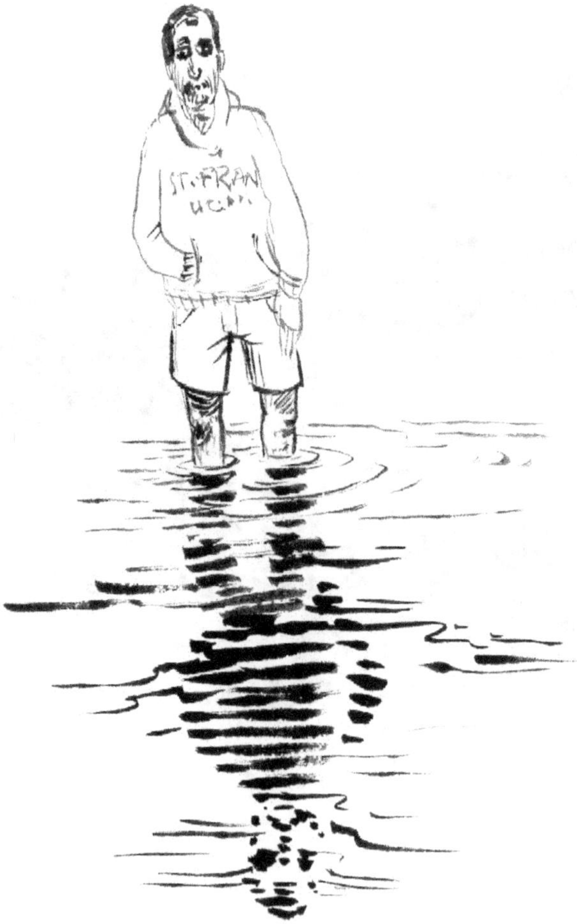
ST. FRAN

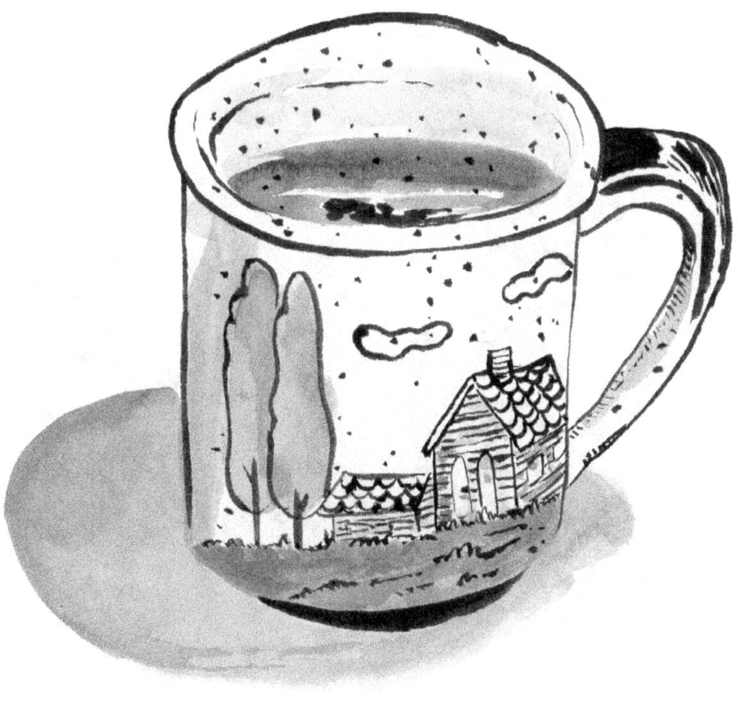

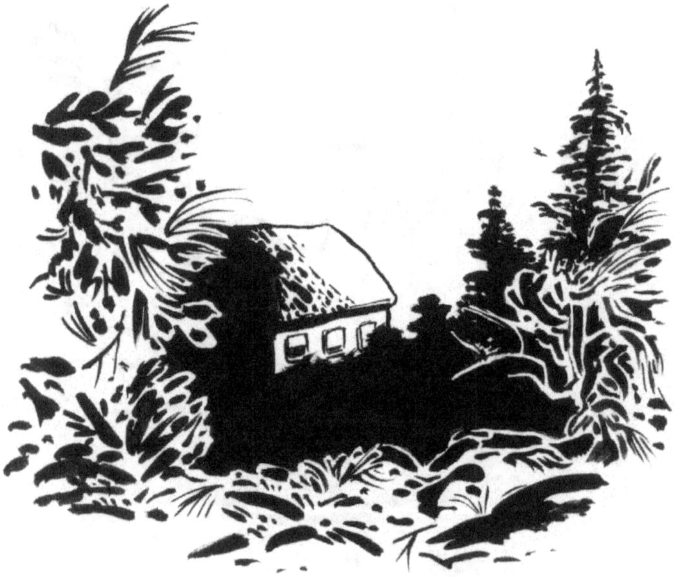

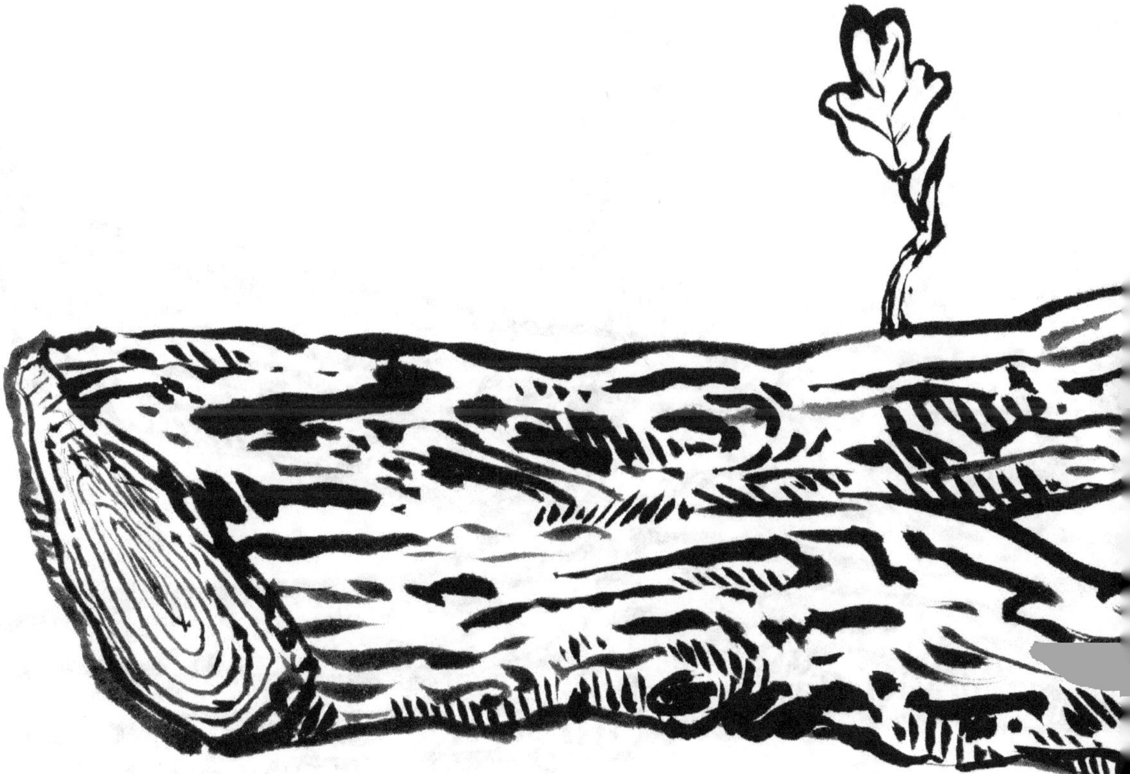

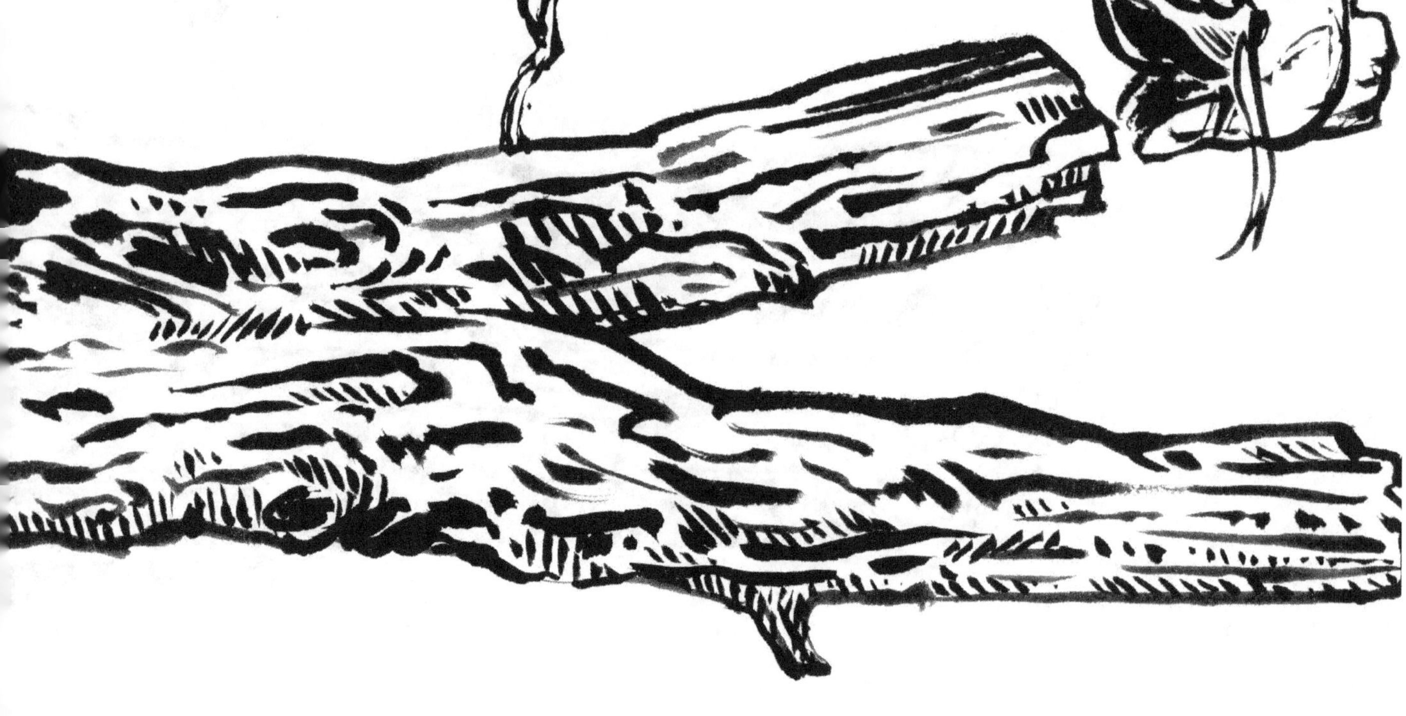

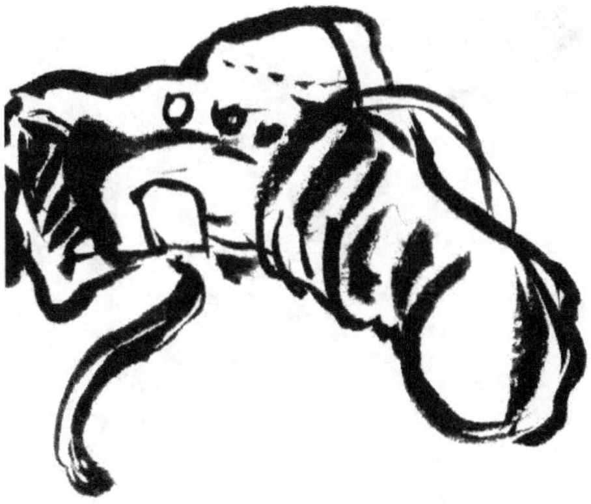

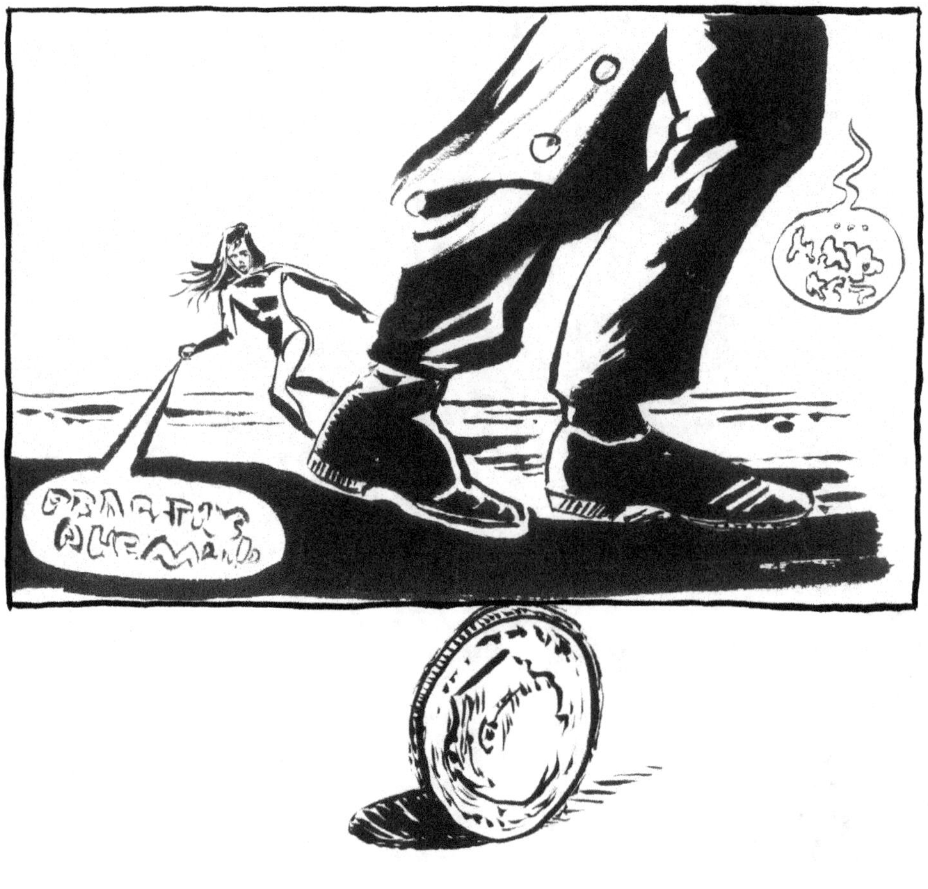

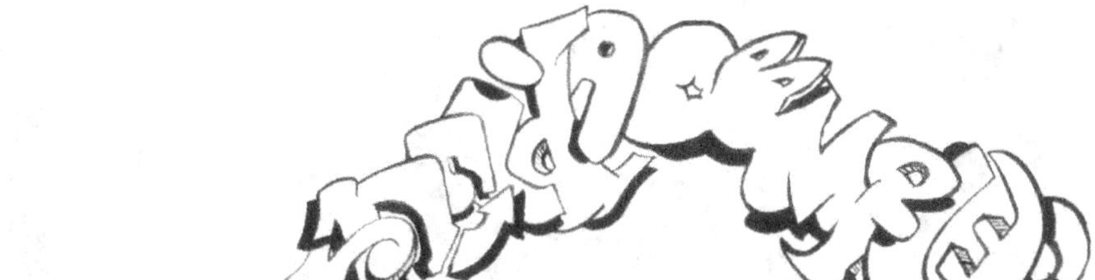

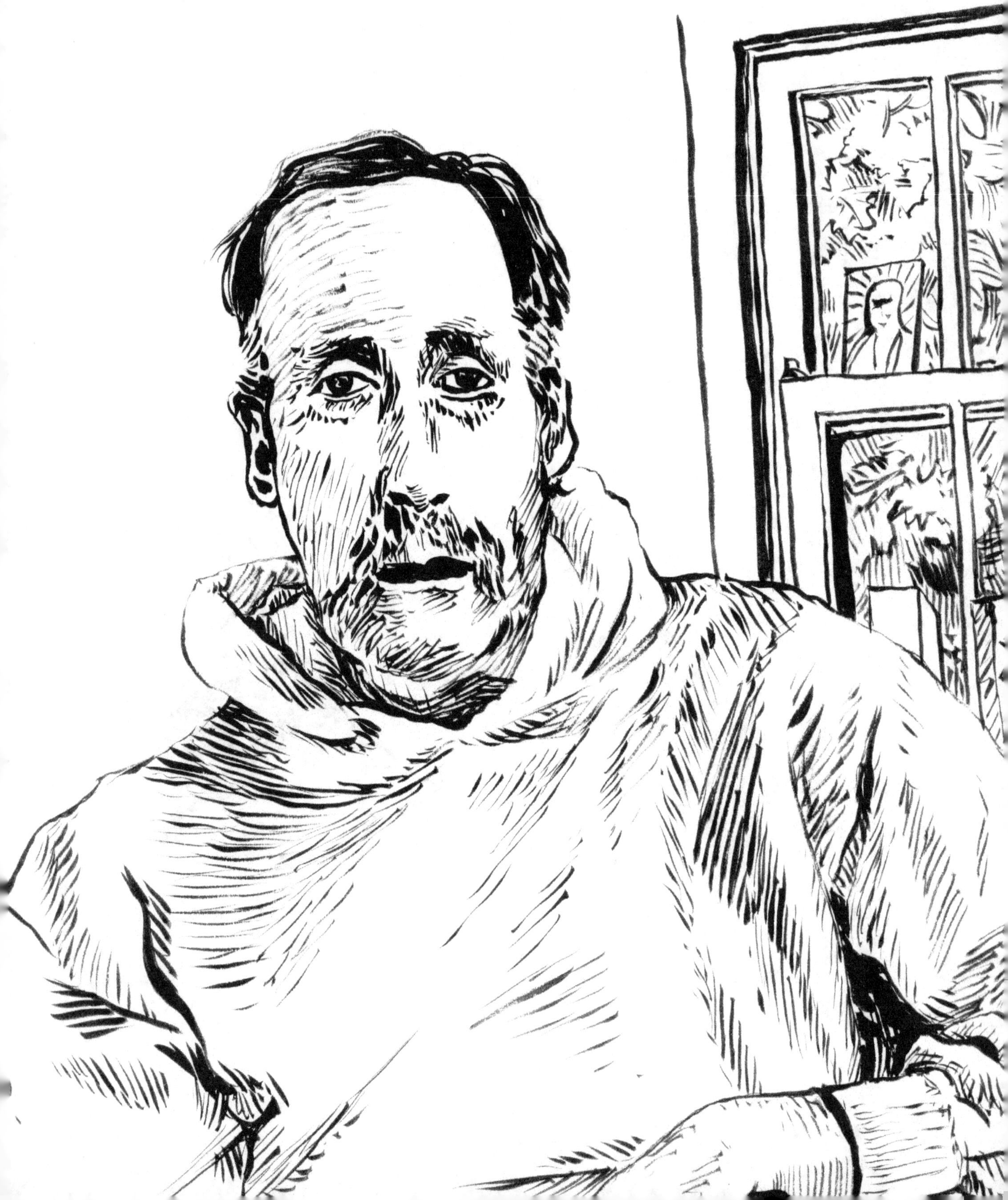

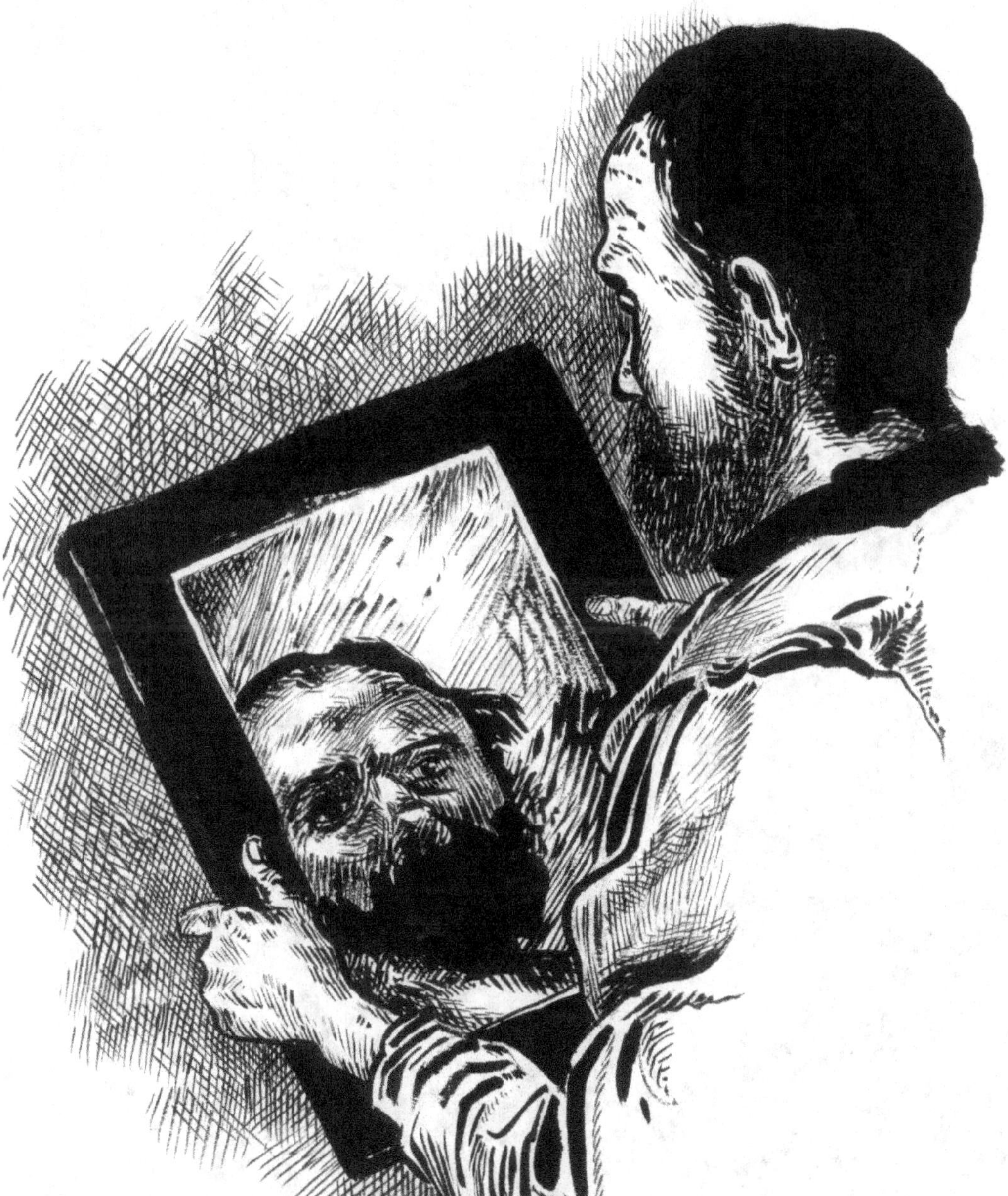

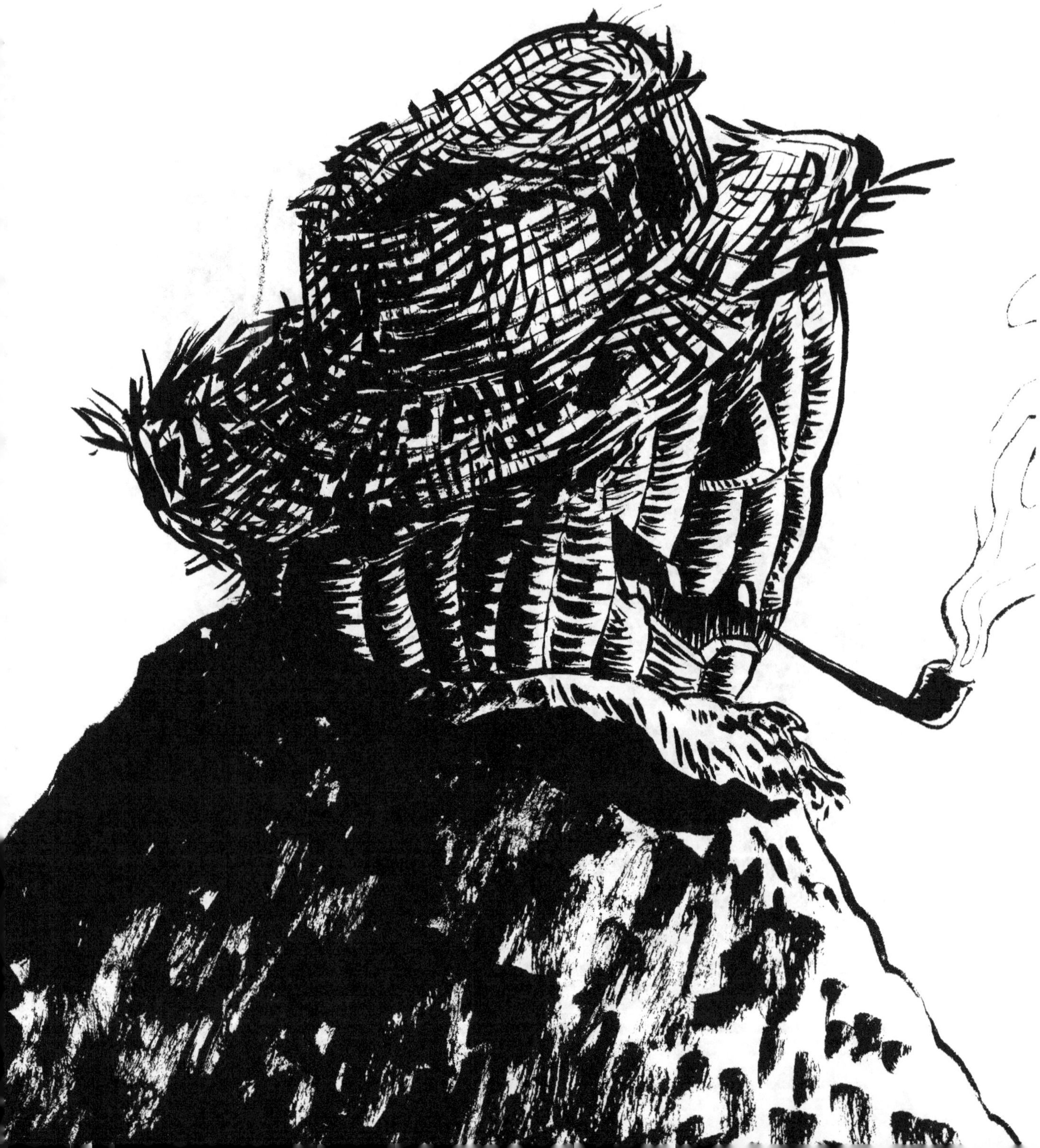

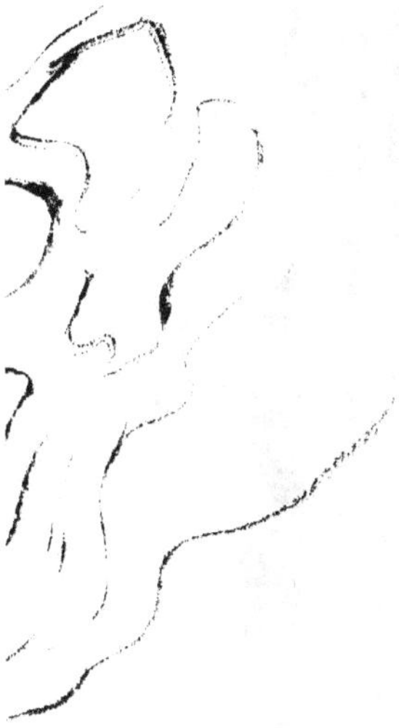

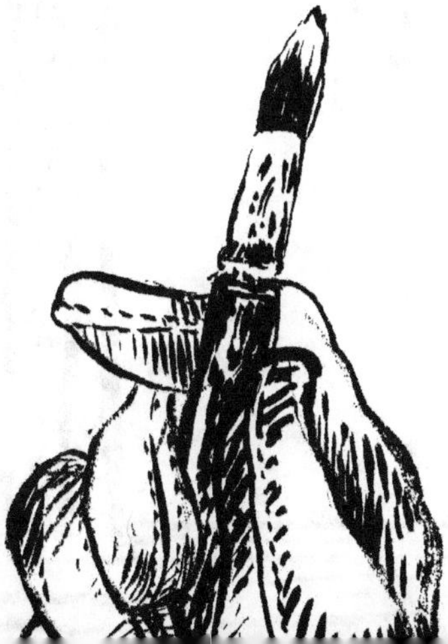

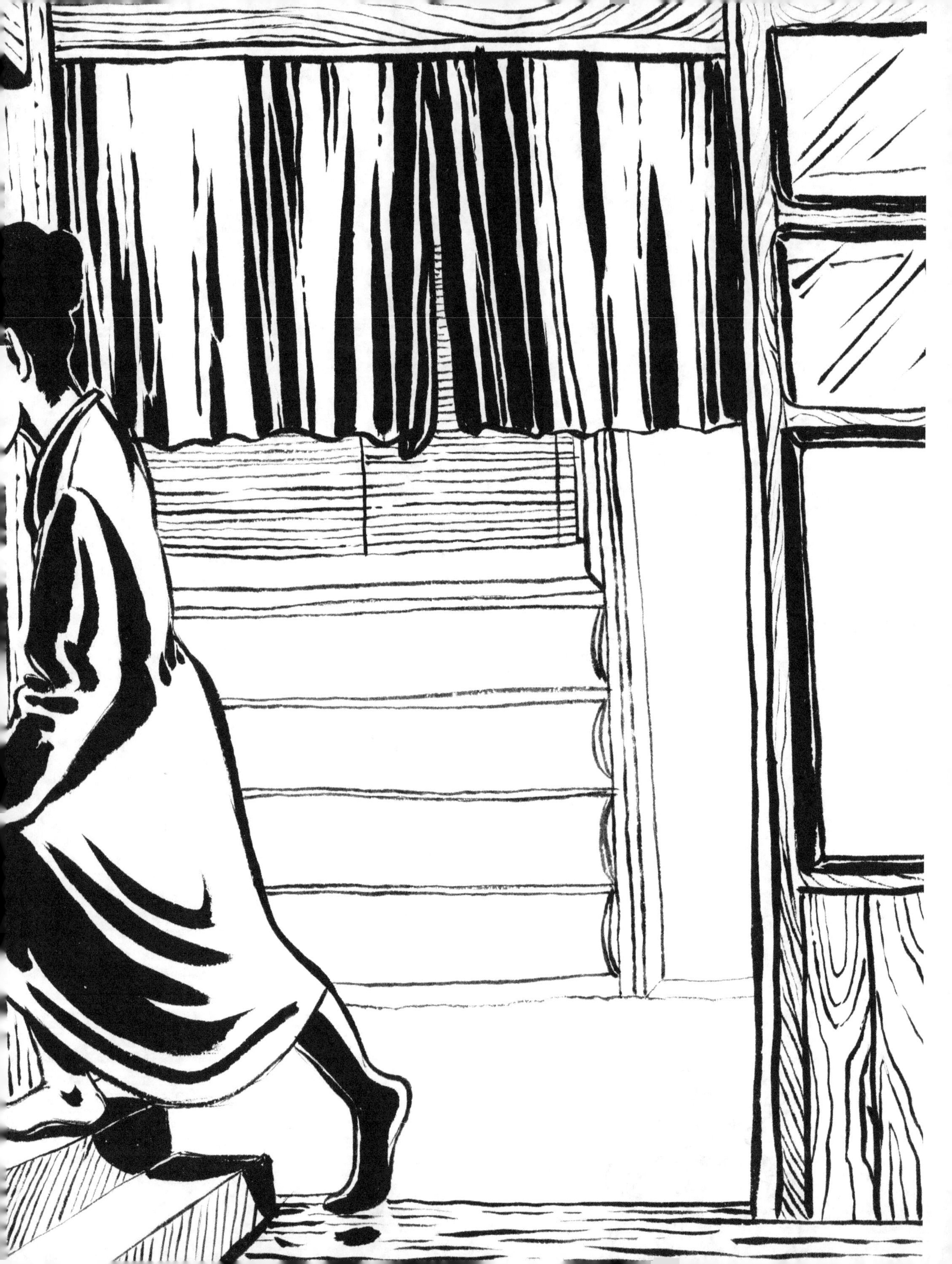

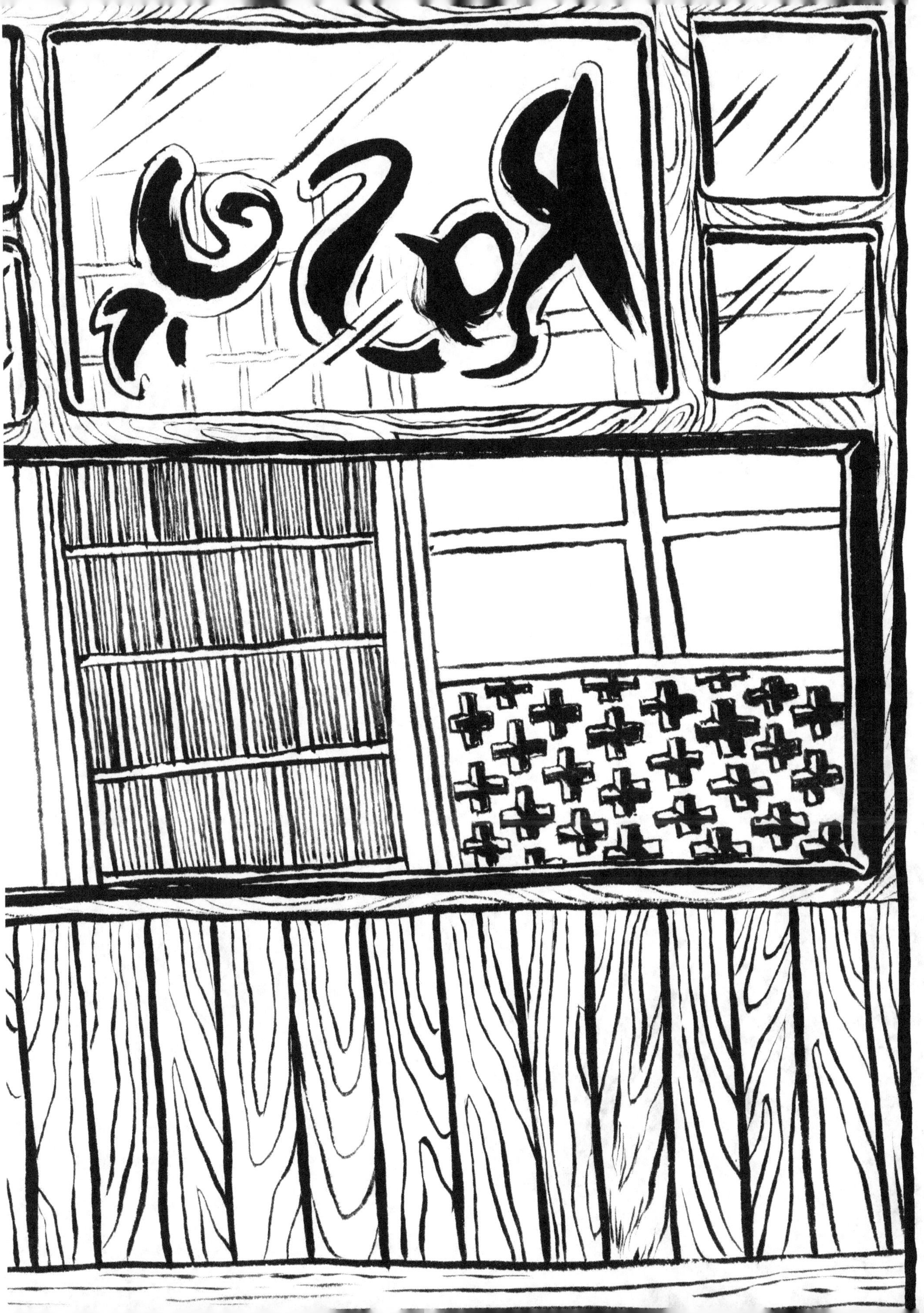
Rossi's

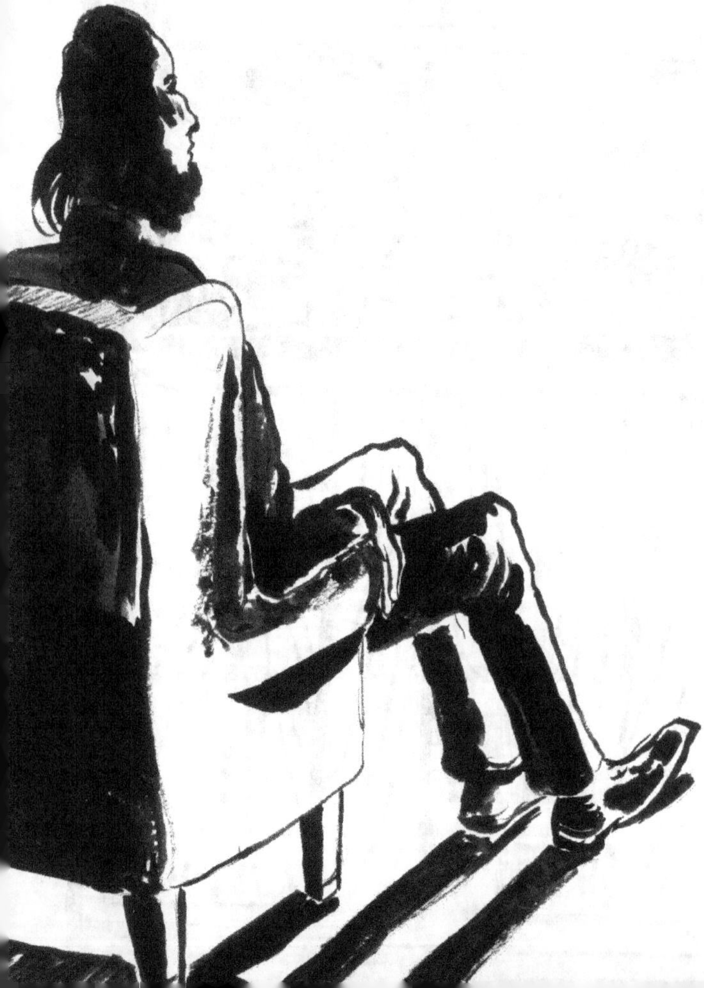

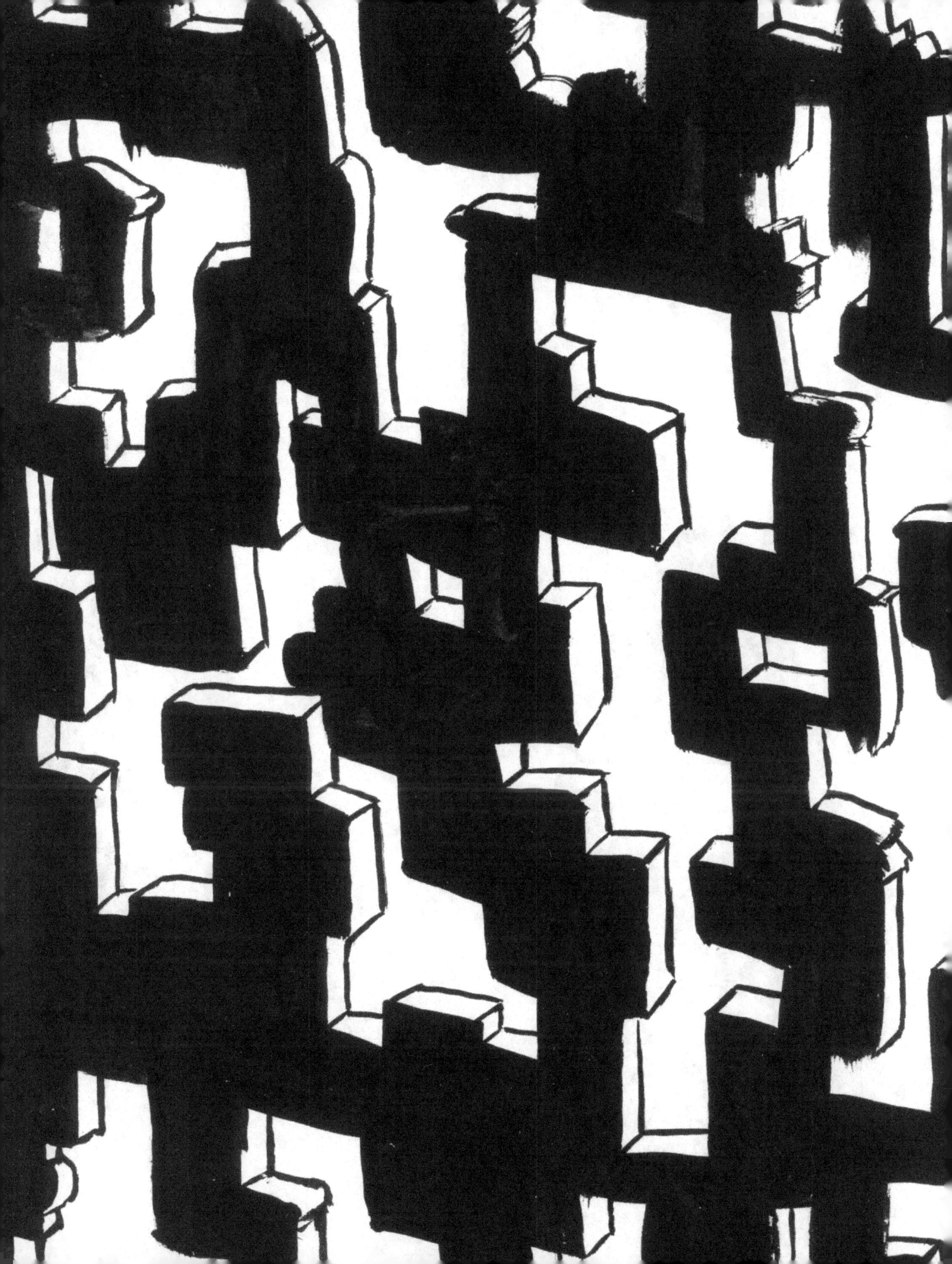

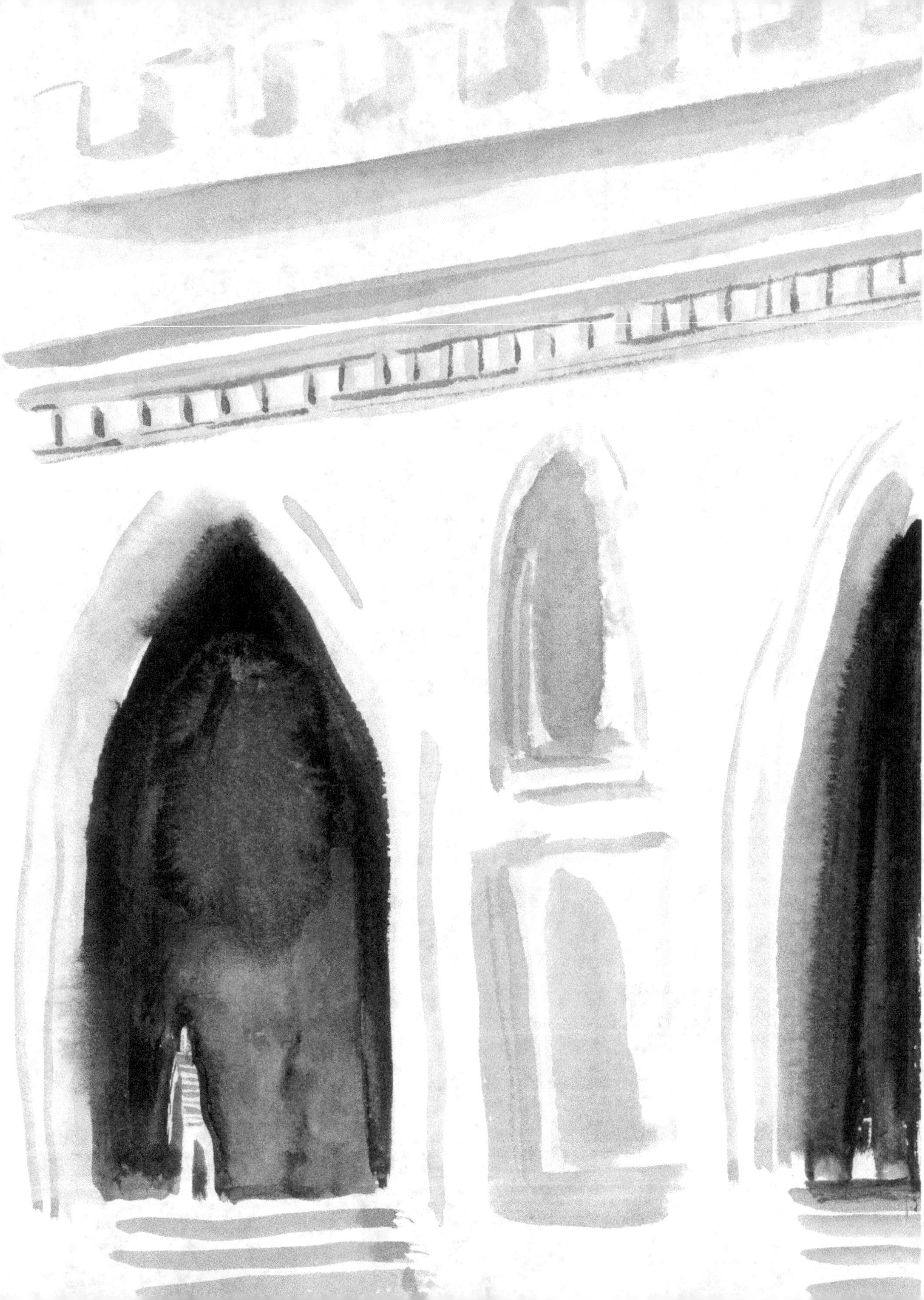

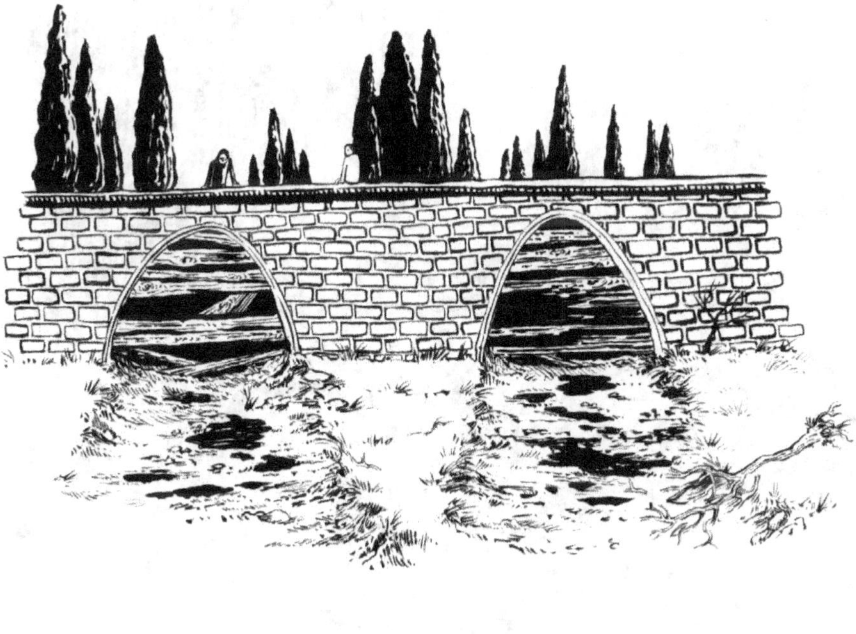

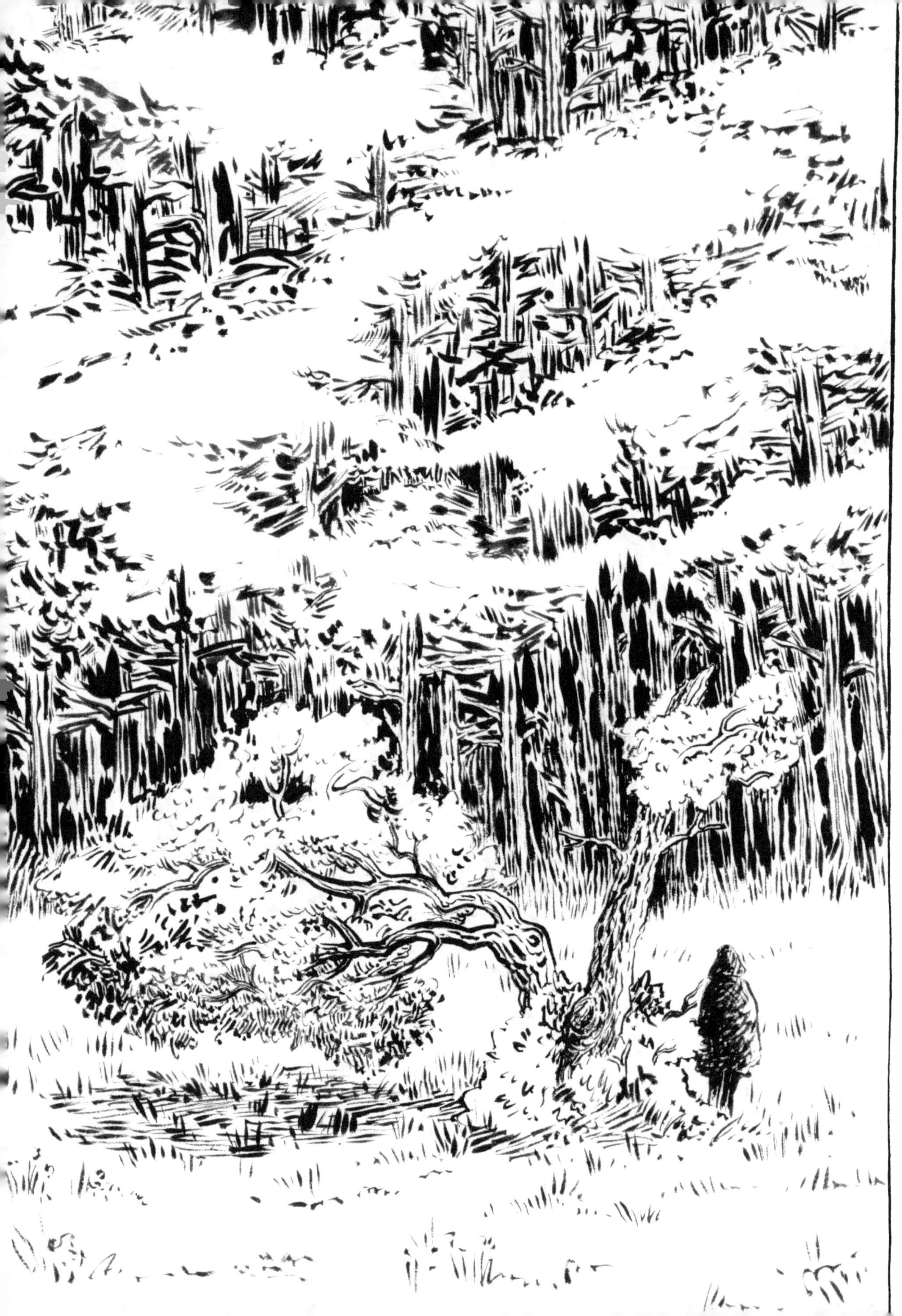

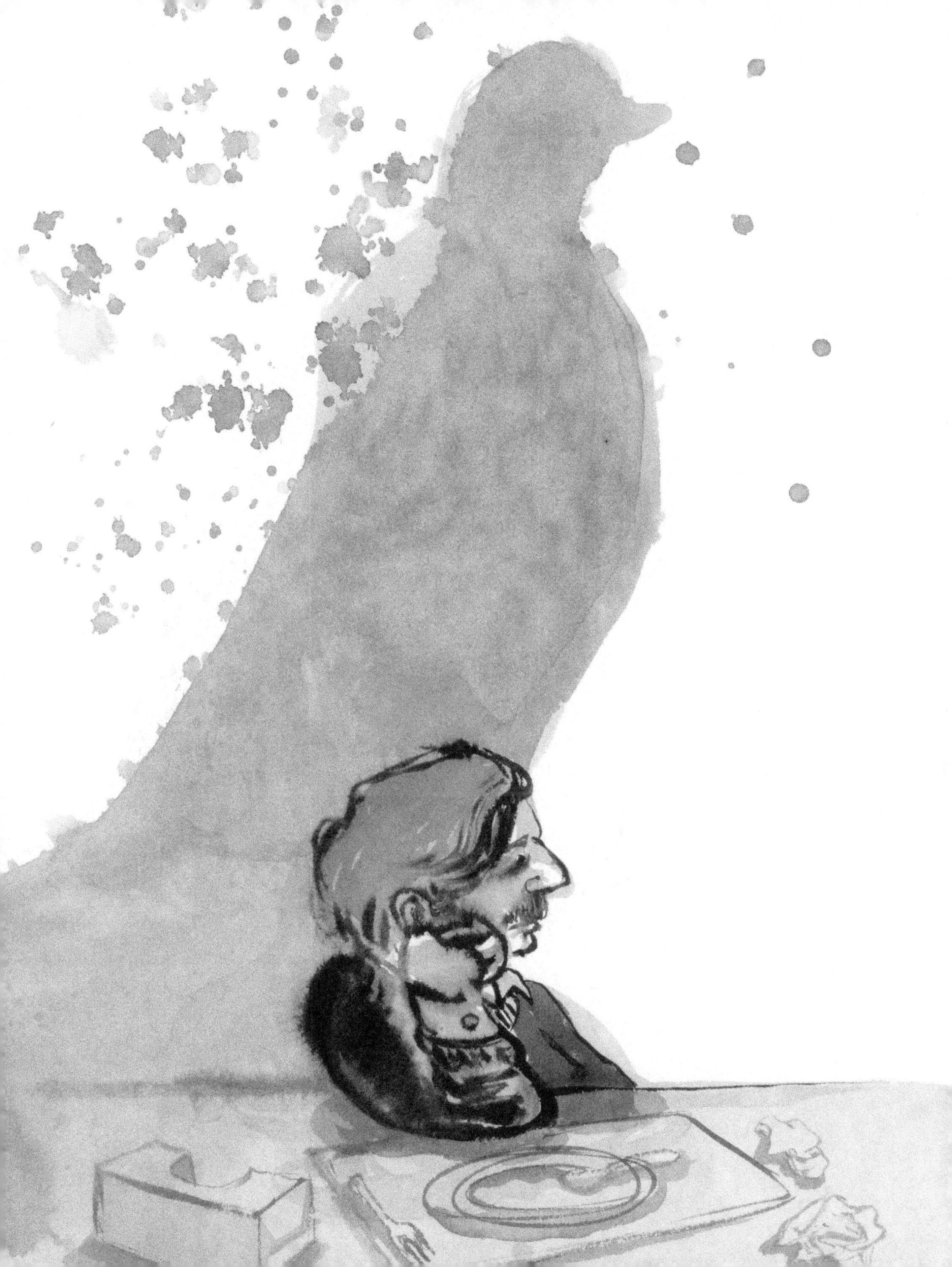

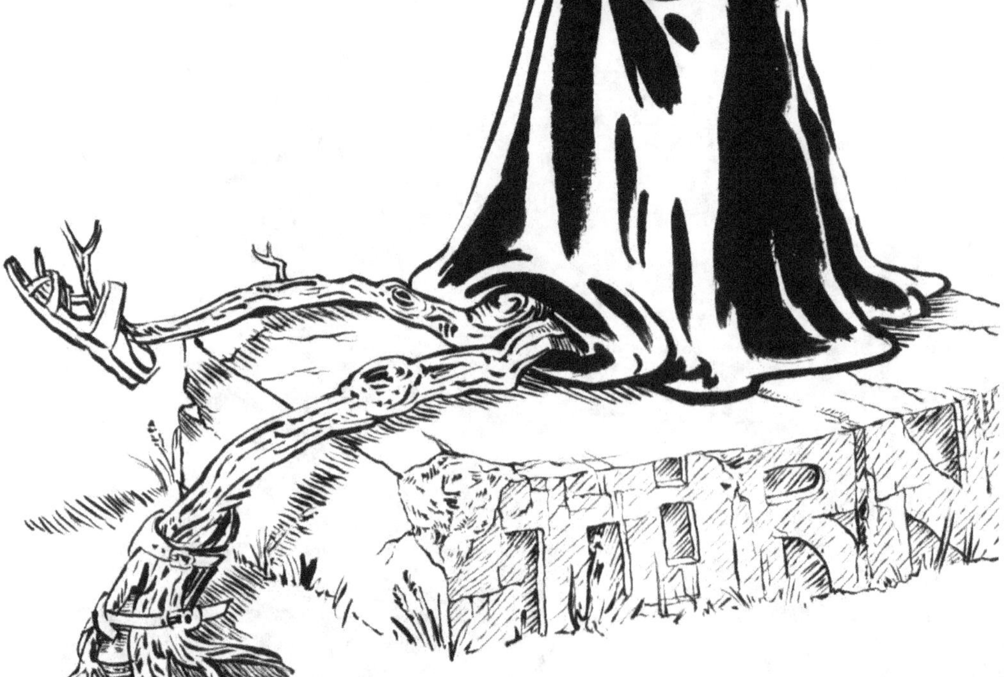

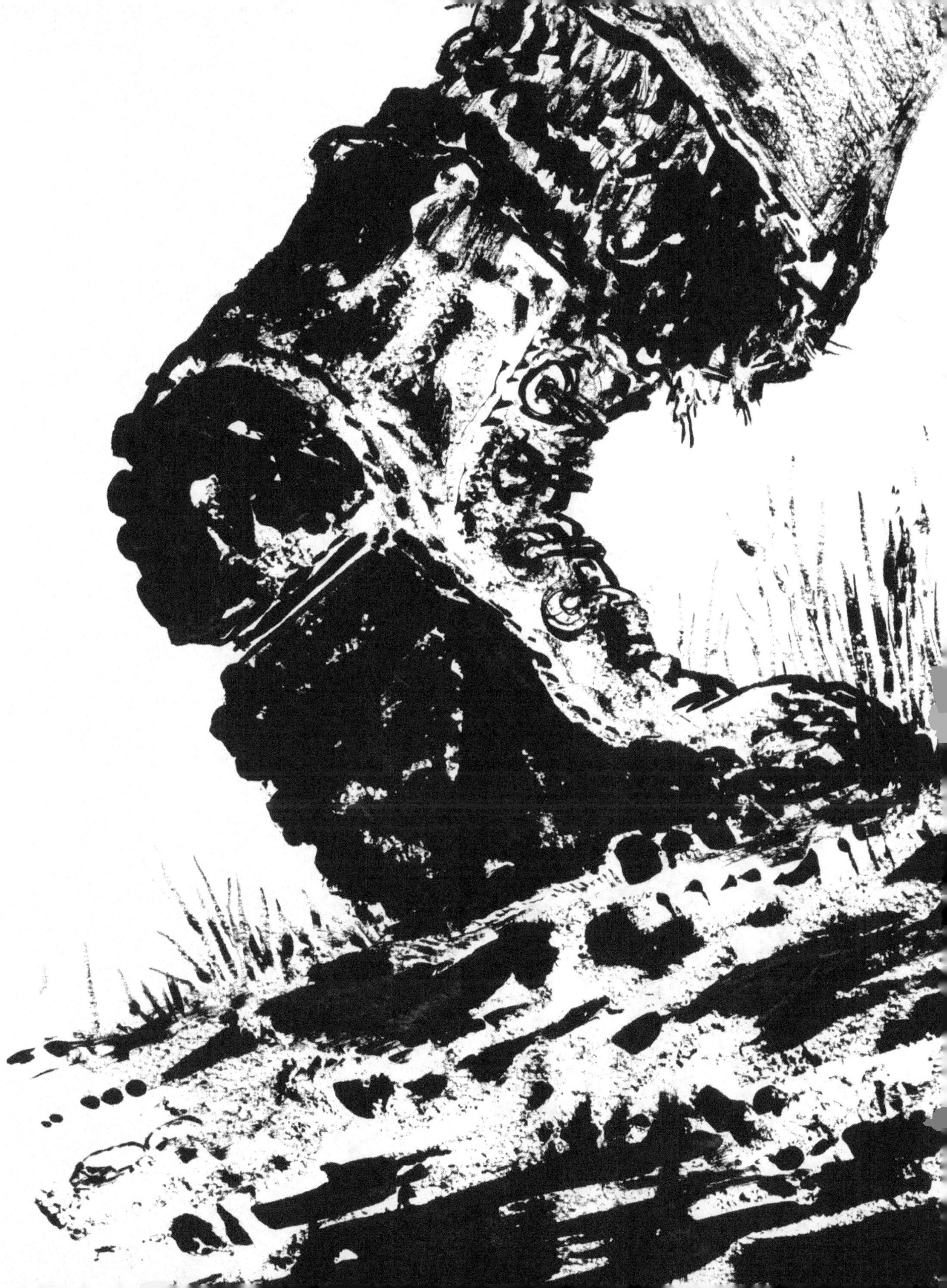

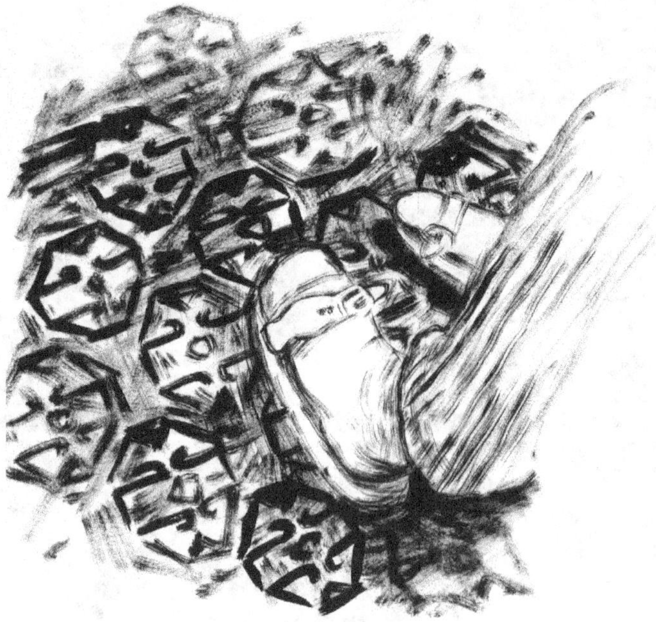

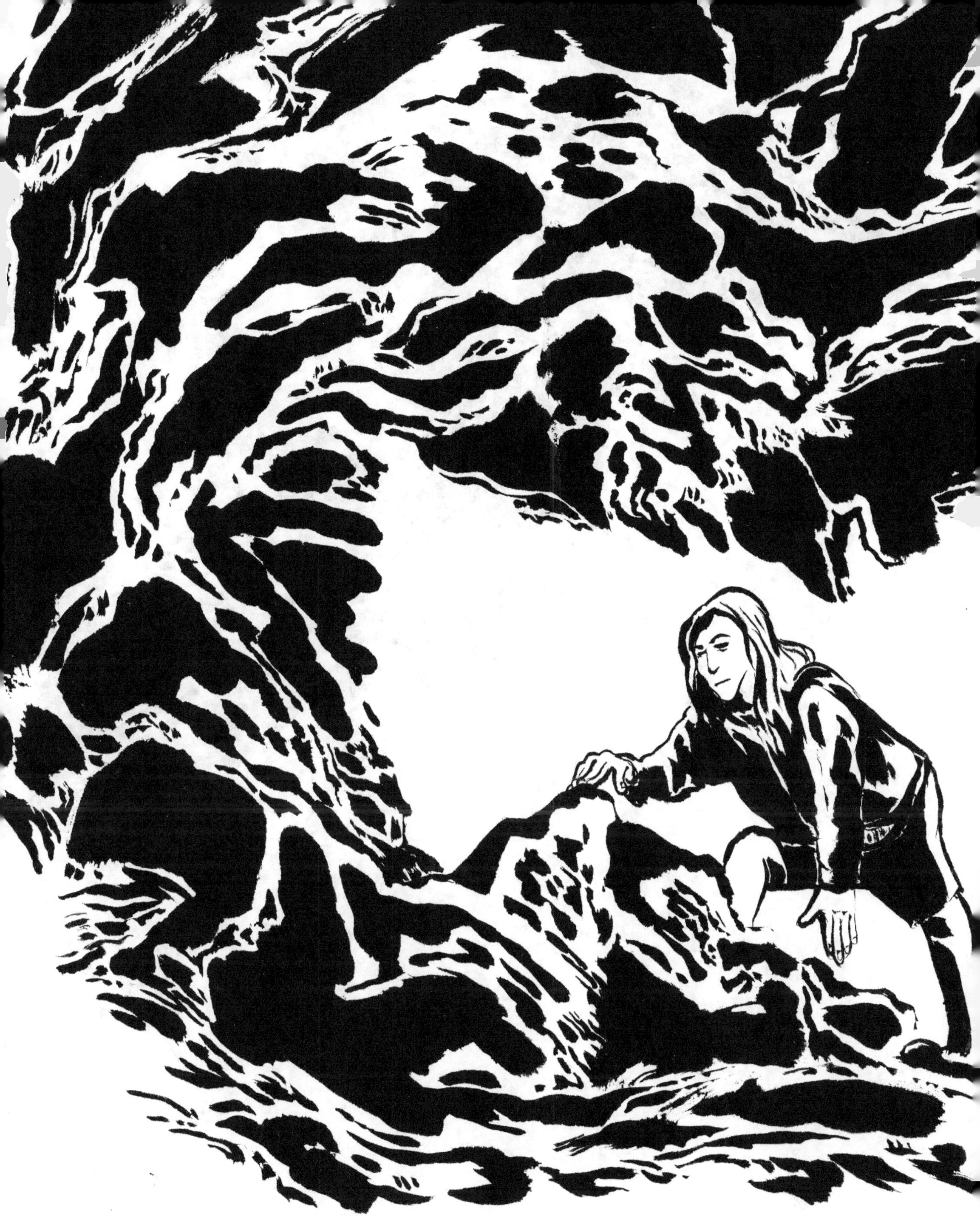

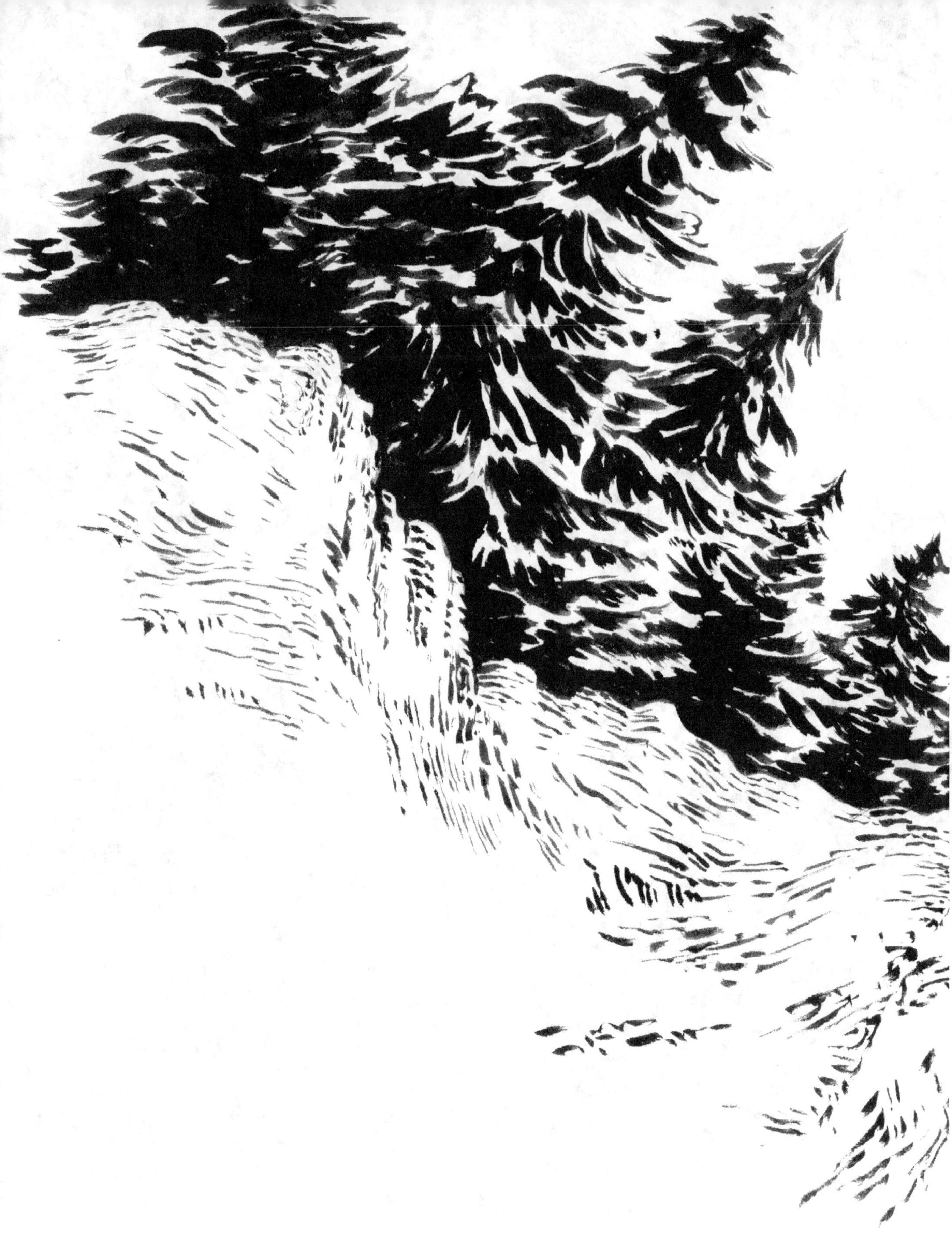

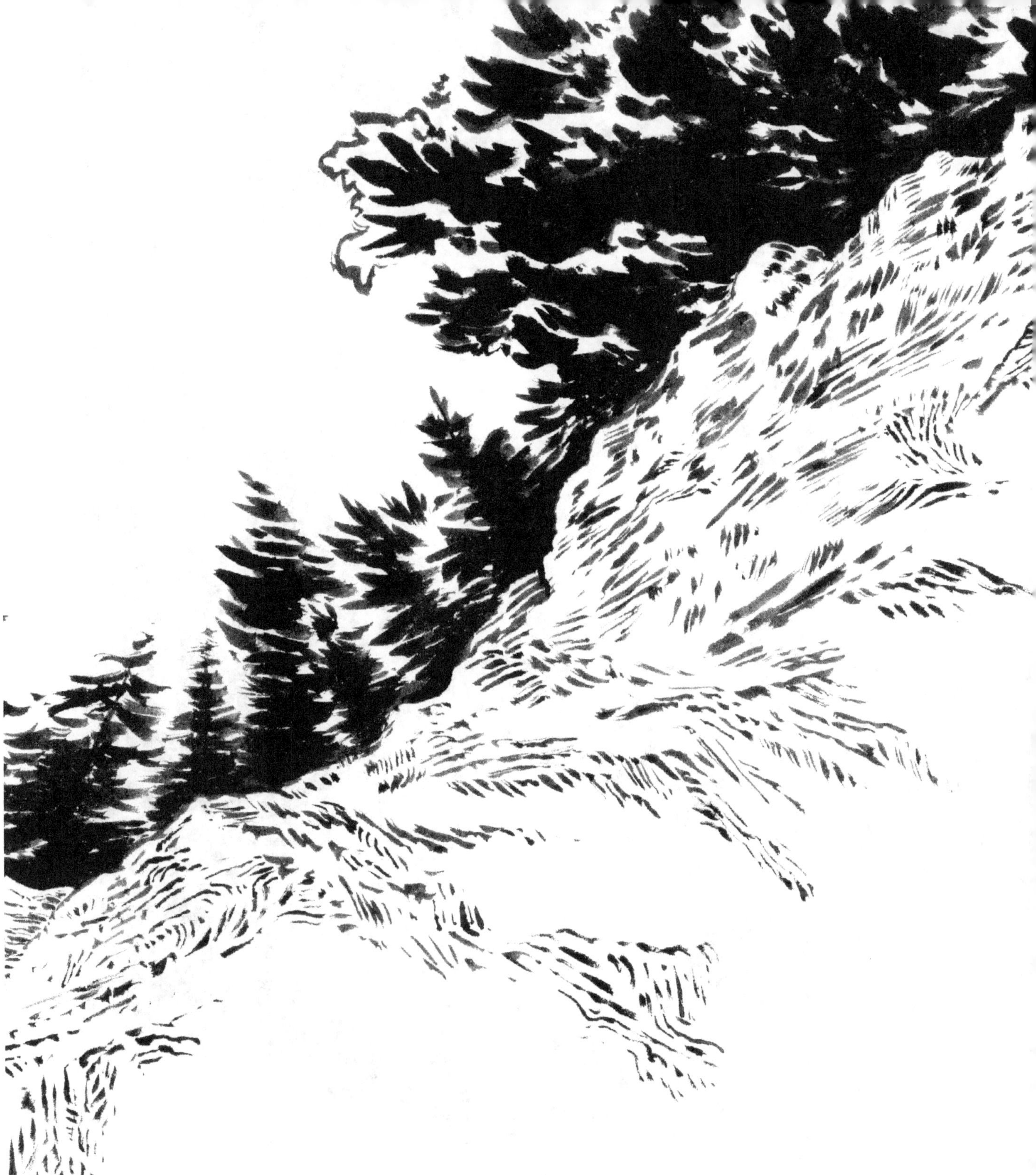

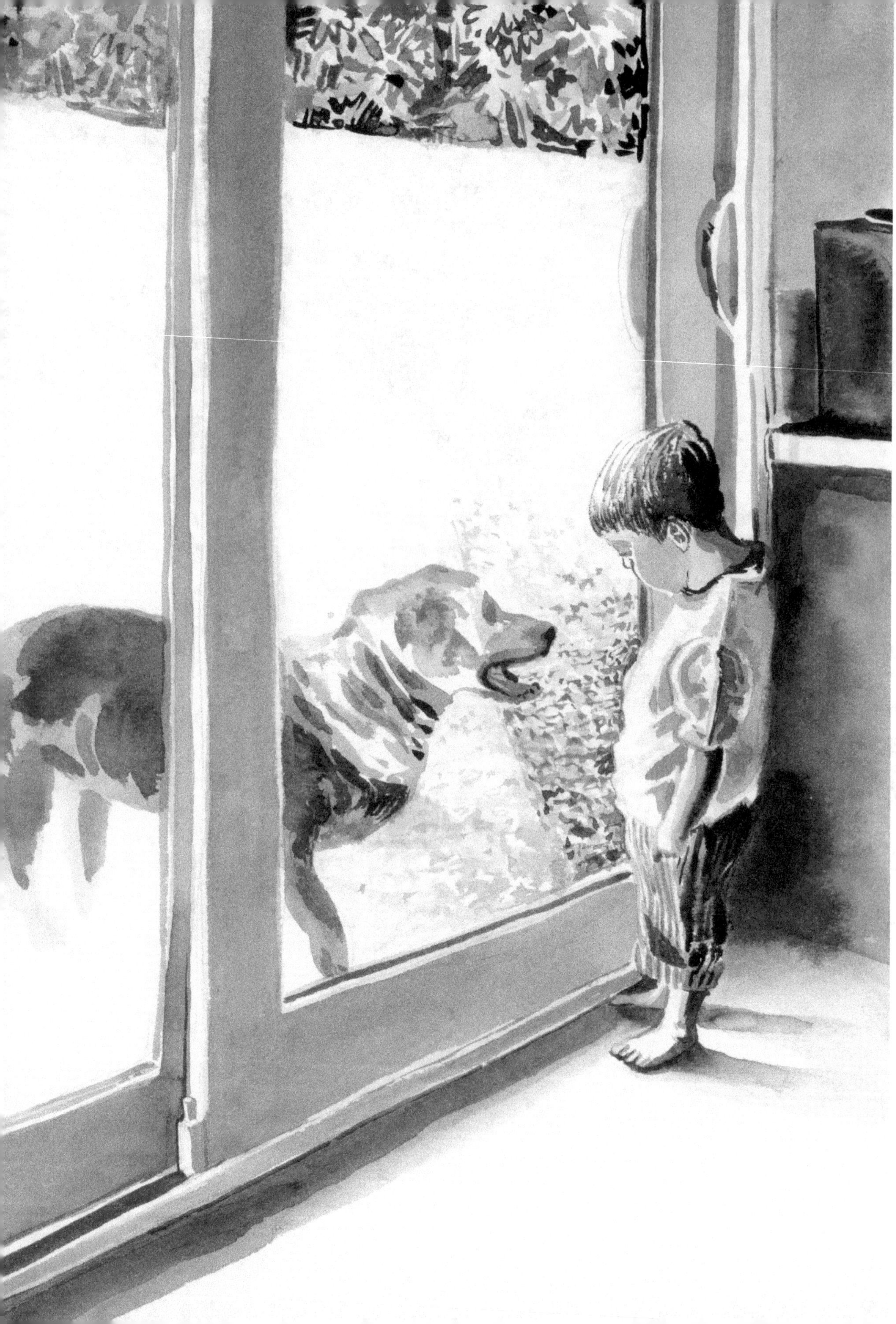

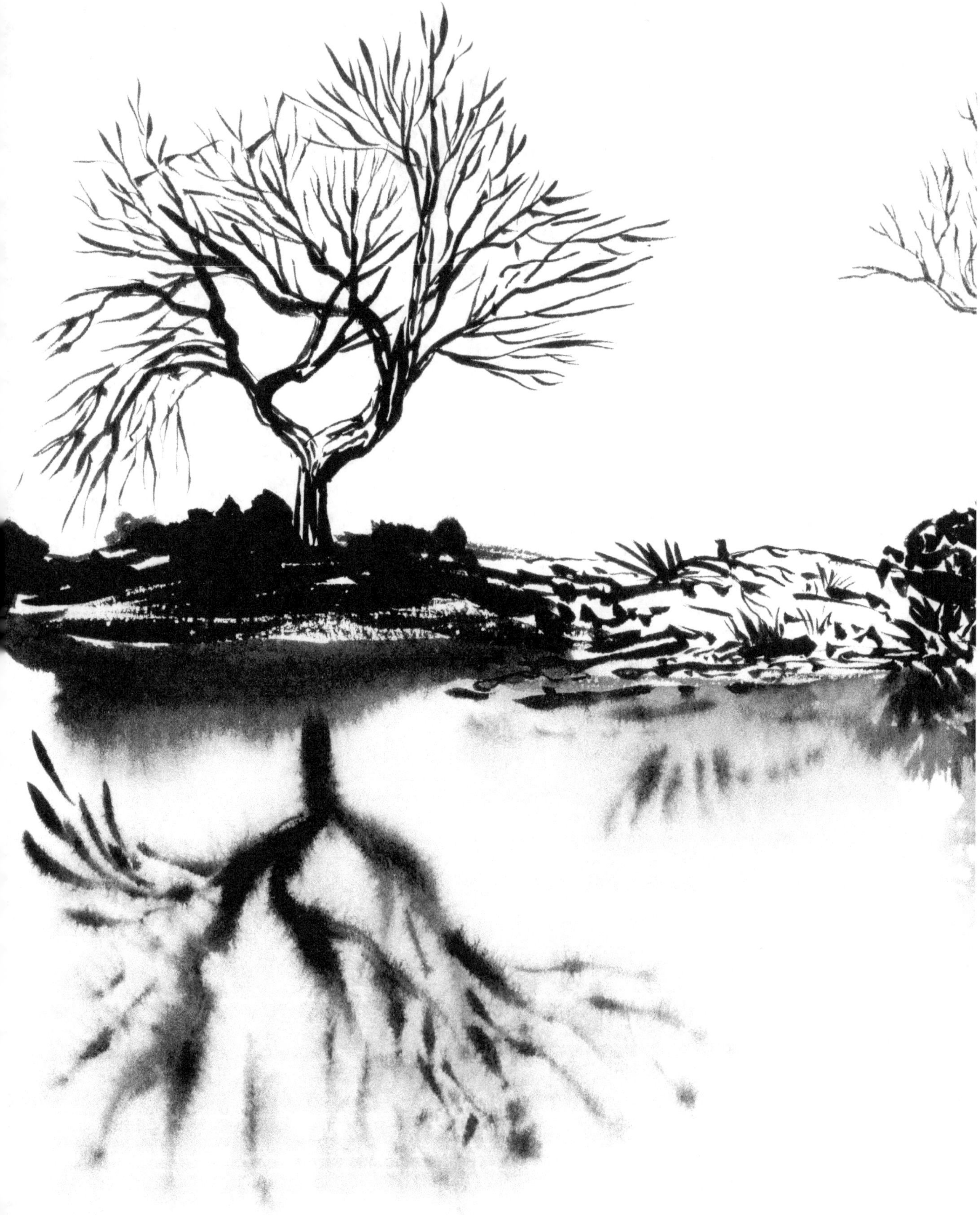

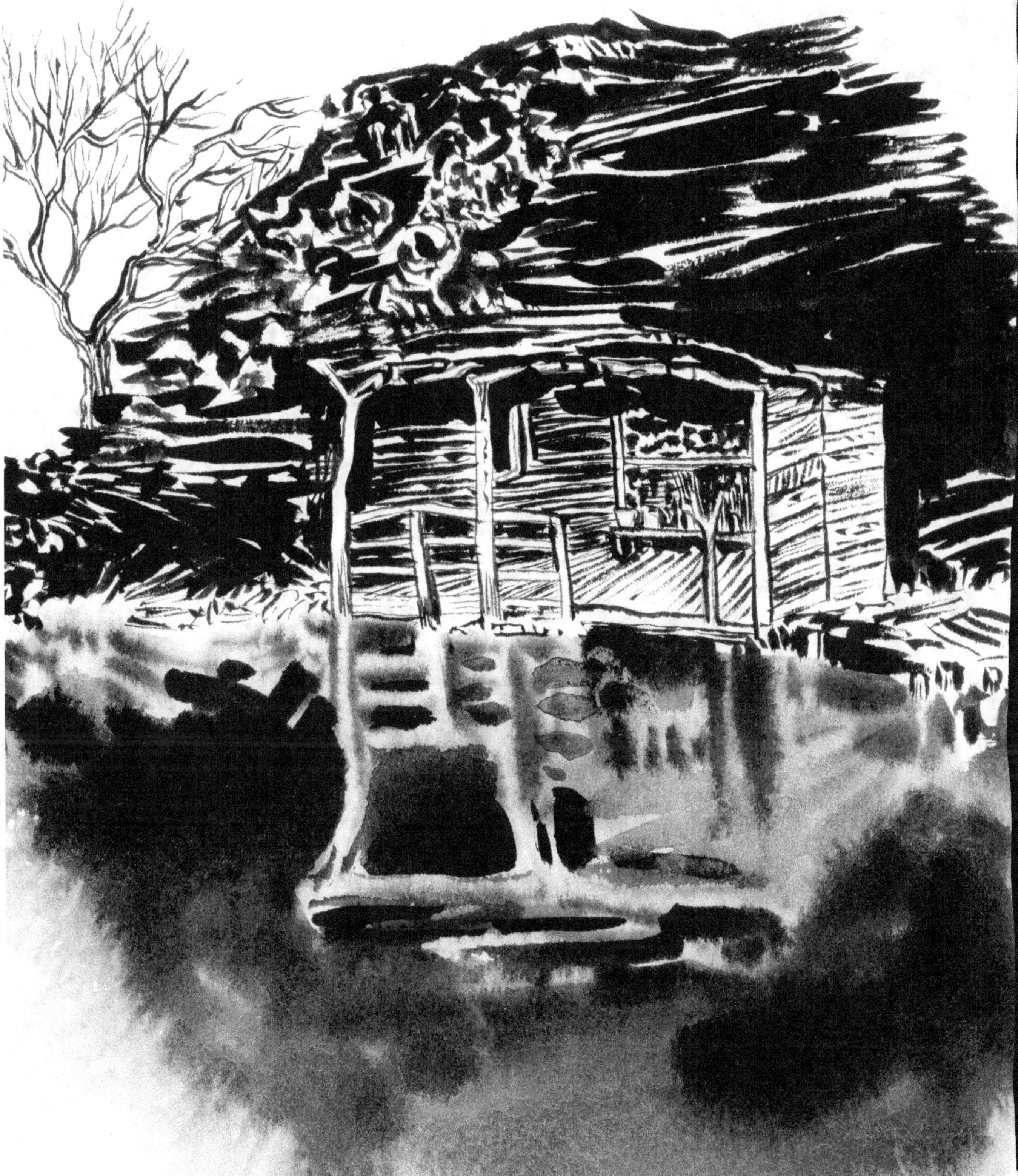

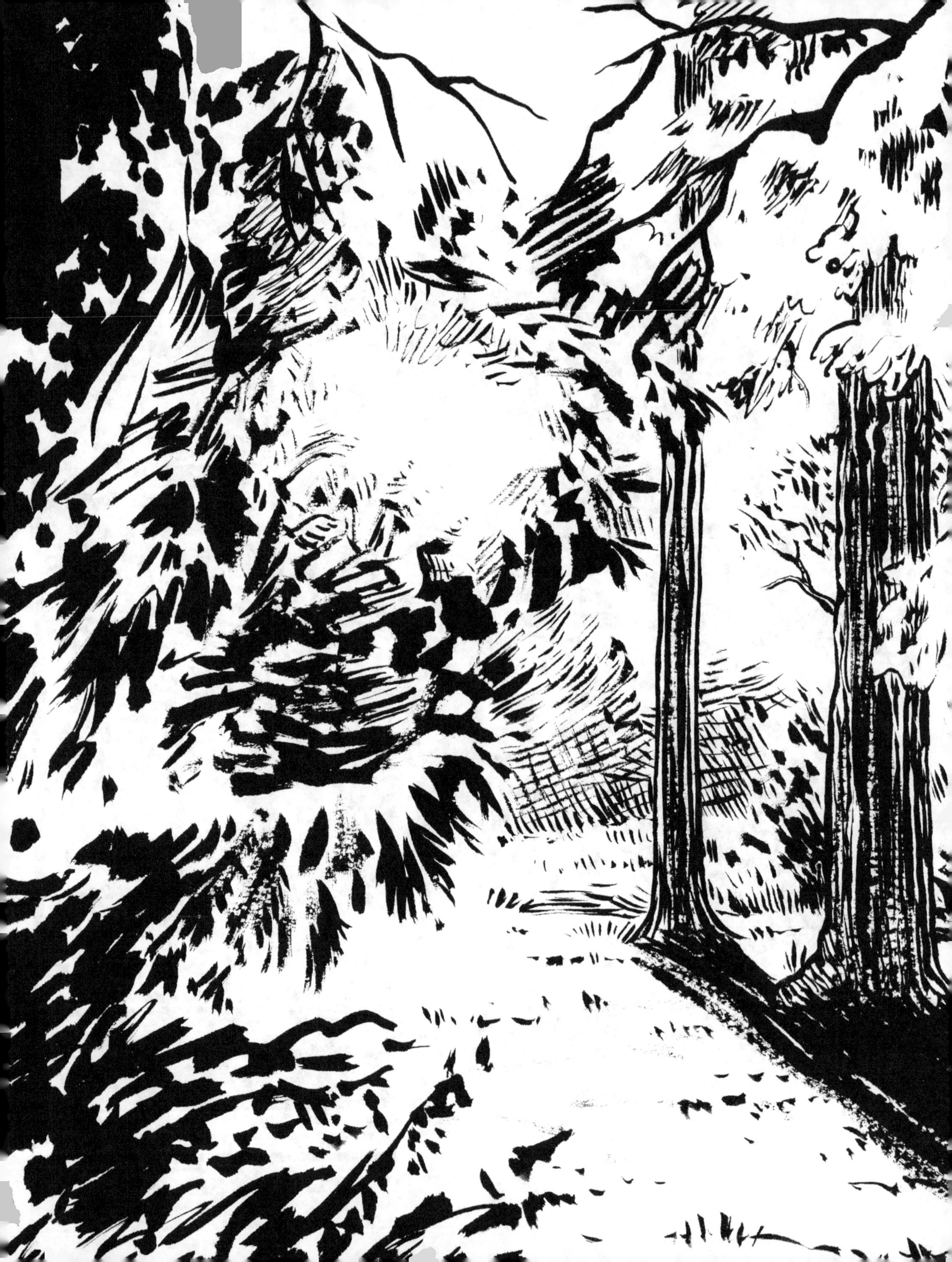

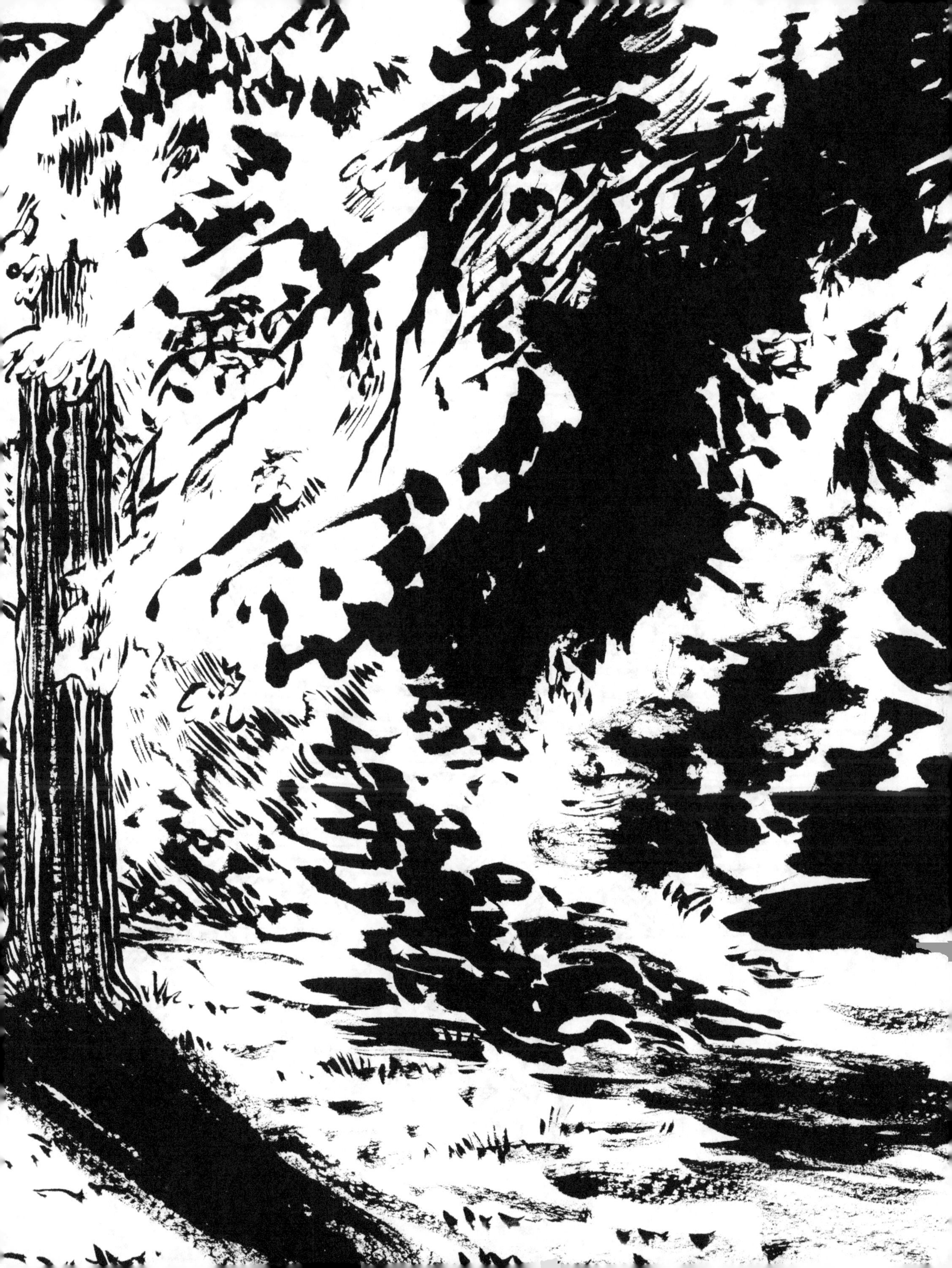

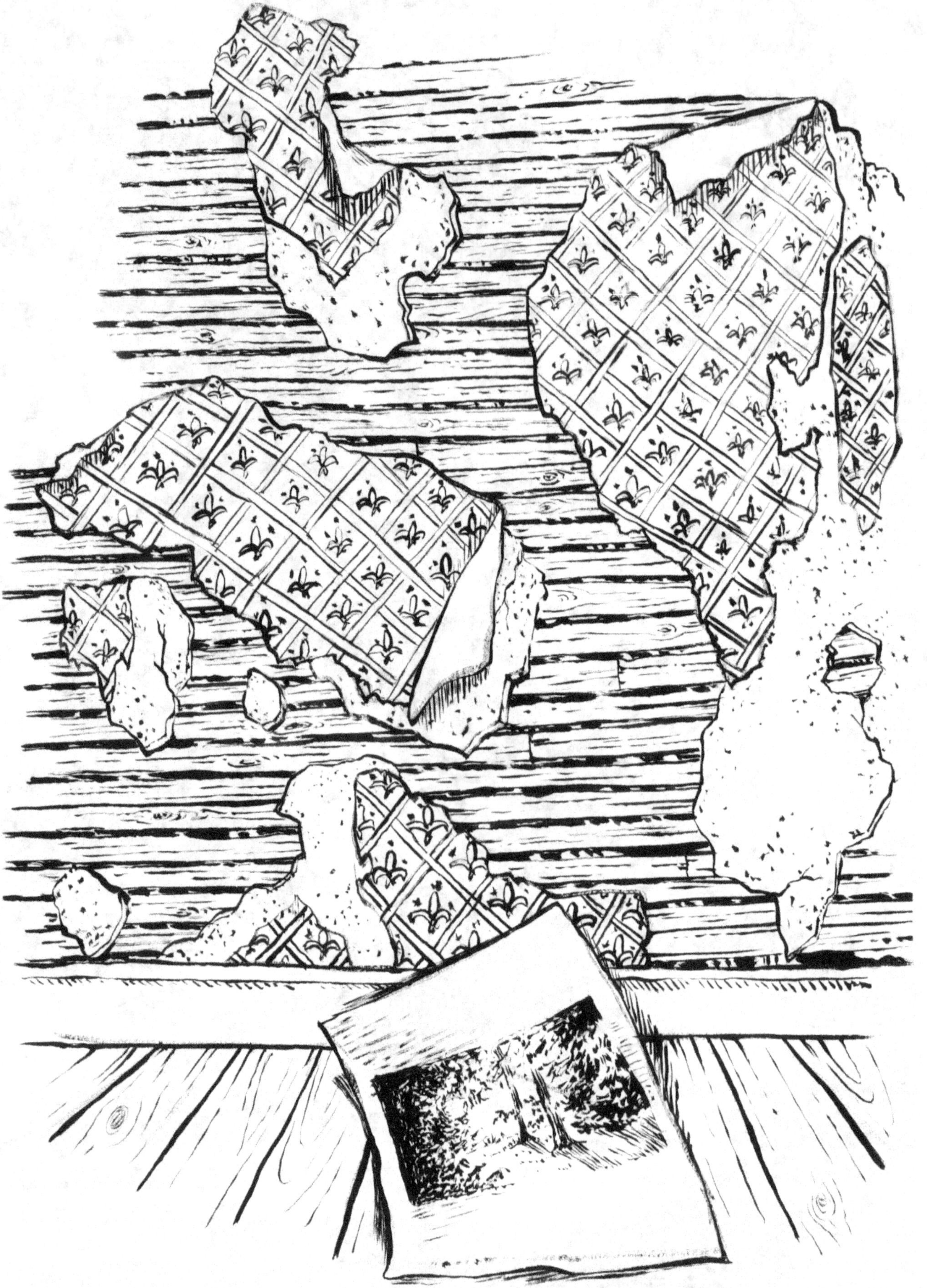

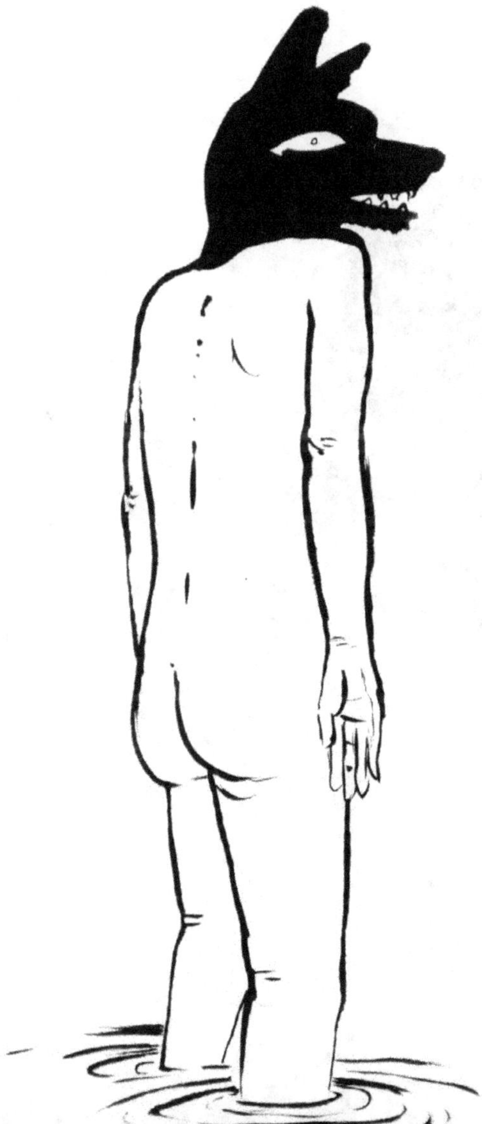

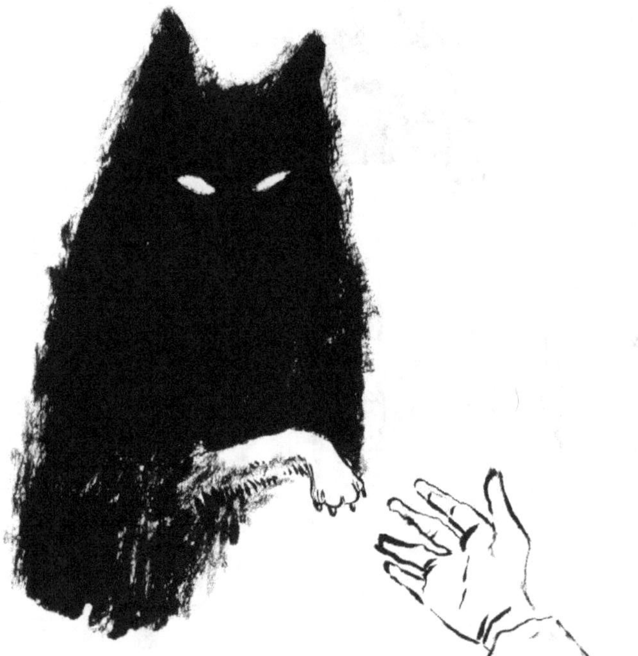

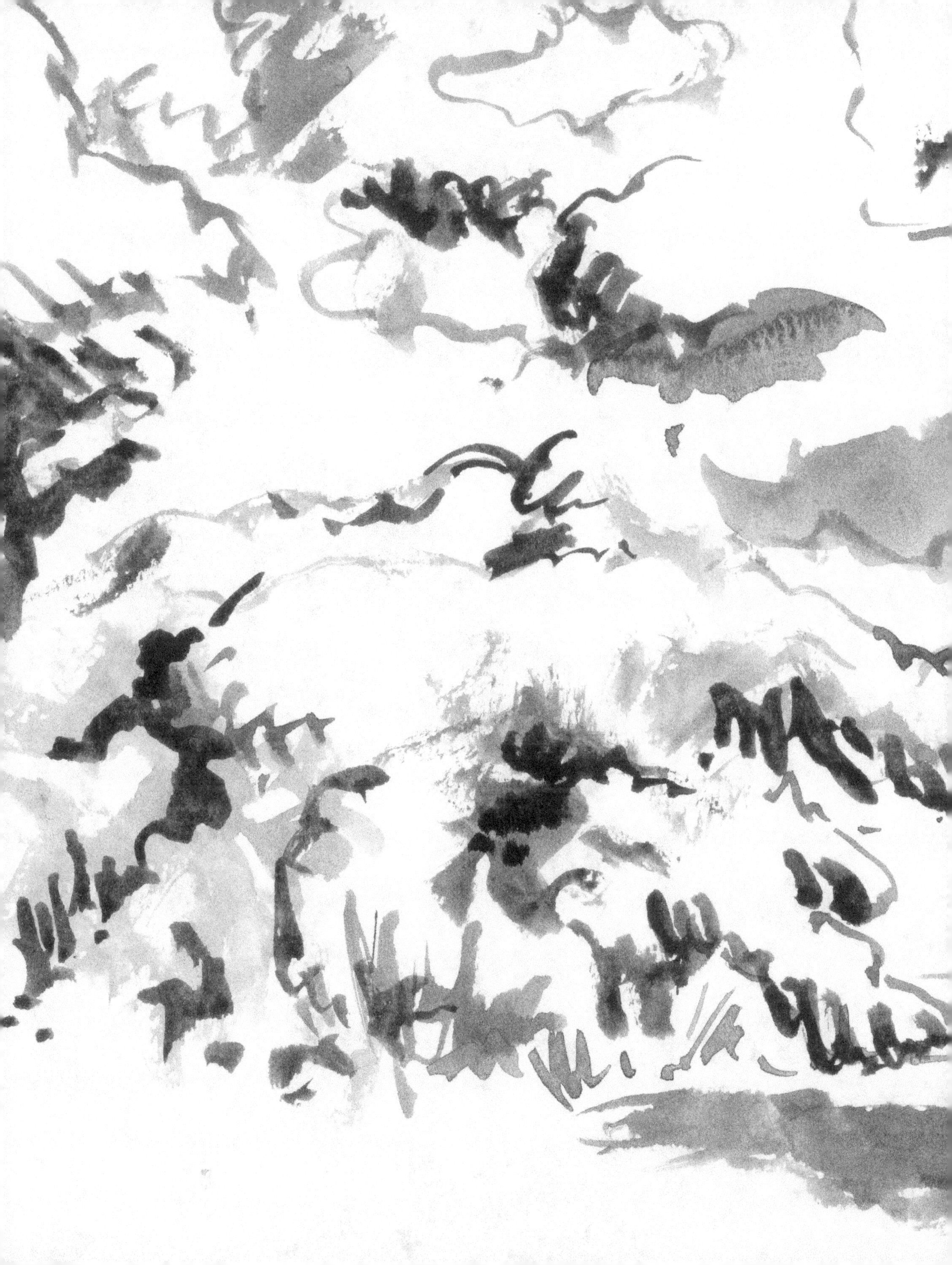

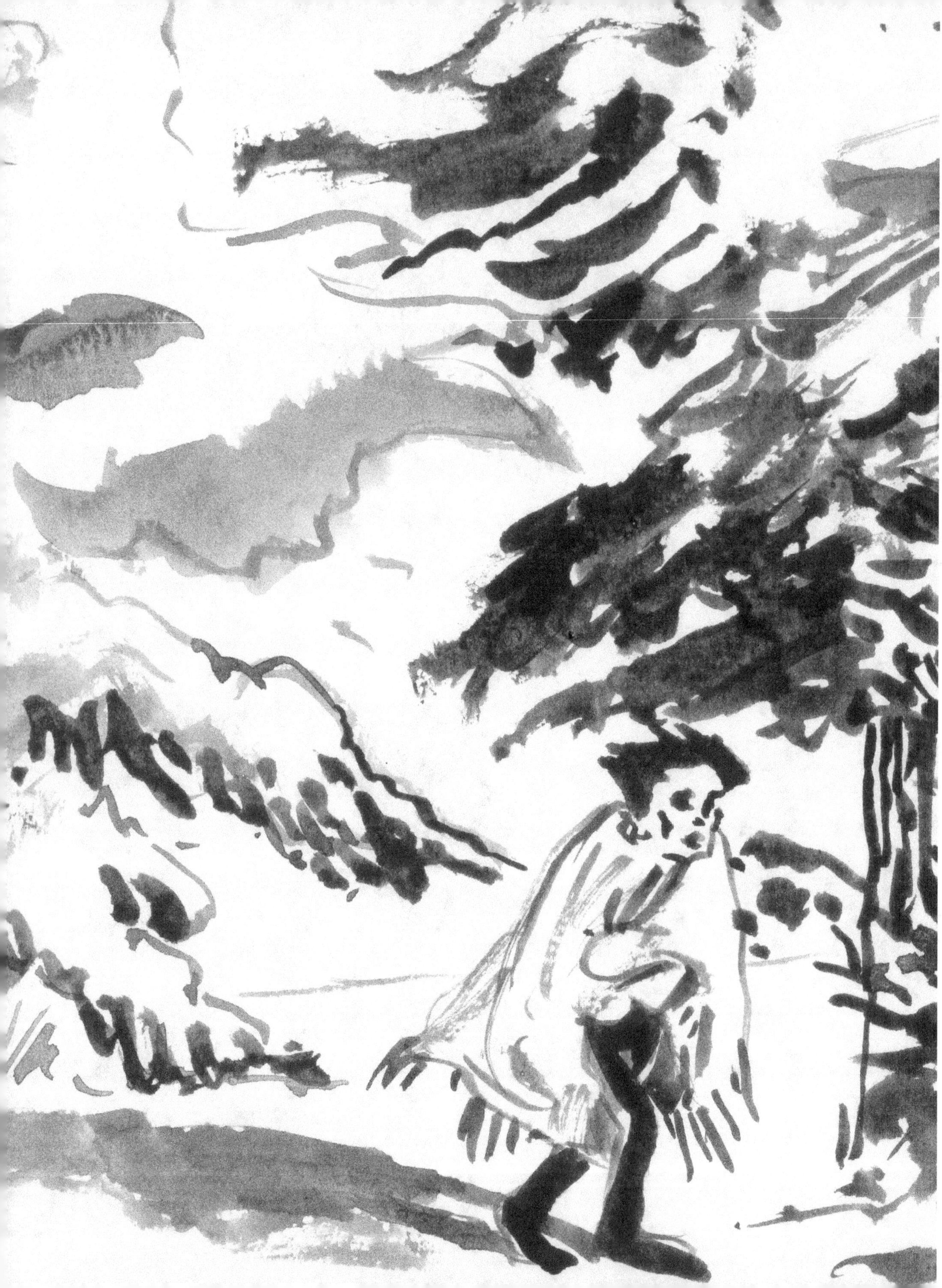

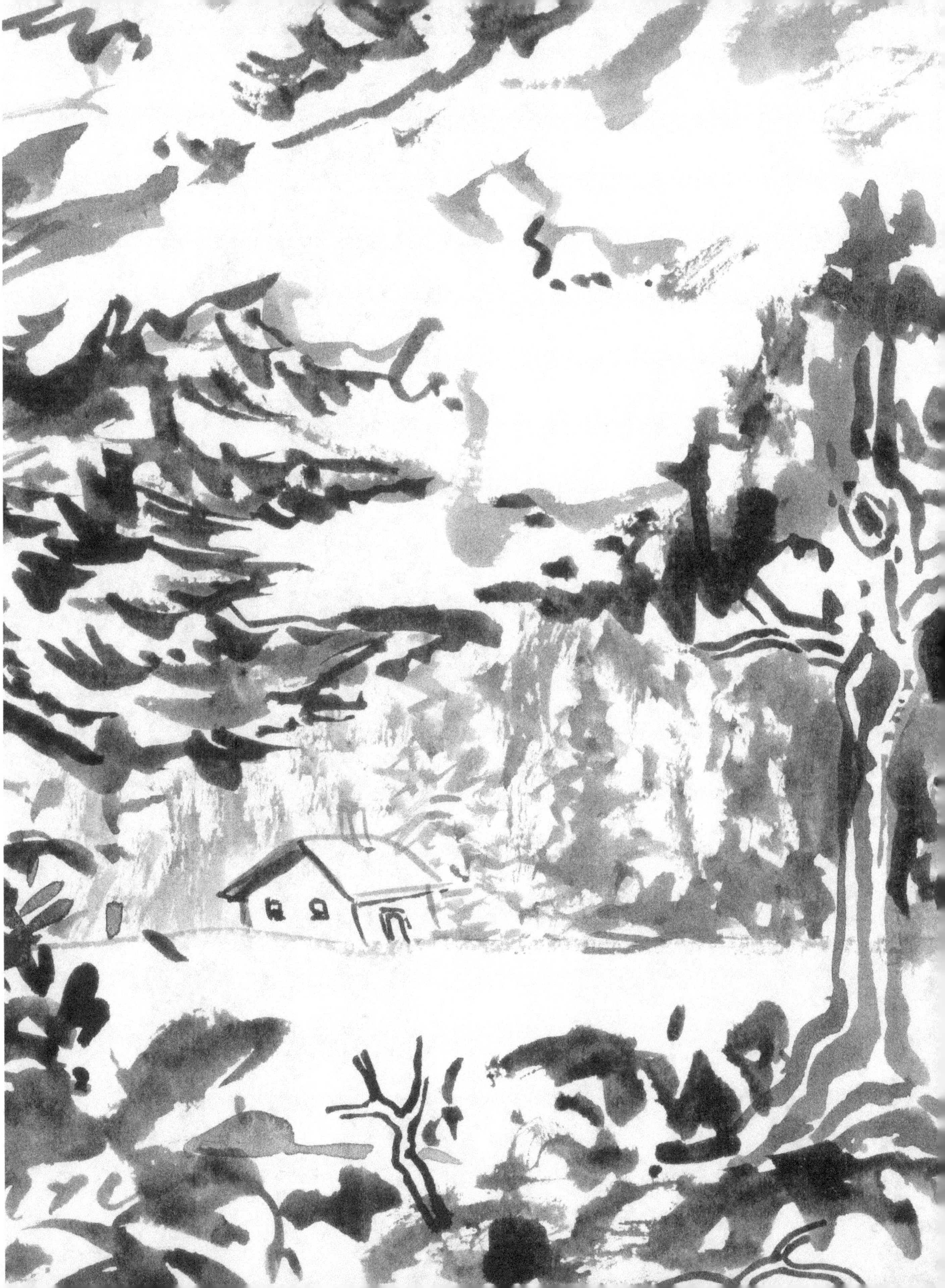

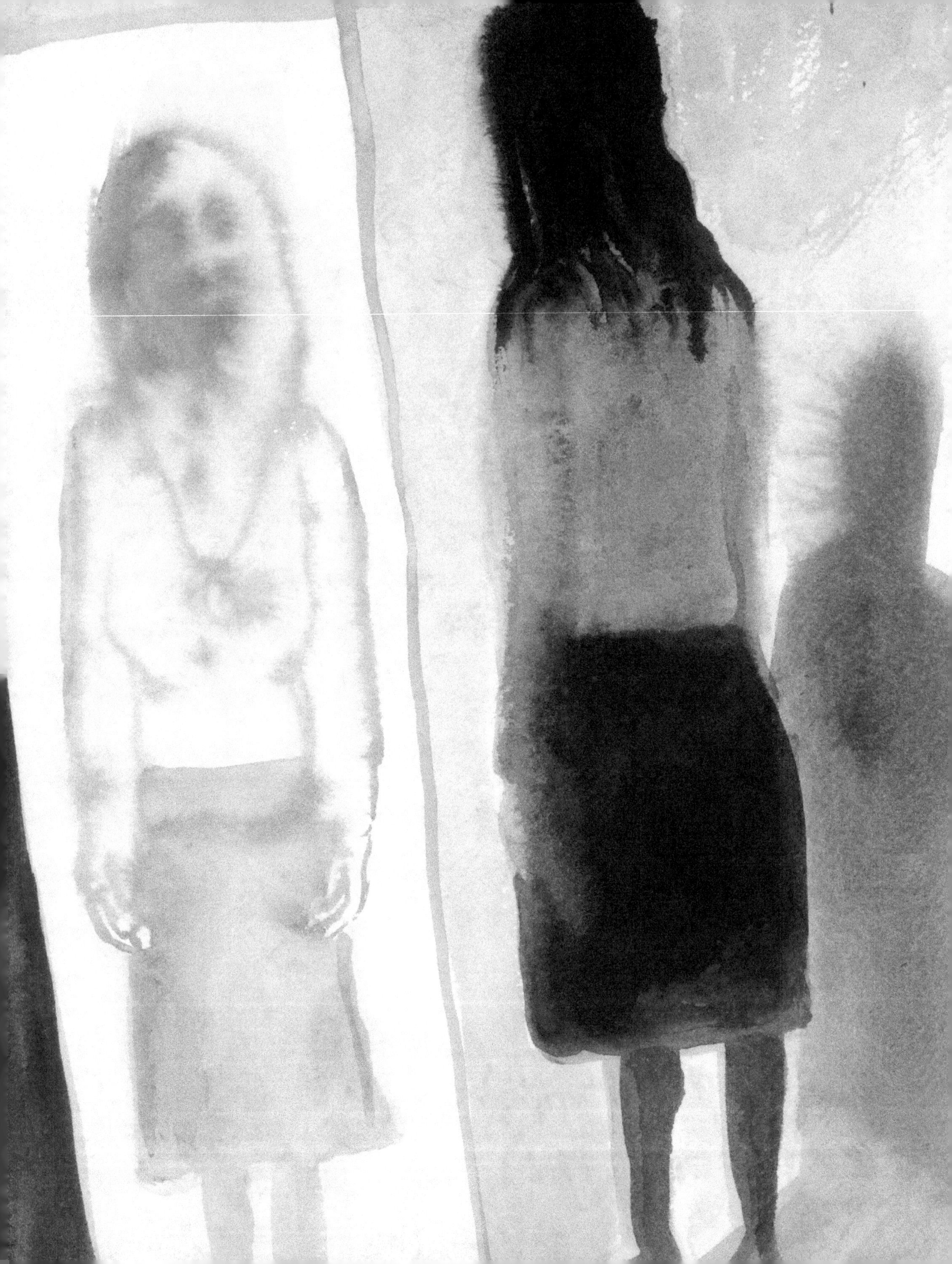

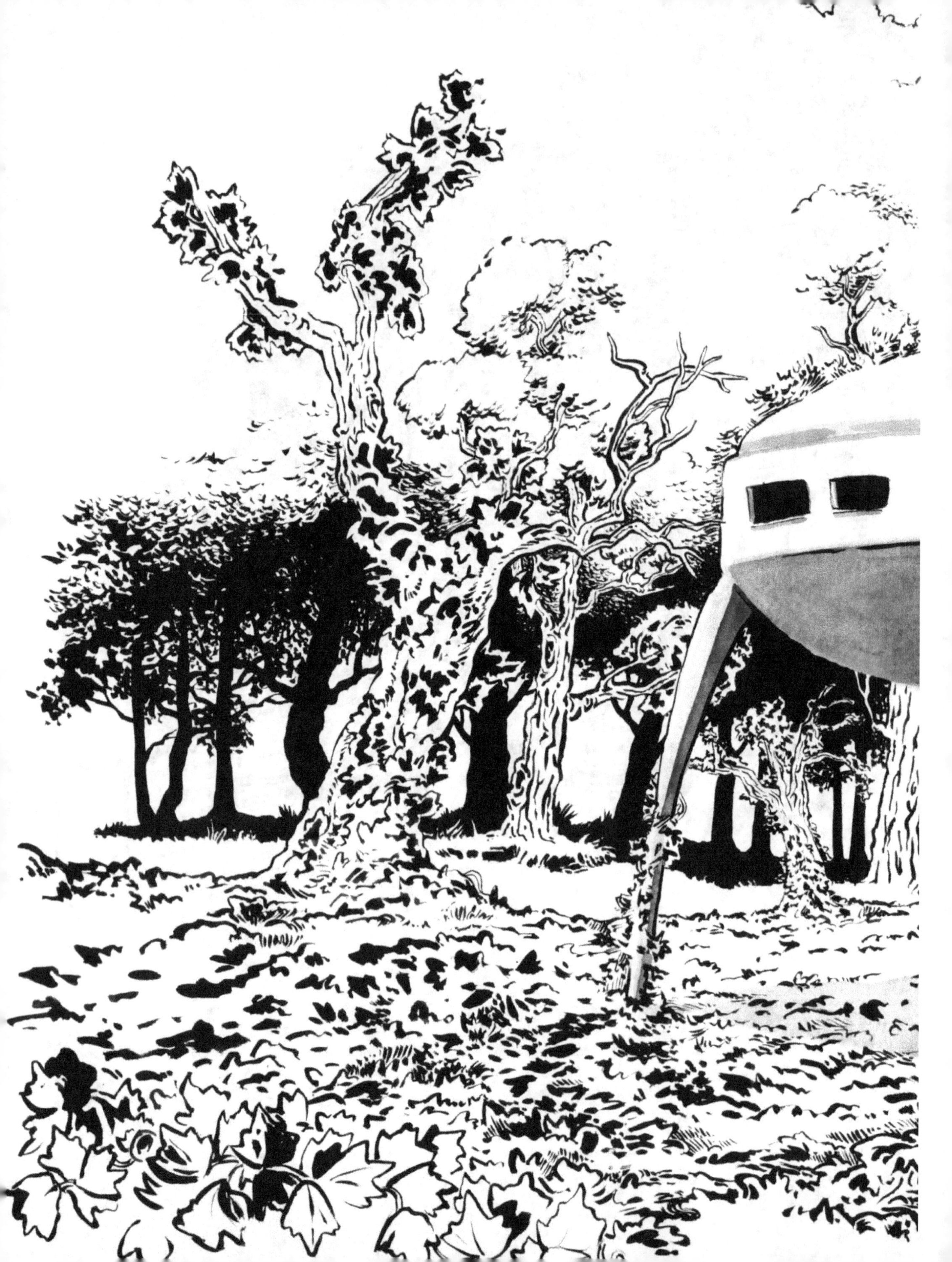

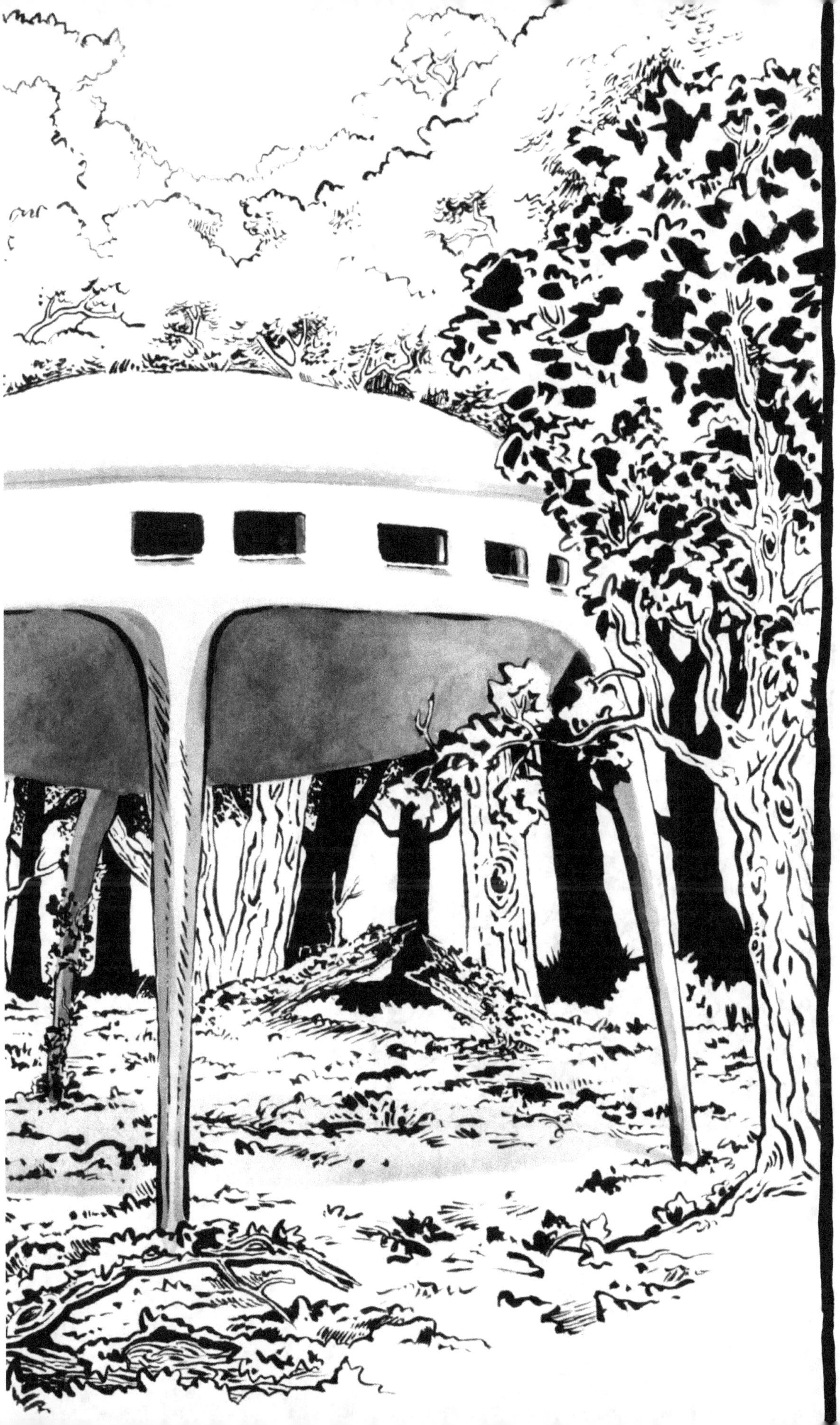

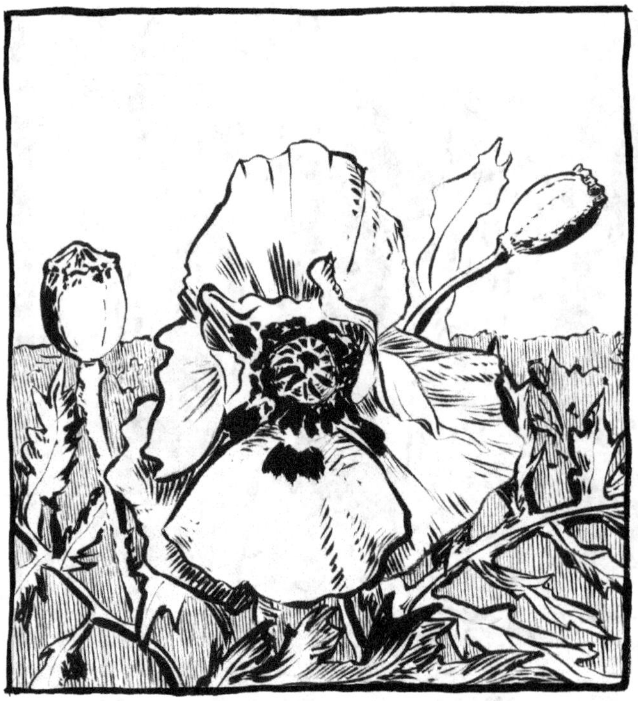

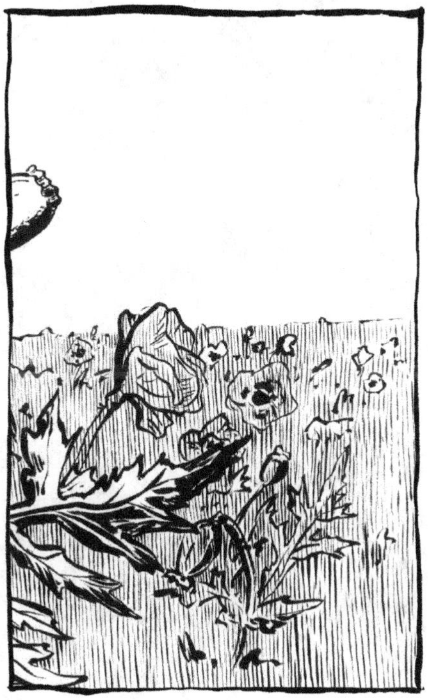

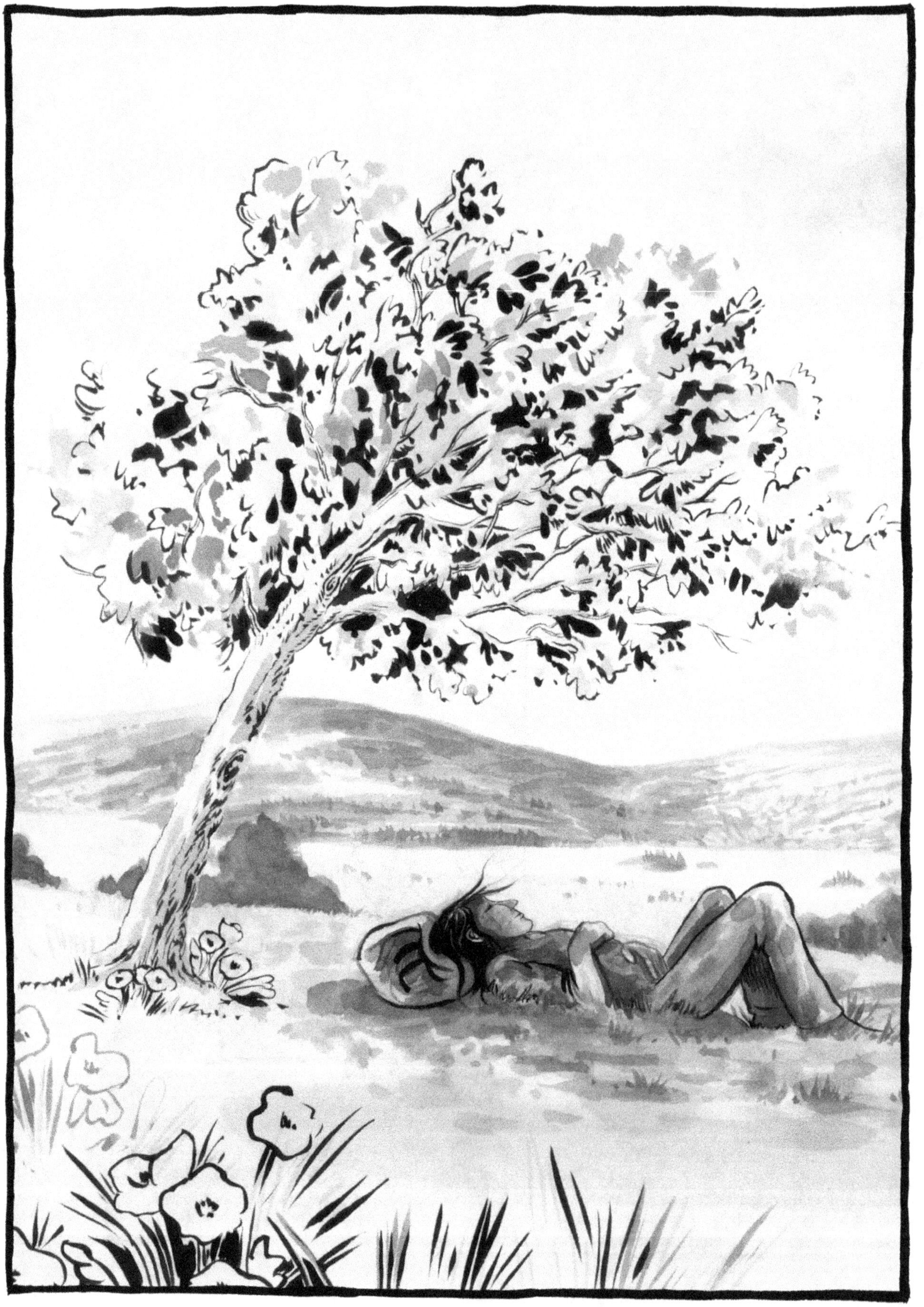

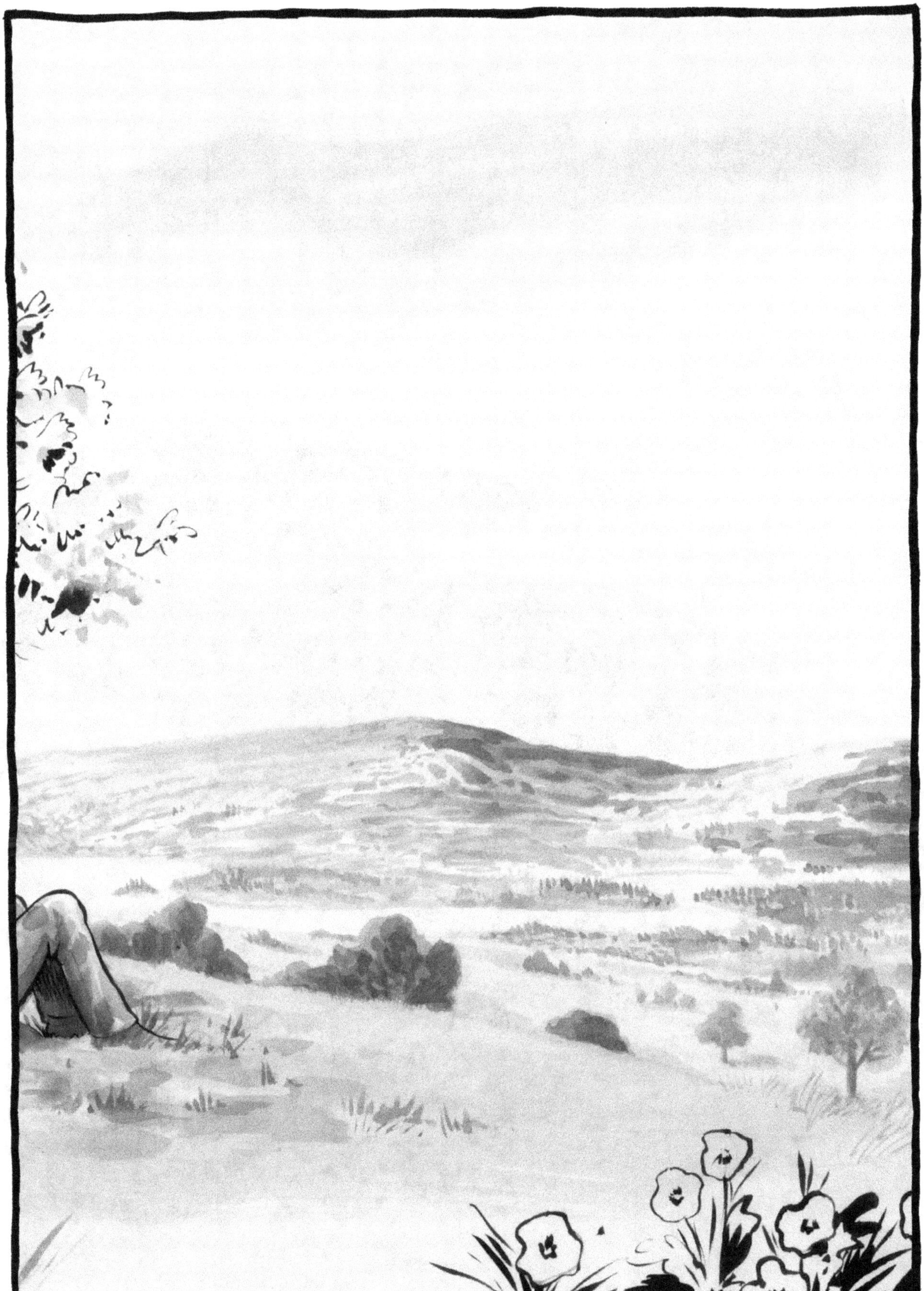

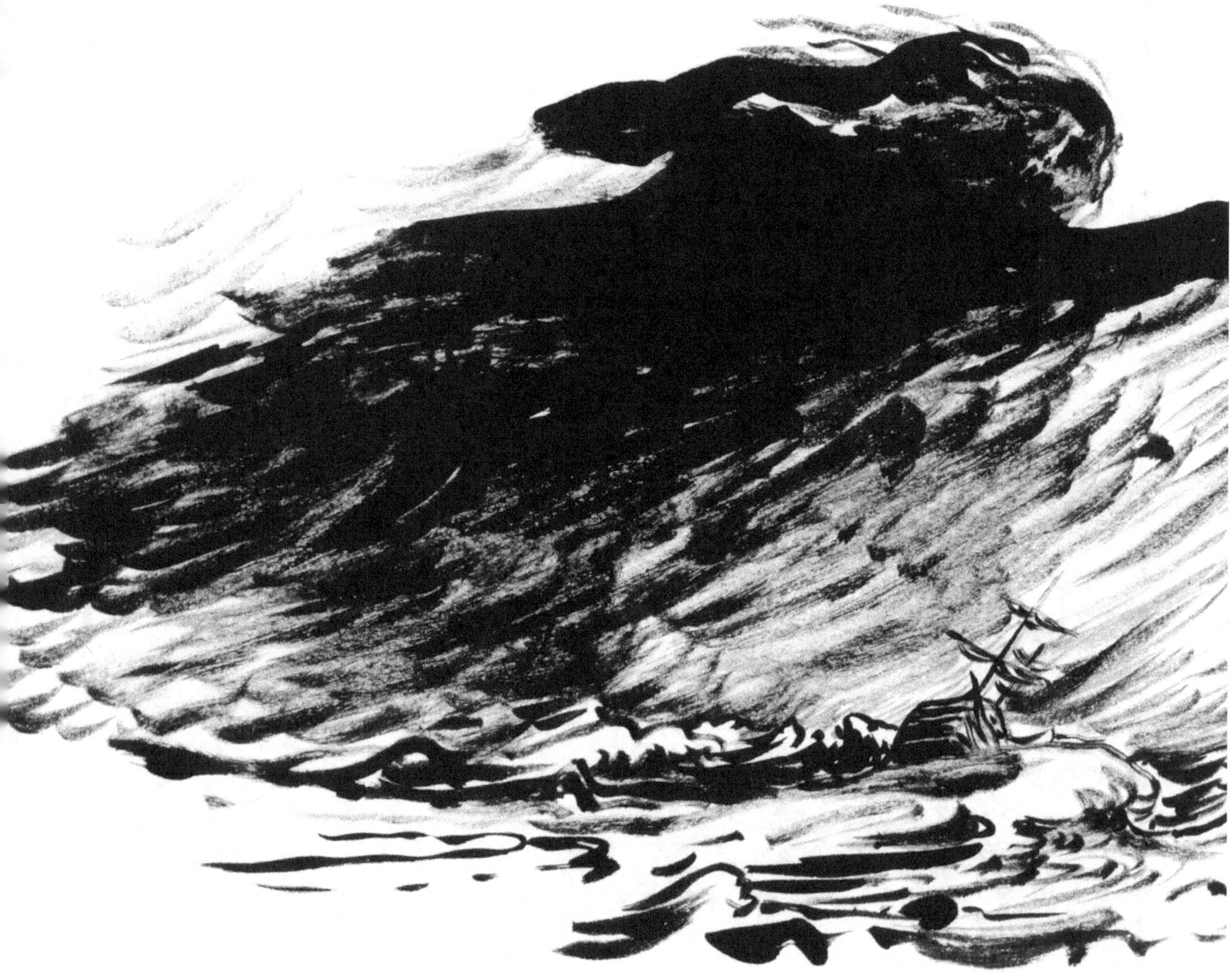

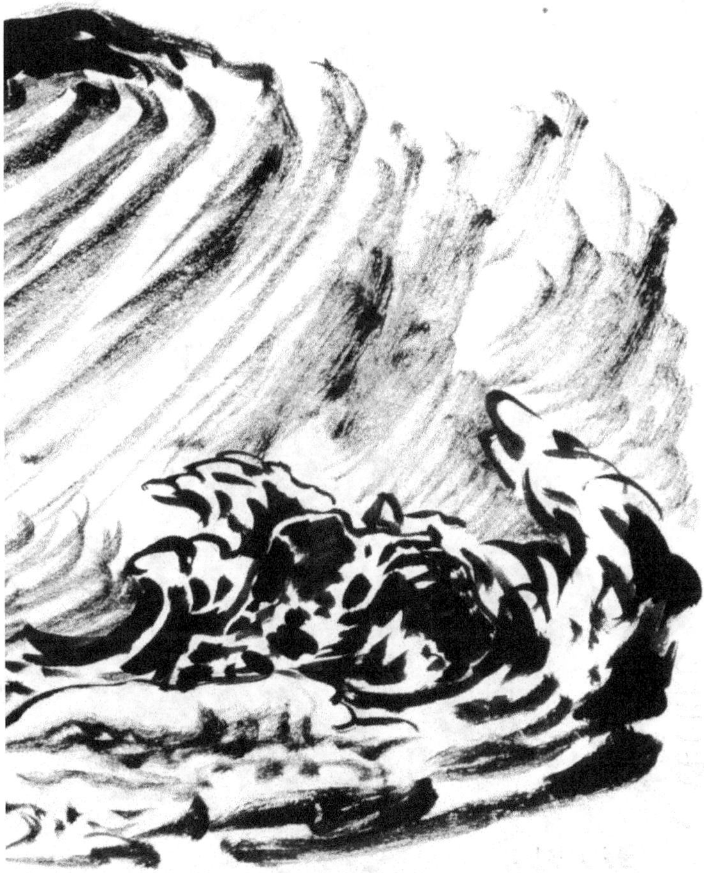

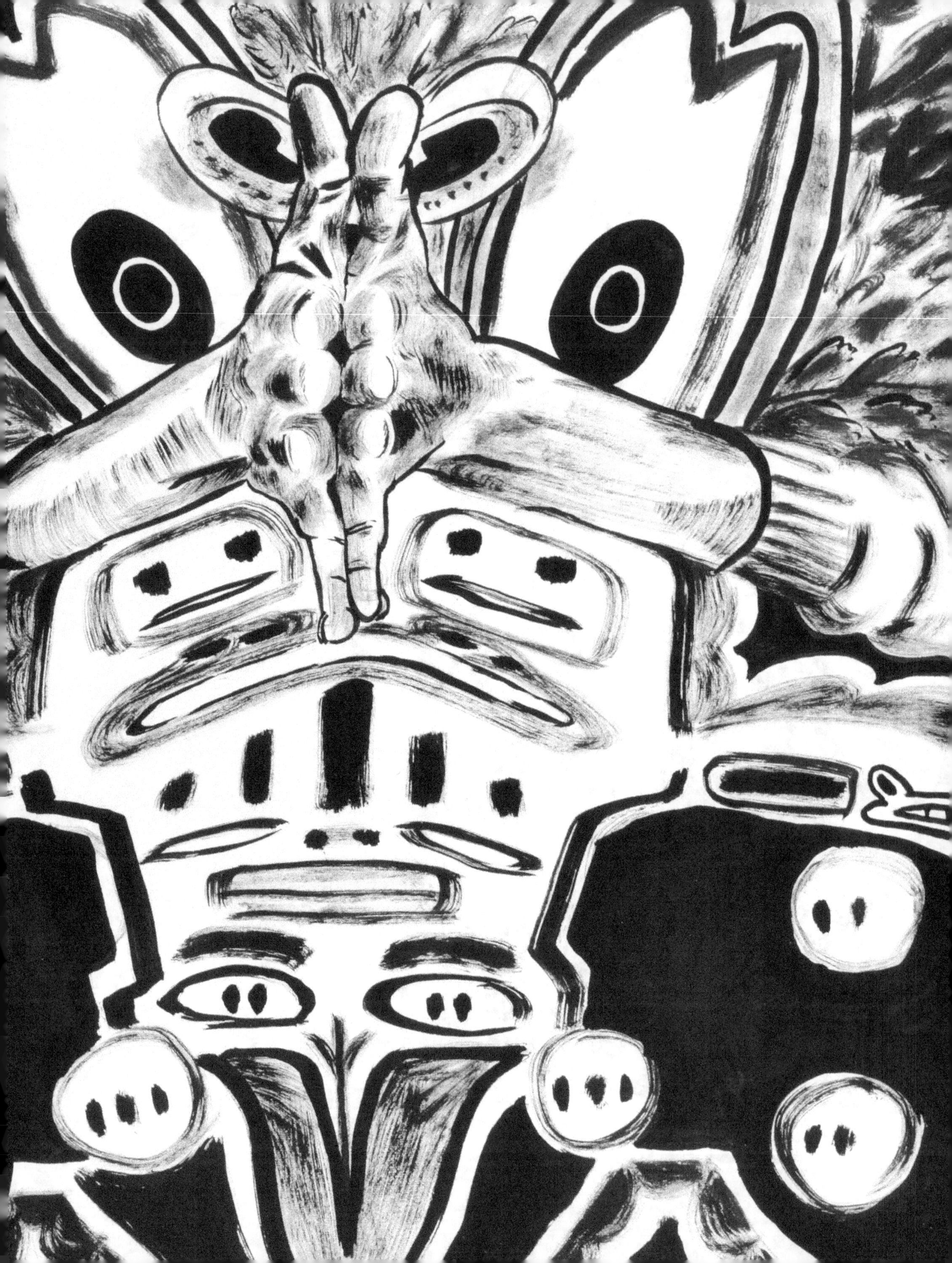

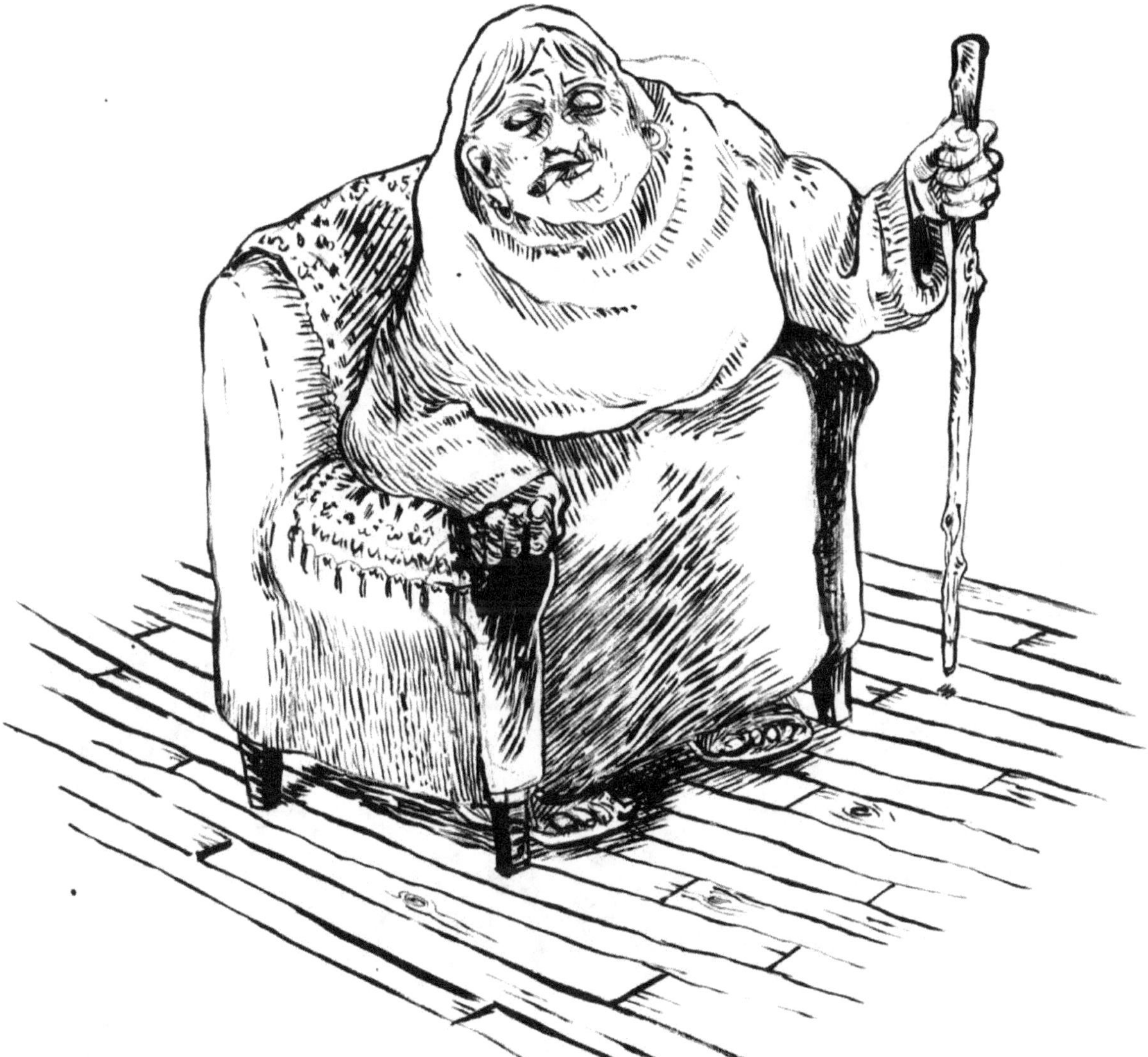

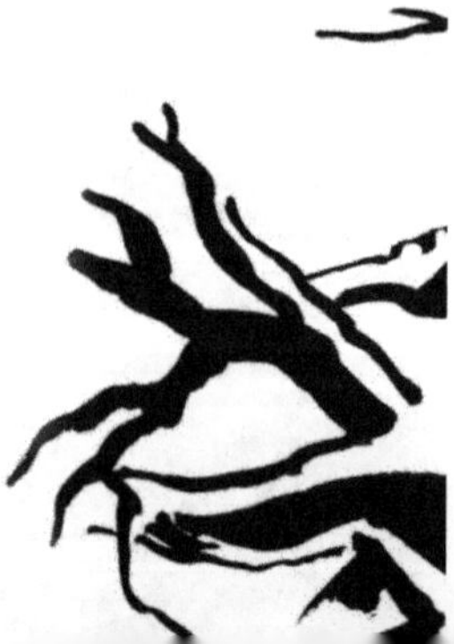

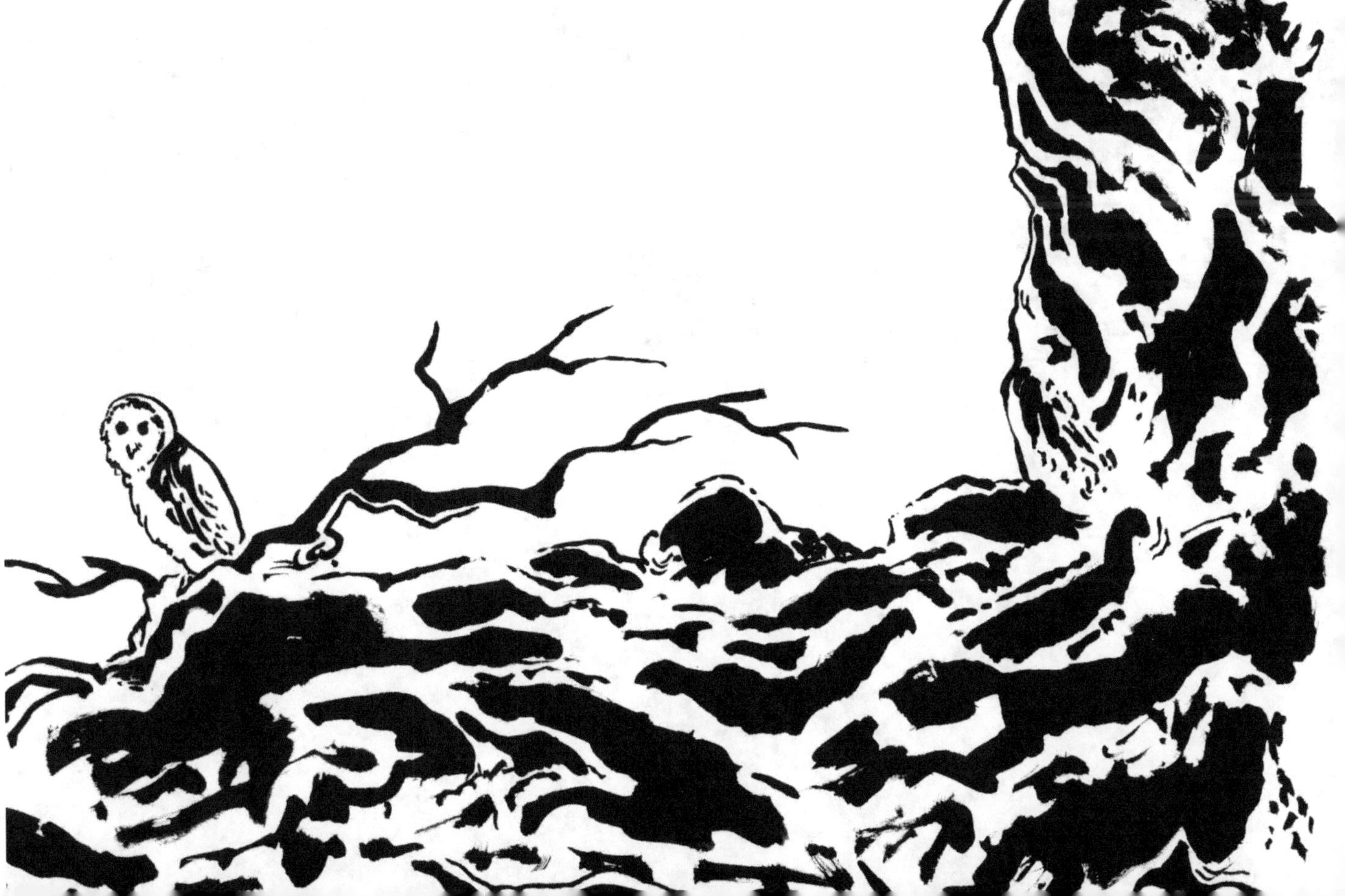

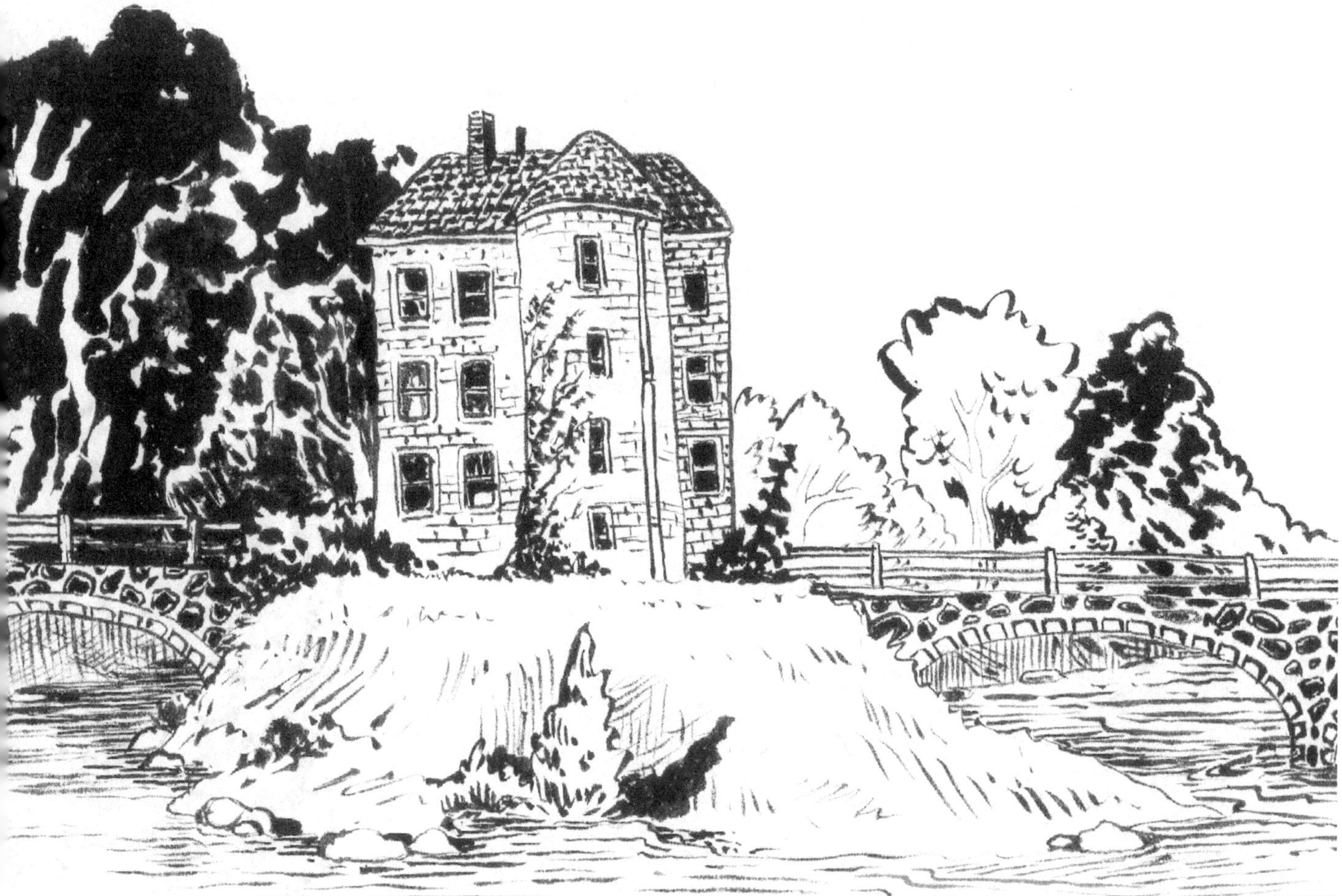

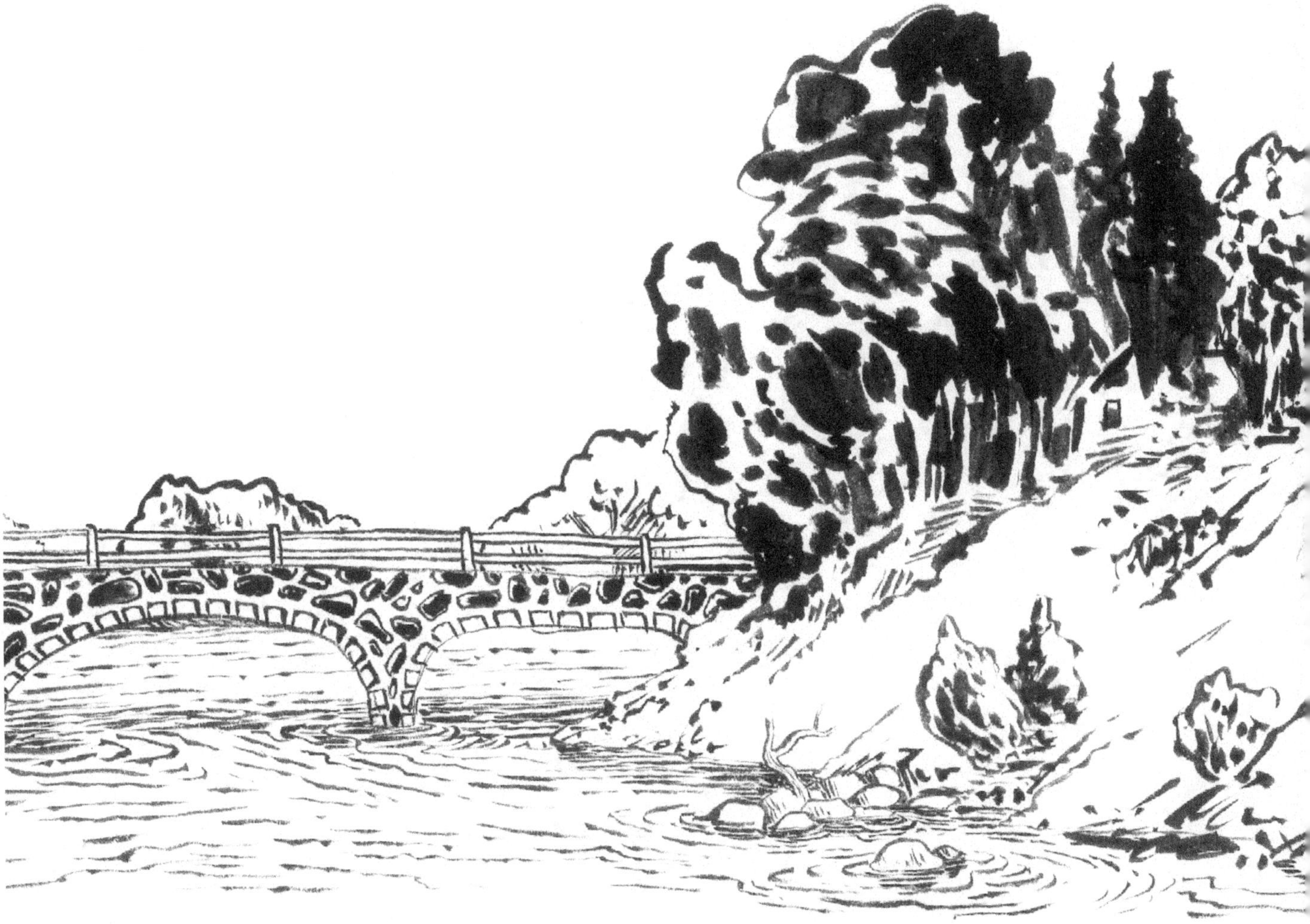

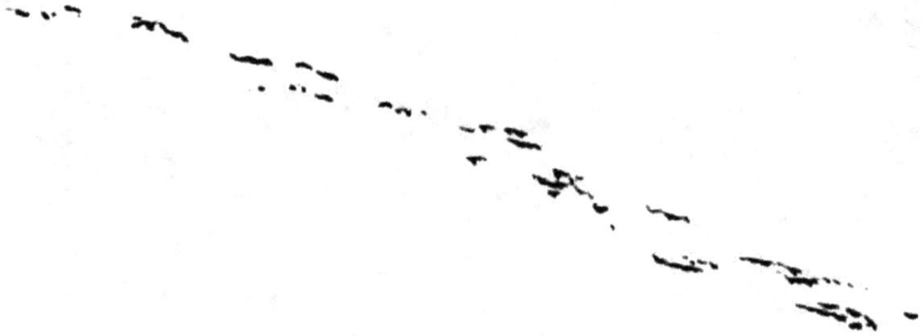

www.ingramcontent.com/pod-product-compliance
Lightning Source LLC
Chambersburg PA
CBHW081001170526
45158CB00010B/2867
9780692303344